SONGS
from the British Drama

BY THE SAME AUTHOR

English Lyrical Poetry (Second printing)
Sea Moods
Lyra Yalensis
Lyra Levis

SONGS

FROM

THE BRITISH DRAMA

EDITED BY EDWARD BLISS REED

Now you talk of music, have you e'er a one that
can play us an old lesson, or sing us an old song.
SHACKERLY MARMION, *The Antiquary*, *Act* 4. 1641.

NEW HAVEN: YALE UNIVERSITY PRESS
London, Humphrey Milford, Oxford University Press
MDCCCCXXV

Table of Contents

	Page
Preface	vii
Songs from the British Drama	1
Notes	257
Some Aspects of Song in the Drama	341
Bibliography	357
Index of Authors	365
Index of Plays, Masques, and Entertainments	368
Index of First Lines	376

Preface

FROM the hundreds of songs to be found in British plays there is an opportunity to make an anthology which the dramatic literature of no other nation can equal; yet though this fact is generally known, such an anthology exists but in part. Robert Bell in his *Songs from the Dramatists, 1854,* pointed the way by bringing together many of the finest lyrics once sung on the stage; his choice, however, was limited and he omitted scores of poems that merit remembrance. In his *Lyrics from the Dramatists of the Elizabethan Age,* 1889, 1891, A. H. Bullen went more thoroughly into this field and recovered many beautiful songs that long had been forgotten; but as his title indicates, he did not confine his selections to songs alone and since he included many lyrical passages from soliloquies and dialogues, one cannot always know what lines in his book were spoken and what were sung.[1] Neither editor made it a rule to print with the songs their stage directions; nor did they give the context which in many cases should be offered the reader if he is to understand the whole intent and effect of the lyric. It is hoped that the present volume may continue and complete the valuable work of these two scholars.

In preparing the text, two general principles have been followed: The word drama has been used in its broadest sense to include not only masques but some of the minor dramatic entertainments offered to Queen Elizabeth and her successors; and secondly, the songs have been taken from plays that have been acted, in all probability; and indeed, for the great majority of them, we have evidence that they were performed. This second method of selection has arbitrarily excluded so many fine songs that they would form a second volume.

As regards the text, all the songs have been taken from the earliest MSS. or from the earliest printed editions of the plays containing them except in some twenty instances where a MS. or play was inaccessible; in such cases, I have relied

[1] This is true, in a lesser degree, of Bell's volume.

upon the most authoritative reprints. The dates appearing
after the titles of printed plays are invariably the dates of publication; the dates of MSS. indicate the years in which they
were made, as accurately as may be ascertained. The acts and
scenes, given after the titles of plays, always refer to the editions whose dates follow immediately and not to modern editions or reprints, which in many cases have not adopted the
original divisions of the plays. Variant readings of the songs
are given in the notes only for the work of the most important
writers and for the most famous lyrics; or whenever these
variations make a distinct change in the thought or style. All
emendations, corrections, and omissions have been recorded.
Except in the first four songs, the spelling has been modern-
ized. So far as the punctuation is concerned, editors and an-
thologists have a tendency to sprinkle these songs with commas
and exclamation points. As a rule, they were carelessly printed
and the original punctuation is often either misleading or
plainly incorrect. It has been followed as closely as the sense
will allow; and, similarly, the original alignment of these
songs has been preferred, for the most part.

The authors are arranged chronologically, as are the anonymous plays with the exception of *Tom Tyler* and *The Thracian Wonder*. The songs of each writer are printed in the order of their publication, one following the other as they do in
their plays. It frequently happens that of two songs the one
first composed may be the one last printed and accordingly
this method of arrangement does not enable the reader to con-
trast at a glance the early and the mature work of any poet;
but the dates of these lyrics are quite uncertain at the best and
to arrange them in even a conjectural order of composition is
out of the question.

When the stage directions are lengthy, they have been
placed in the notes. There also will be found enough of the
context of the songs to enable one to appreciate the purpose of
the dramatists in using them and the way in which they are introduced. In the pages entitled "Some Aspects of Song in the
Drama" is a brief discussion of certain interesting questions
encountered in a study of this subject.

Whenever I have been able to find any information concerning the melodies to which these songs were sung—and a
search through seventeenth-century music books has yielded a

few—I have given it in the notes.[1] Facing page 341 is a most complete picture of the musical instruments used on Shakespeare's stage. Here are the viols, harps, lutes, and recorders mentioned so often in Elizabethan and Jacobean plays.[2] Here we may see the regals, the portable organ that was played in Edwardes' *Damon and Pythias,* 1571; the pandore, or bandore, a wire-strung instrument resembling a lute, used for accompaniments; the theorbo, a large mandolin which the player rested on his knee. Drayton's verses, which the plate illustrated, give the list:

> The trembling Lute some touch, some strain the Viol best
> In sets which there were seen, the music wondrous choice:
> Some likewise there affect the Gamba with the voice,
> To show that England could variety afford.
> Some that delight to touch the sterner, wirey cord,
> The Cythron, the Pandore, and the Theorbo strike:
> The Gittern and the Kit the wandering fiddlers like.
> So were there some again, in this their learned strife,
> Loud instruments that loved; the Cornet and the Fife,
> The Hoboy, Sagbut deep, Recorder and the Flute,
> Even from the shrillest Shawm unto the Cornamute.
> Some blow the Bagpipe up, that plays the country-round:
> The Taber and the Pipe, some take delight to sound.
>
> POLY-OLBION. *The Fourth Song,* p. 63. 1613.

It may be asked upon what principle of selection there have been admitted to this book certain lyrics whose content is insignificant and whose style is the true "rym doggerel." My purpose has been not merely to reprint poems of great charm and beauty too little known, but to explain and illustrate the use of song on the stage. If the poetic quality of certain selections seems too slight to warrant their inclusion, generally it will be found that they were employed in an interesting or an unusual manner, or that they throw some light on the subject

---

[1] I cannot believe that the punctuation offers, except in the most general way, any clue to the music of these songs or the manner in which they were performed. I am utterly unable to follow Mr. Noble in his conclusions based on commas and colons. See his *Shakespeare's Use of Song,* pp. 57, 58, 77, 86, 97, 107.

[2] A note in the MS. of Browne's *Inner Temple Masque* names the instruments for its performance, 1615. "The music was composed of treble violins with all the inward parts, a bass viol, bass lute, sagbut, cornamute, and tabor and pipe."

of singing in the theatre. Should this not be the case, their appearance must be attributed to the customary aberration of an anthologist. On the whole, this collection should do more than to offer certain poems, the flower of what is now a lost art; it should enable the reader to understand how far removed is our emotional yet tuneless drama from the lyric stage of the Tudor and Stuart reigns.

It is a pleasure to acknowledge my indebtedness to the anthologies of Bell and of Bullen, as well as to those scholars whose works appear in the Bibliography. The Notes will show how often I have drawn upon *The Elizabethan Stage* by E. K. Chambers. Assistant Dean Harry Glicksman and Associate Professor F. B. Kaye, former students in my graduate course, have assisted me by criticisms and suggestions in choosing these songs. To W. J. Lawrence I am especially grateful. His wide knowledge of the British drama is equalled only by his generosity in sharing that knowledge with others. I desire to express to the Librarian of the Dyce Collection, South Kensington Museum, and to the authorities of the British Museum and the Bodleian Library my appreciation of many courtesies extended to me while gathering and studying these songs.

I wish to thank the following authors and publishers for their permission to use these lyrics of which they hold the copyrights:

Doubleday, Page and Co., Garden City, N. Y., for "I cannot tell what this love may be" (p. 243); "Prithee, pretty maiden—prithee tell me true" (p. 243); and "When I go out of door" (p. 244), from Acts i and ii of *Patience* by W. S. Gilbert.

Thomas Hardy for "Let's meet again to-night, my Fair" (p. 246), from scene 11 of *The Famous Tragedy of the Queen of Cornwall*, published by The Macmillan Co., New York, and Macmillan and Co., Ltd., London.

The Macmillan Co., New York, and Macmillan and Co., Ltd., London, for "We hadn't been three days at sea before we saw a sail" (p. 247), from Act ii, scene 6, of *Admiral Guinea* by W. E. Henley.

Lady Gregory for "Yesterday travelling Connacht" (p. 248); "It is pitiful and sharp to-day are the wounds of Ireland" (p. 248), from *Dervorgilla*, and "All round my hat I wore a green ribbon" (p. 249), from *The Bogie Man,* published by G. P. Putnam's Sons, New York and London.

William Butler Yeats for "The wind blows out of the gates of the day" (p. 249), from *The Land of Heart's Desire,* published by The Macmillan Co., New York, and Macmillan and Co., Ltd., London.

Laurence Housman and H. Granville-Barker for "How now, everywhere up in air stars stare" (p. 250), from Act ii of *Prunella,* published by Little, Brown and Co., Boston, and Sidgwick and Jackson, Ltd., London.

John Galsworthy for "The windy hours through darkness fly" (p. 251), from Act iii of *The Little Dream,* published by Charles Scribner's Sons, New York, and Gerald Duckworth and Co., Ltd., London.

Gordon Bottomley for "The bird in my heart's a-calling through a far-fled, tear-grey sea" (p. 251), from *The Crier by Night,* published by Small, Maynard and Co., Boston, and Constable and Co., Ltd., London.

Clemence Dane for "Come with me to London" (p. 252) and "If Luck and I should meet" (p. 253), from Act i and Act iii, scene 2, of *Will Shakespeare,* published by The Macmillan Co., New York, and William Heinemann, Ltd., London.

Songs from the British Drama

ANONYMOUS

Theise Songes belonge to the Taylors and Shearemens Pagant.

Song 1.

As I out rode this enderes night,
Of thre joli sheppardes I saw a sight,
And all abowte there fold a star shone bright.
 They sange Terli terlow,
So mereli the sheppards ther pipes can blow.

1. enderes: *last.*

Song 2.

Doune from heaven, from heaven so hie,
Of angeles ther came a great companie,
With mirthe and joy and great solemnitye,
 They sang Terli terlow,
So mereli the sheppards ther pipes can blow.

Song 3.

Lully, lulla, thow littell tine child;
By, by, lully, lullay, thow littell tyne child:
 By, by, lully, lullay.

O sisters too,
How may we do
 For to preserve this day
This pore yongling,
For whom we do singe
 By, by, lully, lullay?

Herod the king,
In his raging
　　Chargid he hath this day
His men of might,
In his owne sight,
　　All yonge children to slay,—

That wo is me,
Pore child for thee,
　　And ever morne and may
For thi parting
Nether say nor singe
　　By, by, lully, lullay.

COVENTRY SHEARMEN AND TAILORS PAGEANT. MS. 1534.

ANONYMOUS

The Good Gossippes Song.

THE flude comes flittinge in full faste,
On everye syde that spreades full farre;
For feare of drowninge I am agaste;
Good gossippes, lett us drawe nere.
And lett us drinke or we departe,
For ofte tymes we have done soe;
For att a draughte thou drinkes a quarte,
And soe will I doe or I goe.
Heare is a pottill full of Malmsine good and stronge;
Itt will rejoyce bouth harte and tonge;
Though Noye thinke us never so longe,
Heare we will drinke alike.

CHESTER PLAYS. THE THIRD PAGEANT OF NOAH'S FLOOD.
MS. Add. 10,305. 1592.

JOHN SKELTON

1460?-1529

Liberty: WITH ye, marry Sirs, thus should it be:
I kissed her sweet and she kissed me;
I danced the darling on my knee;
I garred her gasp, I garred her glee,
With dance on the lea, the lea!
I bassed that baby with heart so free;
    She is the bote of all my bale.
Ah, so! that sigh was far fet!
To love that lovesome I will not let;
My heart is wholly on her set;
I pluckèd her by the patlet;
At my device I with her met;
My fancy fairly on her I set;
    So merrily singeth the nightingale!

MAGNIFICENCE. ll. 2064-2077. [*Circa* 1530.]

4. garred: *made;* glee: *squint.* 6. bassed: *kissed;* baby: *darling.*
7. bote: *cure;* bale: *ill.* 8. fet: *fetched.* 9. let: *cease.* 11. patlet: *ruff.*

JOHN RASTELL

?-1536

*Then the dancers without the hall sing this wise and they
within answer, or else they may say it for need.*

TIME to pass with goodly sport
Our sprits to revive and comfort,
    To pipe, to sing,
    To dance, to spring,
With pleasure and delight
Following Sensual Appetite.

THE NATURE OF THE FOUR ELEMENTS. [*Circa* 1520.]

JOHN BALE, BISHOP OF OSSORY

1495-1563

Dissimulation: WASSAIL, wassail, out of the milk-pail,
Wassail, wassail, as white as my nail,
Wassail, wassail, in snow, frost, and hail,
Wassail, wassail, with partridge and rail,
Wassail, wassail, that much doth avail,
Wassail, wassail, that never will fail.

KING JOHN, ii. MS. [*Circa* 1538.]

JOHN REDFORD

The third song.

*Here Wit, Instruction, Study, and Diligence sing "Welcome,
my own," and Science, Experience, Reason and Confidence
come in at left, and answer every second verse:*

WELCOME, mine own!
Welcome, mine own!

Wit and his Company: O lady dear,
Be ye so near
To be known?
My heart you cheer
Your voice to hear;
Welcome, mine own.

Science and her Company: As ye rejoice
To hear my voice
From me thus blown,
So in my choice
I show my voice
To be your own.

Wit and his Company: Then draw we near
                          To see and hear
                             My love long grown!
                          Where is my dear?
                          Here I appear
                             To see mine own.

Science and her Company: To see and try
                          Your love truly
                             Till death be flown,
                          Lo! here am I,
                          That ye may spy
                             I am your own.

Wit and his Company: Then let us meet,
                          My love so sweet,
                             Half-way here thrown!
Science and her Company: I will not sleet
                          My love to greet.
                             Welcome, mine own.

Wit and his Company: Welcome, mine own!
All sing: Welcome, mine own!

THE PLAY OF WIT AND SCIENCE. MS. [*Circa* 1545.]

R(OBERT?) WEVER

Here entereth Lusty Juventus, or Youth, singing as followeth.

IN a herber green, asleep whereas I lay,
The birds sang sweet in the middes of the day;
I dreamed fast of mirth and play,
    In youth is pleasure, in youth is pleasure.

Methought as I walked still to and fro,
And from her company I could not go;
But when I waked it was not so,
    In youth is pleasure, in youth is pleasure.

Therefore my heart is surely pight
Of her alone to have a sight,
Which is my joy and heart's delight:
    In youth is pleasure, in youth is pleasure.

                    LUSTY JUVENTUS. [*Circa* 1550.]

1. herber: *arbour.* 9. pight: *determined.*

WHY should not youth fulfill his own mind,
As the course of nature doth him bind?
Is not everything ordained to do his kind?
    Report me to you, report me to you.

Do not the flowers spring fresh and gay,
Pleasant and sweet in the month of May?
And when their time cometh, they fade away.
    Report me to you, report me to you.

Be not the trees in winter bare?
Like unto their kind, such they are;
And when they spring, their fruits declare.
    Report me to you, report me to you.

What should youth do with the fruits of age,
But live in pleasure in his passage,
For when time cometh, his lusts will swage.
    Report me to you, report me to you.

                              LUSTY JUVENTUS.
15. swage: *abate.*

NICHOLAS UDALL

1505-1556

The Fourth Song.

I MUN be married a Sunday;
I mun be married a Sunday;
Whosoever shall come that way,
I mun be married a Sunday.

Roister Doister is my name;
Roister Doister is my name;
A lusty brute I am the same,
I mun be married a Sunday.

Christian Custance have I found;
Christian Custance have I found,
A widow worth a thousand pound;
I mun be married a Sunday.

Custance is as sweet as honey;
Custance is as sweet as honey;
I her lamb and she my coney,
I mun be married a Sunday.

When we shall make our wedding feast;
When we shall make our wedding feast,
There shall be cheer for man and beast;
I mun be married a Sunday.
    I mun be married a Sunday, etc.

RALPH ROISTER DOISTER, ii. 3. [1567?]

15. coney: *darling.*

WILLIAM STEVENSON?

Fl. 1550

First a song.

BACK and side go bare, go bare,
  Both foot and hand go cold:
But, belly, God send thee good ale enough,
  Whether it be new or old.

I cannot eat but little meat,
  My stomach is not good:
But sure I think that I can drink
  With him that wears a hood.
Though I go bare, take ye no care,
  I am nothing a-cold;

I stuff my skin so full within
   Of jolly good ale and old.

Back and side go bare, go bare,
   Both foot and hand go cold:
But, belly, God send thee good ale enough,
   Whether it be new or old.

I love no roast but a nutbrown toast,
   And a crab laid in the fire;
A little bread shall do me stead,
   Much bread I not desire:
No frost nor snow, no wind, I trow,
   Can hurt me if I would,
I am so wrapt, and throughly lapt
   Of jolly good ale and old.

Back and side go bare, &c.

And Tib my wife, that as her life
   Loveth well good ale to seek,
Full oft drinks she, till ye may see
   The tears run down her cheeks.
Then doth she trowl to me the bowl,
   Even as a maltworm should,
And saith, "Sweetheart, I took my part
   Of this jolly good ale and old."

Back and side go bare, &c.

Now let them drink, till they nod and wink,
   Even as good fellows should do;
They shall not miss to have the bliss
   Good ale doth bring men to:
And all poor souls that have scoured bowls
   Or have them lustily trowled,
God save the lives of them and their wives,
   Whether they be young or old.

Back and side go bare, &c.

GAMMER GURTON'S NEEDLE, ii. 1575.

W. WAGER

Fl. 1559

*Here entereth Moros, counterfeiting a vain gesture and a fool-
ish countenance, singing the foot of many songs, as fools
were wont.*

BROOM, broom on a hill,
The gentle broom on hill hill:
Broom, broom on Hive hill,
The gentle broom on Hive hill,
The broom stands on Hive Hill a.
¶ Robin lend to me thy bow, thy bow,
Robin the bow, Robin lend to me thy bow a.
¶ There was a maid come out of Kent,
Dainty love, dainty love,
There was a maid came out of Kent,
Dangerous be:
There was a maid came out of Kent,
Fair, proper, small, and gent,
As ever upon the ground went,
For so should it be.
¶ By a bank as I lay, I lay,
Musing on things past, hey how.
¶ Tom a lin and his wife, and his wife's mother,
They went over a bridge all three together,
The bridge was broken and they fell in,
"The Devil go with all," quoth Tom a lin.
¶ Martin Swart and his men, sodledum, sodledum,
Martin Swart and his men, sodledum bell.
¶ Come over the bourn Besse,
My little pretty Besse,
Come over the bourn Besse to me.
¶ The white dove sat on the castle wall,
I bend my bow and shoot her I shall,
I put her in my glove both feathers and all.
I laid my bridle upon the shelf,
If you will any more, sing it your self.

A VERY MERRY AND PITHY COMEDY CALLED THE LONGER THOU
LIVEST, THE MORE FOOL THOU ART. [*Circa* 1559?]

13. gent: *gentle.* 24. bourn: *small stream, brook.*

Moros: ¶ I HAVE a pretty titmouse
         Come picking on my toe.
All III   Gossip with you I purpose
the same: To drink before I go.
Moros: ¶ Little pretty nightingale
         Among the branches green,
All III   Give us of your Christmas ale,
the same: To the honour of St. Stephen.
Moros: ¶ Robin redbreast with his notes
         Singing aloft in the quere
All III   Warneth to get you fresh coats
the same: For winter then draweth near.
Moros: ¶ My bridle lieth on the shelf,
         If you will have any more,
         Vouchsafe to sing it your self,
         For here you have all my store.

THE LONGER THOU LIVEST.

10. quere: *choir.*

ANONYMOUS

Tom Tyler cometh in singing.

THE proverb reporteth, no man can deny,
That wedding and hanging is destiny.

I am a poor tiler in simple array,
And get a poor living, but eightpence a day,
My wife as I get it, doth spend it away;
     And I cannot help it, she saith; wot ye why?
     For wedding and hanging is destiny.

I thought when I wed her, she had been a sheep,
At board to be friendly, to sleep when I sleep.
She loves so unkindly, she makes me to weep;
     But I dare say nothing, God wot, wot ye why?
     For wedding and hanging is destiny.

Besides this unkindness whereof my grief grows,
I think few tilers are matched with such shrows;
Before she leaves brawling, she falls to deal blows

Which early and late doth cause me cry
That wedding and hanging is destiny.

The more that I please her, the worse she doth like me,
The more I forbear her, the more she doth strike me,
The more that I get her, the more she doth glike me;
  Woe worth this ill fortune that maketh me cry
  That wedding and hanging is destiny.

If I had been hanged when I had been married,
My torments had ended, though I had miscarried;
If I had been warned, then would I have tarried;
  But now all too lately I feel and cry
  That wedding and hanging is destiny.

TOM TYLER AND HIS WIFE. 1661.

14. shrows: *shrews.* 20. glike: *mock.*

TOM Tiler, Tom Tiler
More morter for Tom Tiler.

Strife sing- As many as match themselves with shrowes,
eth this staff: May hap to carry away the blows,
        Tom Tiler, Tom Tiler.
  As many a tide both ebbs and flows,
  So many a misfortune comes and goes,
        Tom Tiler, Tom Tiler.

Tipple sing- Though Tilers climb the house to tile,
eth this staff: They must come down another while,
        Tom Tiler, Tom Tiler.
  Though many a one do seem to smile,
  When geese do wink, they mean some guile,
        Tom Tiler, Tom Tiler.

Sturdy sing- Though Tom be stout, and Tom be strong,
eth this staff: Though Tom be large, and Tom be long,
        Tom Tiler, Tom Tiler.
  Tom hath a wife will take no wrong
  But teach her Tom another song.
        Tom Tiler, Tom Tiler.

TOM TYLER AND HIS WIFE.

The Mill a, the Mill a,
So merrily goes the merry Mill a.

LET us sip, and let it flip,
  And go which way it will a,
Let us trip, and let us skip,
  And let us drink our fill a.
Take the cup, and drink all up,
  Give me the can to fill a:
Every sup, and every cup,
  Hold here, and my good will a.
Gossip mine, and gossip thine,
  Now let us gossip still a:
Here is good wine, this ale is fine,
  Now drink of which you will a.
Round about, till all be out,
  I pray you let us swill a:
This jelly grout, is jelly and stout,
  I pray you stout it still a.
Let us laugh, and let us quaff,
  Good drinkers think none ill a:
Here is your bag, here is your staff,
  Be packing to the mill a.

                    TOM TYLER AND HIS WIFE.

17. jelly: *jolly, good;* grout: *small beer;* stout: *having "body."*

ANONYMOUS

A Song to the tune of "Heart's Ease."

SING care away, with sport and play,
  Pastime is all our pleasure;
If well we fare, for nought we care,
  In mirth consists our treasure.

What doth avail, far hence to sail
  And lead our life in toiling,
Or to what end should we here spend
  Our days in irksome moiling?

It is the best, so live at rest
And tak't as God doth send it,
To haunt each wake, and mirth to make
And with good fellows spend it.

Nothing is worse than a full purse
To niggards and to pinchers;
They always spare and live in care,
There's no man loves such flinchers.

The merry man with cup and can
Lives longer than doth twenty;
The miser's wealth doth hurt his health,
Examples we have plenty.

'Tis a beastly thing to lie musing
With pensiveness and sorrow;
For who can tell that he shall well
Live here until the morrow?

In card and dice our comfort lies,
In sporting and in dancing,
Our minds to please and live at ease,
And sometime to use prancing.

With Bess and Nell we love to dwell
In kissing and in haking;
But whoopho, holly, with trolly lolly!
To them we'll now be walking.

MISOGONUS, ii. 2. MS. 1560-1577.

30. haking: *idling.*

LEWIS WAGER

Fl. 1560

HEY dery, dery, with a lusty dery,
Hoigh mistress Mary, I pray you be merry.

Your pretty person we may compare to Lais,
A morsel for princes and noble kings,
In beauty you excell the fair lady Thais,

You exceed the beautiful Helen in all things,
To behold your face who can be weary?
  Hoigh mistress Mary, I pray you be merry.

The hair of your head shineth as fine gold,
Your eyes as gray as glass and right aimiable,
Your smiling countenance so lovely to behold,
To us all is most pleasant and delectable,
Of your commendations who can be weary?
  Huffa mistress Mary, I pray you be merry.

Your lips as ruddy as the red rose,
Your teeth as white as ever was the whale's bone,
So clean, so sweet, so fair, so good, so fresh, so gay,
In all Jewry truly at this day there is none.
With a lusty voice sing we Hey dery dery.
  Huffa mistress Mary, I pray you be merry.

THE LIFE AND REPENTANCE OF MARY MAGDALENE. 1566.

16. whale's bone: *ivory*.

JOHN PHILLIP

Fl. 1565

The nurse singeth.

LULLA by baby, lulla by baby,
Thy nurse will tend thee, as duly as may be.

Be still my sweet sweeting, no longer do cry,
  Sing lulla by baby, lulla by baby:
Let dolors be fleeting, I fancy thee aye,
  To rock and to lull thee, I will not delay me.
  Lulla by baby, etc.

What creature now living would hasten thy woe,
  Sing lulla by, lulla by, lulla by baby:
See for thy relieving, the time I bestow,
  To dance, and to prance thee, as prett'ly as may be.
  Lulla by baby, etc.

The Gods be thy shield, and comfort in need,
  Sing lulla by, lulla by, lulla by baby:
They give thee good fortune and well for to speed,
  And this to desire, I will not delay me.
Lulla by baby, etc.

THE COMEDY OF PATIENT AND MEEK GRISSELL. [*Circa* 1566.]

JOHN PICKERING

*Haltersick entereth and singeth this song to the tune of "Have
over the water to Floride" or "Selengers round."*

FAREWELL, adieu, that courtly life,
  To war we tend to go;
It is good sport to see the strife
  Of soldiers in a row.
    How merrily they forward march
    These enemies to slay:
    With hey trim and trixie too,
    Their banners they display.

Now shall we have the golden cheats,
  When others want the same;
And soldiers have full many feats
  Their enemies to tame:
    With cocking here, and booming there,
    They break their foes array;
    And lusty lads amid the fields
    Their ensigns do display.

The drum and flute play lustily,
  The trumpet blows amain,
And venturous knights courageously
  Do march before their train:
    With spears in rest so lively drest,
    In armour bright and gay;
    With hey trim and trixie too,
    Their banners they display.

A NEW INTERLUDE OF VICE, CONTAINING THE HISTORY OF
  HORESTES. 1567.

9. cheats: *booty.* 13. cocking: *fighting.*

*Enter Ægisthus and Clytemnestra, singing this song to the
tune of "King Solomon."*

Ægisthus: AND was it not a worthy sight
Of Venus' child, king Priam's son:
To steal from Greece a lady bright,
For whom the wars of Troy begun?
Naught fearing danger that might fall,
    Lady, lady,
        From Greece to Troy he went with all,
        My dear Lady.

Clytemnestra: When Paris first arrived there,
Where as dame Venus worshiped is,
And blustering Fame abroad did bear
His lively fame, she did not miss
To Helena for to repair,
    Her for to tell
        Of praise and shape so trim and fair,
        That did excell.

Ægisthus: Her beauty caused Paris pain,
And bare chief sway within his mind:
Nothing was able to restrain
His will, some way forth for to find
Whereby he might have his desire,
    Lady, lady:
        So great in him was Cupid's fire,
        My dear lady!

Clytemnestra: And eek as Paris did desire,
Fair Helena for to possess:
Her heart, inflamèd with like fire,
Of Paris love desired no less,
And found occasion him to meet
    In Cytheron,
        Where each of them the other did greet
        The feast upon.

Ægisthus: If that in Paris Cupid's shaft,
O Clytemnestra, took such place
That time ne way he never left,

Till he had got her comely grace,
  I think my chance not ill to be,
    Lady, lady,
      That ventured life to purchase ye,
      My dear lady.

Clytemnestra: King Priam's son loved not so sore
  The Greecian dame, thy brother's wife:
  But she his person esteemed more,
  Not, for his sake, saving her life;
  Which caused her people to be slain,
    With him to fly,
    And he requite[d] her love again
    Most faithfully.

Ægisthus: And as he recompense[d] again
  The fair queen Helen for the same:
  So, while I live, I will take pain
  My will always to yours to frame,
  Sith that you have vouchsafe[d] to be
    Lady, lady,
    A queen and lady unto me,
    My dear lady.

Clytemnestra: And as she loved him best, while life
  Did last, so tend I you to do,
  If that devoid of war and strife
  The gods shall please to grant us to,
  Sith you vouchsafest me for to take,
    O my good knight,
    And me thy lady for to make,
    My heart's delight.

                                        HORESTES.

Enter the Vice, singing this song to the tune of "The Painter."

    STAND back, ye sleeping Jacks at home,
      And let me go.
    You lie, sir knave; am I a mome?
      Why say you so?

Tut, tut, you dare not come in field,
For fear you should the ghost up yield.
With blows he goes, the gunshot fly,
It fears, it sears, and there doth lie.

A hundred in a moment be
    Destroyèd quite:
Sir sauce, in faith, if you should see
    The gunshot light,
To quake for fear you would not stint,
When as by force of gunshot's dint
The ranks in ray are took away,
As pleaseth fortune oft to play.

But in this stour who bears the fame
    But only I?
Revenge, Revenge will have the name,
    Or he will die.
I spare no wight, I fear none ill,
But with this blade I will them kill;
For when mine ear is set on fire,
I rap them, I snap them, that is my desire.

Farewell, adieu, to wars I must
    In all the haste.
My cousin Cutpurse will, I trust,
    Your purse well taste;
But to it, man, and fear for nought;
Me say to thee, it is well fraught
With ruddocks red: be at a beck,
Beware thy face, break not thy neck.

                                HORESTES.

1. Jacks: *knaves.* 3. mome: *fool.* 11. sauce: *impudent.* 13. stint: *cease.* 15. ray: *array, line.* 17. stour: *battle.* 31. ruddocks: *money, gold.*

Enter the Vice, singing this song.

A NEW master, a new!
No longer I may
Abide: by this day
    Horestes now doth rue.

A new master, a new!
And was it not ill
His mother to kill?
   I pray you, how say you?

A new master, a new!
Now it's too late
To shut the gate:
   Horestes gins to rue.

HORESTES.

ANONYMOUS

Enter Lust like a gallant, singing this song.

HEY ho, care away, let the world pass,
For I am as lusty as ever I was,
In flowers I flourish as blossoms in May,
Hey ho, care away: hey ho, care away.

THE TRIAL OF TREASURE. 1567.

AM not I in blessed case,
Treasure and pleasure to possess?
I would not wish no better place,
If I may still have wealthiness,
And to enjoy in perfect peace,
   My lady, lady.
My pleasant pleasure shall increase,
   My dear lady.

Helen may not compared be,
Nor Cressida that was so bright,
These cannot stain the shine of thee,
Nor yet Minerva of great might.
Thou passest Venus far away,
   Lady, lady,
Love thee I will both night and day,
   My dear Lady.

My mouse, my nobs, my coney sweet,
My hope and joy, my whole delight,
Dame Nature may fall at thy feet,
And may yield to thee her crown of right.
I will thy body now embrace,
   Lady, lady,
And kiss thy sweet and pleasant face,
   My dear Lady.

THE TRIAL OF TREASURE.

17. nobs: *darling.*

THOMAS INGELEND

SPITE of his spite, which that in vain
Doth seek to force my fantasy,
I am professed for loss or gain
To be thine own assuredly.
   Wherefore let my father spite and spurn,
   My fantasy will never turn.

Although my father of busy wit
Doth bable still, I care not tho;
I have no fear, nor yet will flit,
As doth the water to and fro.

For I am set and will not swerve,
Whom spiteful speech removeth nought.
And since that I thy grace deserve,
I count it is not dearly bought.

This minion here, this mincing trull,
Doth please me more a thousand fold
Than all the earth that is so full
Of precious stones, silver and gold.

Whatsoever I did, it was for her sake,
It was for her love, and only pleasure;
I count it no labour such labour to take,
In getting me so high a treasure.
   Wherefore let my father spite and spurn,
   My fantasy will never turn.

THE DISOBEDIENT CHILD. [*Circa* 1569.]

8. tho: *then.*

ANONYMOUS

Idleness Singeth.

COME, come, lie down, and thou shalt see
None like to me to entertain
Thy bones and thee oppressed with pain.
Come, come and ease thee in my lap,
And if it please thee, take a nap;
A nap that shall delight thee so
That fancies all will thee forego.
By musing still, what canst thou find
But wants of will and restless mind?
A mind that mars and mangles all,
And breedeth jars to work thy fall;
Come, gentle Wit, I thee require,
And thou shalt hit thy chief desire,
Thy chief desire, thy hoped pray,
First ease thee here, and then away!

THE MARRIAGE OF WIT AND SCIENCE, iv. 4. *Circa* 1570.

14. pray: *prayer.*

ULPIAN FULWELL

Fl. 1575

Philip Fleming singeth these four lines following.

TROLL the bowl and drink to me, and troll the bowl again,
And put a brown toast in the pot, for Philip Fleming's brain.
And I shall toss it to and fro, even round about the house a:
Good hostess now let it be so, I drinks them all carouse a.

LIKE WILL TO LIKE. 1568.

1. troll: *pass about.*

GOOD hostess, lay a crab in the fire and broil a mess of souse a:
That we may toss the bowl to and fro, I drinks them all carouse a.

And I will pledge Tom Tosspot 'till I be drunk as a mouse a:
Whoso will drink to me all day, I will pledge them all carouse a.
Then we will not spare for any cost, so long as we be in
   house a:
Then, hostess, fill the pot again, for I pledge them all carouse a.

LIKE WILL TO LIKE.

GEORGE WAPULL

Fl. 1576

The Song.

WE have great gain, with little pain,
And lightly spend it too:
We do not toil, nor yet we moil,
As other poor folks do.
   We are winners all three,
   And so will we be,
   Wherever that we come a:
   For we know how,
   To bend and bow,
   And what is to be done a.

To kneel and crouch, to fill the pouch,
We are full glad and fain:
We ever still, even at our will,
Are getters of great gain.
   We are winners etc.

It is our will, to poll and pill,
All such as do us trust:
We bear in hand, good friends to stand,
Though we be most unjust.
   We be winners etc.

Full far abouts, we know the routes
Of them that riches had:
Whom through deceit, as fish to bait,
We made their thrift forth gad.
  We are winners etc.

THE TIDE TARRIETH NO MAN. 1576.

16. poll and pill: *plunder and pillage.* 18. bear in hand: *deceive.*
24: gad: *wander.*

The Song.

THOUGH Wastefulness and Wantoness,
Some men have us two named:
Yet Pleasantness and Pliantness,
Our names we have now framed.
For as I one is pleasant, to kiss and to cully,
The other is pliant as ever was holly.
    As youth would it have,
    So will we be brave.

To live in bliss, we will not miss,
What care we for mens sayings:
What joy is this, to sport and kiss,
But hurt comes in delayings.
The one is full ready to the others becking,
Between us there is neither chiding, nor checking.
    As youth will it have etc.

Full brave and full fine, we pass the time,
Take time while time is biding:
What joy is thine, the same is mine,
My mind shall not be sliding.
Our goods are our own, why should we spare,
Or for time to come, why should we care.
    As youth would it have etc.

THE TIDE TARRIETH NO MAN.

5. cully: *fondle.*

ANONYMOUS

Here entereth the mariners with a song.

LUSTILY, lustily, let us sail forth,
The wind trim doth serve us, it blows at the North.

All things we have ready, and nothing we want,
To furnish our ship that rideth hereby:
Victuals and weapons, they be nothing scant,
Like worthy mariners ourselves we will try.
        Lustily, lustily etc.

Her flags be new trimmed set flaunting aloft,
Our ship for swift swimming, Oh she doth excell:
We fear no enemies, we have escaped them oft;
Of all ships that swimmeth, she bareth the bell.
        Lustily, lustily. etc.

And here is a master excelleth in skill,
And our master's mate, he is not to seek:
And here is a boatswain will do his good will,
And here is a shipboy, we never had the leek.
        Lustily, lustily. etc.

If fortune then fail not, and our next voyage prove,
We will return merrily, and make good cheer,
And hold all together as friends linked in love;
The cans shall be filled with wine, ale and beer.
        Lustily, lustily. etc.

A PLEASANT COMEDY CALLED COMMON CONDITIONS. [*Circa* 1576.]

14. to seek: *without skill.* 16. leek: *like.*

ANONYMOUS

Money: As light as a fly,
In pleasant jollity:
With mirth and melody,
Sing money, money, money.

Money the minion, the spring of all joy,
Money, the medicine that heals each annoy,
Money, the jewel that man keeps in store,
Money, the idol that women adore.
That money am I, the fountain of bliss,
Whereof whoso tasteth, doth never amiss.
Money, money, money.
Sing money, money, money.

THE CONTENTION BETWEEN LIBERALITY AND PRODIGALITY, i. 5. 1602.

5. minion: *darling*.

Prodigality: THE princely heart, that freely spends,
Relieves full many a thousand more,
He getteth praise, he gaineth friends,
And people's love procures therefore.
But pinching fist, that spareth all,
Of due relief the needy robs,
Nought can be caught, where nought doth fall,
There comes no good of greedy cobs.
This issue therefore do I make:
The best deserver draw the stake.

Tenacity: Whilst thou dost spend with friend and foe,
At home che hold the plough by th' tail:
Che dig, che delve, che zet, che zow,
Che mow, che reap, che ply my flail.
A pair of dice is thy delight,
Thou liv'st for most part by the spoil:
I truly labour day and night,
To get my living by my toil:
Chill therefore sure this issue make,
The best deserver draw the stake.

LIBERALITY AND PRODIGALITY, ii. 4.

8. cobs: *misers.* 12. che: *I.* 13. zet: *set, plant;* zow: *sow.* 19. chill: *I will.*

NICHOLAS BRETON

1545?-1626?

*The three men's song, sung the third morning under Her
Majesty's gallery window.*

IN the merry month of May,
In a morn, by break of day,
Forth I walked by the woodside,
Whenas May was in her pride.
There I spied all alone
Phillida and Corydon.
Much ado there was, God wot,
He would love, and she would not.
She said, never man was true:
He said, none was false to you.
He said, he had loved her long:
She said, love should have no wrong.
Corydon would kiss her then;
She said, maids must kiss no men
Till they did for good and all.
Then she made the shepherd call
All the heavens to witness truth,
Never loved a truer youth.
Thus with many a pretty oath,
Yea and nay, and faith and troth,
Such as silly shepherds use,
When they will not love abuse,
Love, which had been long deluded,
Was with kisses sweet concluded:
And Phillida with garlands gay,
Was made the Lady of the May.

THE HONORABLE ENTERTAINMENT GIVEN TO THE QUEEN'S
MAJESTY IN PROGRESS, AT ELVETHAM IN HAMPSHIRE, BY
THE RIGHT HONORABLE THE EARL OF HERTFORD. 1591.

SIR WALTER RALEIGH?

1552?-1618

The Third Song.

Now what is love I pray thee tell:
It is the fountain and the well,
Where pleasure and repentance dwell,
It is perhaps the sansing bell
That rings all in to heaven and hell:
And this is love, and this is love, as I hear tell.

Now what is love I pray you show:
A thing that creeps and cannot go:
A prize that passeth to and fro,
A thing for me, a thing for moe,
And he that proves shall find it so,
And this is love, and this is love, sweet friends, I trow.

THOMAS HEYWOOD'S RAPE OF LUCRECE. 1608.

4. sansing bell: *sanctus bell.* 8. go: *walk.* 10. moe: *more, many.*

ANONYMOUS

Victoria setteth open the casement of her window and with her lute in her hand playeth, and singeth this ditty.

IF love be like the flower that in the night,
When darkness drowns the glory of the skies,
Smells sweet, and glitters in the gazer's sight,
But when the gladsome sun begins to rise,
  And he that views it, would the same embrace,
  It withereth, and loseth all his grace:

Why do I love and like the cursed tree,
Whose buds appear, but fruit will not be seen:
Why do I languish for the flower I see,
Whose root is rot, when all the leaves be green?
  In such a case it is a point of skill
  To follow chance, and love against my will.

FEDELE AND FORTUNIO OR THE TWO ITALIAN GENTLEMEN, i. 2.
Circa 1584.

ANTHONY MUNDAY

1553?-1633

From under the stage, the third antique.

3 Antique: You that seek to sunder love,
    Learn a lesson ere you go;
    And as others pains do prove,
       So abide yourselves like woe.
For I find, and you shall feel
Self same turn of Fortune's wheel:
    Then if wrong be repaid,
    Say deservèd mends is made.

         Exit into the Castle.

JOHN A KENT AND JOHN A CUMBER, iii. MS. 1594.

8. mends: *amends.*

    The fourth out of a tree, if possible it may be.

4 Antique: You stole my love; fie upon ye, fie,
    You stole my love, fie, fie a.
Guessed you but what a pain it is to prove,
    You for your love would die a;
    And henceforth never longer
    Be such a crafty wronger:
But when deceit takes such a fall,
Then farewell sly devise and all.
You stole my love; fie upon ye, fie.
You stole my love, fie, fie a.

         Exit into the Castle.

JOHN A KENT AND JOHN A CUMBER, iii.

*The boy trips round about Oswen and Amery, sing[ing in]
chime and they, the one after the other, lay them [down]
using very sluggish gestures; the ladies amazed [look] about
them.*
    Song to the music within.

SLEEP sweetly, sleep sweetly, sweetly take rest,
Till each go with her choice, where she likes best.

Ladies, cheer up your despairing minds,
    For your friends are near,
That will answer true love in due kind;
    Then never more fear.

JOHN A KENT AND JOHN A CUMBER, iv. 1.

The Song of Robin Hood and his Huntsmen.

Now wend we together, my merry men all,
    Unto the forest side-a:
And there to strike a buck or a doe,
    Let our cunning all be tried-a.

Then go we merrily, merrily on,
    To the greenwood to take our stand,
Where we will lie in wait for our game,
    With our bent bows all in our hand.

What life is there like to Robin Hood?
    It is so pleasant a thing-a:
In merry Sherwood he spends his days,
    As pleasantly as a king-a.

No man may compare with Robin Hood,
    With Robin Hood, Scathlock and John:
Their like was never, nor never will be,
    If in case that they were gone.

They will not away from merry Sherwood,
    In any place else to dwell:
For there is neither city nor town,
    That likes them half so well.

Our lives are wholly given to hunt,
    And haunt the merry green wood:
Where our best service is daily spent
    For our master Robin Hood.

METROPOLIS CORONANTA, THE TRIUMPHS OF ANCIENT DRAPERY.
1615.

ANTHONY MUNDAY?

Weep, weep, ye woodmen wail,
  Your hands with sorrow wring:
Your master Robin Hood lies dead,
  Therefore sigh as you sing.
Here lie his primer and his beads,
  His bent bow and his arrows keen,
His good sword and his holy cross,
  Now cast on flowers fresh and green.
And as they fall, shed tears and say
  Wella, well-a-day, wella, well-a-day:
Thus cast ye flowers and sing,
  And on to Wakefield take your way.

The Death of Robert, Earl of Huntington, Other
Wise Called Robin Hood of Merry Sherwood.
Scene 5. 1601.

5. primer: *book of prayers or devotions.*

JOHN LYLY

1554?-1606

Granichus: O for a bowl of fat canary,
  Rich Palermo, sparkling sherry,
  Some nectar else, from Juno's dairy,
  O these draughts would make us merry.

Psyllus: O for a wench, (I deal in faces,
  And in other daintier things,)
  Tickled am I with her embraces,
  Fine dancing in such fairy rings.

Manes: O for a plump fat leg of mutton,
  Veal, lamb, capon, pig, and coney.
  None is happy but a glutton,
  None an ass but who wants money.

Chorus: Wines, indeed, and girls are good,
But brave victuals feast the blood,
For wenches, wine and lusty cheer,
Jove would leap down to surfeit here.

ALEXANDER AND CAMPASPE, i. 3. 1632.

Song by Apelles

CUPID and my Campaspe played
At cards for kisses, Cupid payed;
He stakes his quiver, bow, and arrows,
His Mother's doves, and team of sparrows,
Loses them too; then down he throws
The coral of his lip, the rose
Growing on's cheek (but none knows how),
With these, the crystal of his brow,
And then the dimple of his chin:
All these did my Campaspe win.
At last, he set her both his eyes;
She won, and Cupid blind did rise.
O Love! has she done this to Thee?
What shall, Alas!, become of me?

ALEXANDER AND CAMPASPE, iii. 5.

Trico Singeth.

WHAT bird so sings, yet so does wail?
O 'tis the ravished Nightingale.
Jug, jug, jug, jug, tereu, she cries,
And still her woes at midnight rise.
Brave prick song! who is't now we hear?
None but the Lark so shrill and clear;
How at heaven's gates she claps her wings,
The morn not waking till she sings.
Hark, hark, with what a pretty throat
Poor Robin red-breast tunes his note;
Hark how the jolly Cuckoos sing
Cuckoo, to welcome in the spring.
Cuckoo, to welcome in the spring.

ALEXANDER AND CAMPASPE, v. 1.

Criticus: MERRY knaves are we three-a.
Molus: When our songs do agree-a.
Calypho: O now I well see-a,
        What anon we shall be-a.
Criticus: If we ply thus our singing,
Molus: Pots must then be flinging.
Calypho: If the drink be but stinging.
Molus: I shall forget the rules of grammar,
Calypho: And I the pit-apat of my hammer.
Chorus: To the tap-house then lets gang, and roar,
        Call hard, 'tis rare to vamp a score,
        Draw dry the tub, be it old or new,
        And part not till the ground look blue.

SAPHO AND PHAO, ii. 3. 1632.

O CRUEL Love! on thee I lay
My curse, which shall strike blind the day:
Never may sleep with velvet hand
Charm thine eyes with sacred wand;
Thy jailers shall be hopes and fears,
Thy prison-mates, groans, sighs and tears;
Thy play, to wear out weary times,
Fantastic passions, vows, and rimes;
Thy bread be frowns, thy drink be gall,
Such as when you Phao call,
The bed thou liest on by despair;
Thy sleep, fond dreams; thy dreams, long care;
Hope (like thy fool) at thy bed's head,
Mocks thee, till madness strike thee dead;
As Phao, thou doest me, with thy proud eyes,
In thee poor Sapho lives, for thee she dies.

SAPHO AND PHAO, iii. 3.

The Song in making of the Arrows.

Vulcan: My shag-hair Cyclops, come let's ply
        Our Lemnian hammers lustily.
        By my wife's sparrows,
        I swear these arrows

Shall singing fly
Through many a wanton's eye.
These headed are with golden blisses,
These silver ones feathered with kisses;
    But this of lead
    Strikes a clown dead,
    When in a dance
    He falls in a trance,
To see his black-brow lass not buss him,
And then whines out for death t' untruss him.
So, so: our work being done, let's play,
Holiday, boys, cry holiday.

SAPHO AND PHAO, iv. 3.

Watch: STAND: who goes there?
    We charge you appear
    'Fore our constable here,
    (In the name of the Man in the Moon.)
    To us billmen relate,
    Why you stagger so late,
    And how you come drunk so soon.
Pages: What are ye, scabs?
Watch: The watch:
    This is the constable.
Pages: A patch.
Constable: Knock 'em down unless they all stand;
    If any run away,
    'Tis the old watchman's play,
    To reach him a bill of his hand.
Pages: O gentlemen, hold,
    Your gowns freeze with cold,
    And your rotten teeth dance in your head.
Epiton: Wine nothing shall cost ye;
Samias: Nor huge fires to roast ye;
Dares: Then soberly let us be led.
Constable: Come, my brown bills, we'll roar,
    Bounce loud at tavern door.
Omnes: And i' th' morning steal all to bed.

ENDYMION, iv. 2. 1632.

Song by Fairies.

The Fairies dance, and with a song pinch him, and he falleth asleep, they kiss Endymion and depart.

Omnes: PINCH him, pinch him, black and blue,
         Saucy mortals must not view
         What the queen of stars is doing,
         Nor pry into our fairy wooing.
1 *Fairy:*   Pinch him blue.
2 *Fairy:*   And pinch him black.
3 *Fairy:*   Let him not lack
         Sharp nails to pinch him blue and red,
         Till sleep has rocked his addlehead.
4 *Fairy:* For the trespass he hath done,
         Spots o'er all his flesh shall run.
         Kiss Endymion, kiss his eyes,
         Then to our midnight heidegyes.

                        ENDYMION, iv. 3.

13. heidegyes: *frolics, revels.*

Omnes: ROCKS, shelves, and sands and seas, farewell.
         Fie! who would dwell
         In such a hell
         As is a ship, which (drunk) does reel,
         Taking salt healths from deck to keel.
Robin: Up were we swallowed in wet graves,
Dick: All soust in waves,
Rafe: By Neptune's slaves.
Omnes: What shall we do being tossed to shore?
Robin: Milk some blind tavern, and there roar.
Rafe: 'Tis brave, my boys, to sail on land,
         For being well manned
         We can cry "Stand."
Dick: The trade of pursing ne'er shall fail,
         Until the hangman cries "Strike sail."
Omnes: Rove then no matter whither,
         In fair or stormy weather.
         And as we live, let's die together,
         One hempen caper, cuts a feather.

                 GALATHEA, i. 4. 1632.

Cupid, Telusa, Eurota, Larissa, enter singing.

Telusa: O YES, O yes! if any maid
   Whom leering Cupid has betrayed
   To frowns of spite, to eyes of scorn,
   And would in madness now see torn
All 3: The boy in pieces, let her come
   Hither, and lay on him her doom.
Eurota: O yes, O yes! has any lost
   A heart which many a sigh hath cost,
   Is any cozened of a tear
   Which, as a pearl, disdain does wear?
All 3: Here stands the thief; let her but come
   Hither, and lay on him her doom.
Larissa: Is any one undone by fire,
   And turned to ashes through desire?
   Did ever any lady weep,
   Being cheated of her golden sleep?
   Stolen by sick thoughts!—the pirate's found,
   And in her tears he shall be drowned.
All 3: Read his indictment, let him hear
   What he's to trust to: Boy, give ear.

          GALATHEA, iv. 2.

A Song of Daphne to the Lute.

Apollo: MY Daphne's hair is twisted gold,
   Bright stars a-piece her eyes do hold,
   My Daphne's brow enthrones the Graces,
   My Daphne's beauty stains all faces;
   On Daphne's cheek grow rose and cherry,
   On Daphne's lip a sweeter berry;
   Daphne's snowy hand but touched does melt,
   And then no heavenlier warmth is felt;
   My Daphne's voice tunes all the spheres,
   My Daphne's music charms all ears.
   Fond am I thus to sing her praise:
   These glories now are turned to bays.

        MIDAS, iv. 1. 1632.

(He pipes, then sings)

Pan: Pan's Syrinx was a girl indeed,
     Though now she's turned into a reed;
     From that dear reed Pan's pipe does come,
     A pipe that strikes Apollo dumb;
     Nor flute, nor lute, nor gittern can
     So chant it as the pipe of Pan:
     Cross-gartered swains and dairy girls
     With faces smug and round as pearls,
     When Pan's shrill pipe begins to play,
     With dancing wear out night and day:
     The bagpipe's drone his hum lays by,
     When Pan sounds up his minstrelsy.
     His minstrelsy! O base! this quill,
     Which at my mouth with wind I fill,
     Puts me in mind, though her I miss,
     That still my Syrinx' lips I kiss.

MIDAS, iv. 1.

(They sing all)

Sing to Apollo, god of day,
Whose golden beams with morning play,
And make her eyes so brightly shine,
Aurora's face is called divine.
Sing to Phœbus and that throne
Of diamonds which he sits upon.
     Io, pæans let us sing
     To Physic's and to Poesy's king.

Crown all his altars with bright fire,
Laurels bind about his lyre,
A Daphnean coronet for his head,
The Muses dance about his bed;
When on his ravishing lute he plays,
Strew his temple round with bays.
     Io, pæans let us sing
     To the glittering Delian king.

MIDAS, v. 3.

Memphio and Stellio singing.

Memphio: O CUPID! monarch over kings,
Wherefore hast thou feet and wings?
It is to show how swift thou art,
When thou woundest a tender heart,
Thy wings being clipped, and feet held still,
Thy bow so many could not kill.

Stellio: It is all one in Venus' wanton school,
Who highest sits, the wise man or the fool:

Fools in love's college
Have far more knowledge
To read a woman over,
Than a neat prating lover.

Nay, 'tis confessed
That fools please women best.

MOTHER BOMBIE, iii. 2. 1632.

Rixula: FULL hard I did sweat,
When hemp I did beat.
Then thought I of nothing but hanging,
The hemp being spun,
My beating was done,
Then I wished for a noise
Of crack-halter boys,
On those hempen strings to be twanging.
Long looked I about,
The City throughout,
4 Pages: And found no such fiddling varlets.
Rixula: Yes, at last coming hither,
I saw four together.
4 Pages: May thy hemp choke such singing harlots.
Rixula: "To whit to whoo," the owl does cry,
"Phip, phip," the sparrows as they fly,
The goose does hiss, the duck cries quack,
"A rope" the parrot, that holds tack.
4 Pages: The parrot and the rope be thine.
Rixula: The hanging yours, but the hemp mine.

MOTHER BOMBIE, iii. 4.

6. noise: *a band of musicians.* 18. holds tack: *holds its own with anyone.*

THOMAS WATSON

1557?-1592

The ditty of the Six Virgins Song.

WITH fragrant flowers we strew the way
And make this our chief holiday:
For though this clime were blest of yore,
Yet was it never proud before.
    O beauteous Queen of second Troy,
    Accept of our unfeigned joy.

Now the air is sweeter than sweet balm,
And satyrs dance about the palm:
Now earth, with verdure newly dight,
Gives perfect sign of her delight.
    O beauteous Queen of second Troy,
    Accept of our unfeigned joy.

Now birds record new harmony,
And trees do whistle melody:
Now every thing that nature breeds
Doth clad itself in pleasant weeds.
    O beauteous Queen of second Troy,
    Accept of our unfeigned joy.

THE HONORABLE ENTERTAINMENT GIVEN TO THE QUEEN'S MAJESTY
IN PROGRESS, AT ELVETHAM IN HAMPSHIRE, BY THE RIGHT HONOR-
ABLE THE EARL OF HERTFORD. 1591.

THOMAS LODGE

1558?-1625

BEAUTY, alas! where wast thou born,
Thus to hold thyself in scorn?
Whenas Beauty kissed to woo thee,
Thou by Beauty dost undo me:
    Heigh-ho, despise me not.

I and thou in sooth are one,
Fairer thou, I fairer none:
Wanton thou, and wilt thou, wanton,
Yield a cruel heart to plant on?
Do me right, and do me reason,
Cruelty is cursed treason.
  Heigh-ho, I love, heigh-ho, I love,
  Heigh-ho, and yet he eyes me not.

A LOOKING GLASS FOR LONDON AND ENGLAND. 1594.

GEORGE PEELE

1558?-1596

The Song. A Quire within and without.

Gods: O IDA, O Ida, O Ida, happy hill,
     This honour done to Ida, may it continue still.
Muses: Ye country gods, that in this Ida wonne,
     Bring down your gifts of welcome,
       For honour done to Ida.
Gods: Behold in sign of joy we sing,
     And signs of joyful welcome bring,
       For honour done to Ida.
Muses: The Muses give you melody to gratulate this chance,
     And Phœbe, chief of Sylvan chase, commands you
       all to dance.
Gods The round in a circle our sportance must be,
dance: Hold hands in a hornpipe all gallant in glee.
Muses: Reverence, reverence, most humble reverence.
Gods: Most humble reverence.

THE ARRAIGNMENT OF PARIS. A PASTORAL, i. 3. 1584.

3. wonne: *dwell.*

Pallas, Juno and Venus enter, Rhanis leading the way. Pan alone sings.

THE God of shepherds, and his mates,
With country cheer salute your states,
Fair, wise and worthy as you be,
And thank the gracious ladies three,
For honour done to Ida.

(The birds sing)

THE ARRAIGNMENT OF PARIS, i. 4.

They sing; and while Œnone singeth, he pipeth.

Œnone: FAIR and fair and twice so fair,
As fair as any may be:
The fairest shepherd on our green,
A love for any lady.

Paris: Fair and fair and twice so fair,
As fair as any may be:
Thy love is fair for thee alone,
And for no other lady.

Œnone: My love is fair, my love is gay,
As fresh as bin the flowers in May,
And of my love my roundelay,
My merry, merry, merry roundelay
Concludes with Cupid's curse:
They that do change old love for new,
Pray Gods they change for worse.

Ambo simul: They that do change, &c.
Œnone: Fair and fair, &c.
Paris: Fair and fair, &c. Thy love is fair, &c.
Œnone: My love can pipe, my love can sing,
My love can many a pretty thing,
And of his lovely praises ring
My merry merry roundelays: Amen to Cupid's curse:
They that do change, &c.

Paris: They that do change, &c.
Ambo: Fair and fair, &c.

THE ARRAIGNMENT OF PARIS, i. 5.

Colin, the enamoured shepherd, singeth his passion of love.

The song.

O GENTLE love, ungentle for thy deed,
  Thou makest my heart
  A bloody mark
With piercing shot to bleed.
Shoot soft sweet love, for fear thou shoot amiss,
  For fear too keen
  Thy arrows been,
And hit the heart where my beloved is.
Too fair that fortune were, nor never I
  Shall be so blest
  Among the rest
That love shall seize on her by sympathy.
That since with Love my prayers bear no boot,
  This doth remain
  To cease my pain,
I take the wound, and die at Venus' foot.

     THE ARRAIGNMENT OF PARIS, iii. 1.

Œnone singeth as she sits.

Œnone's Complaint.

MELPOMENE, the muse of tragic songs,
With mournful tunes, in stole of dismal hue,
Assist a silly nymph to wail her woe,
And leave thy lusty company behind.

Thou luckless wreath, becomes not me to wear
The poplar tree for triumph of my love.
Then as my joy, my pride of love, is left,
Be thou unclothed of thy lovely green.

And in thy leaves my fortune written be,
And them some gentle wind let blow abroad,
That all the world may see how false of love
False Paris hath to his Œnone been.

     THE ARRAIGNMENT OF PARIS, iii. 3.

The Shepherds bring in Colin's hearse singing.

WELLADAY. Welladay:
Poor Colin, thou art going to the ground,
The love whom Thestylis hath slain,
Hard heart, fair face, fraught with disdain,
Disdain in love a deadly wound.
Wound her, sweet Love, so deep again,
That she may feel the dying pain
Of this unhappy shepherds swain,
And die for love as Colin died, as Colin died.

THE ARRAIGNMENT OF PARIS, iii. 5.

Thestylis singeth and the Shepherds reply.

THE strange effects of my tormented heart,
Whom cruel love hath woeful prisoner caught,
Whom cruel hate hath unto bondage brought,
Whom wit no way of safe escape hath taught,
Enforce me say in witness of my smart:
There is no pain to foul disdain in hardy suits of love.
Shep.:   There is no pain &c.
Thest.: Cruel farewell. *Shep.:* Cruel farewell.
Thest.: Most cruel thou, of all that nature framed.
Shep.:   Most cruel &c.
Thest.: To kill thy love with thy disdain.
Shep.:   To kill thy love with thy disdain.
Thest.: Cruel disdain, so live thou named.
Shep.:   Cruel disdain &c.
Thest.: And let me die of Iphis' pain.
Shep.:   A life too good for thy disdain.
Thest.: Sith this my stars to me allot,
           And thou my love hast all forgot. *Exit Thest.*
Shep.:   And thou &c.

The shepherds carry out Colin.

The grace of this song is in the Shepherds' echo to her verse.

THE ARRAIGNMENT OF PARIS, iii. 5.

6. to: *compared with.*

His golden locks time hath to silver turned;
    O time too swift, O swiftness never ceasing!
His youth 'gainst time and age hath ever spurned,
    But spurned in vain; youth waneth by increasing:
Beauty, strength, youth, are flowers but fading seen;
Duty, faith, love, are roots, and ever green.

His helmet now shall make a hive for bees,
    And lover's sonnets turned to holy psalms,
A man-at-arms must now serve on his knees,
    And feed on prayers, which are age his alms:
But though from court to cottage he depart,
His saint is sure of his unspotted heart.

And when he saddest sits in homely cell,
    He'll teach his swains this carol for a song:
"Blessed be the hearts that wish my sovereign well,
    Cursed be the souls that think her any wrong!"
Goddess, allow this agèd man his right,
To be your beadsman now that was your knight.

                              POLYHYMNIA. 1590.

WHAT thing is love? for (well I wot) love is a thing.
It is a prick, it is a sting,
It is a pretty, pretty thing;
It is a fire, it is a coal,
Whose flame creeps in at every hole;
And as my wit doth best devise,
Love's dwelling is in ladies' eyes:
From whence do glance love's piercing darts,
That make such holes into our hearts;
And all the world herein accord
Love is a great and mighty lord,
And when he list to mount so high,
With Venus he in heaven doth lie,
And evermore hath been a god
Since Mars and she played even and odd.

                    THE HUNTING OF CUPID. [1591?]

Coridon and Melampus' Song.

A Song to be sung for a wager—a dish of damsons new gathered off the trees.

Cor.: MELAMPUS, when will love be void of fears?
Mel.: When jealousy hath neither eyes nor ears.
Cor.: Melampus, when will love be thoroughly shrieved?
Mel.: When it is hard to speak, and not believed.
Cor.: Melampus, when is love most malcontent?
Mel.: When lovers range and bear their bows unbent.
Cor.: Melampus, tell me when love takes least harm?
Mel.: When swains' sweet pipes are puffed, and trulls are warm.
Cor.: Melampus, tell me when is love best fed?
Mel.: When it has sucked the sweet that ease hath bred.
Cor.: Melampus, when is time in love ill-spent?
Mel.: When it earns meed and yet receives no rent.
Cor.: Melampus, when is time well-spent in love?
Mel.: When deeds win meed, and words love-works do prove.

THE HUNTING OF CUPID (ENGLAND'S HELICON, 1600).

WHENAS the rye reach to the chin,
And chopcherry, chopcherry ripe within,
Strawberries swimming in the cream,
And schoolboys playing in the stream;
Then O, then O, then O, my true love said,
'Till that time come again,
She could not live a maid.

THE OLD WIVES TALE. 1595.

Enter the harvest men a-singing, with this song double repeated.

All ye that lovely lovers be, pray you for me,
Lo here we come a-sowing, a-sowing,
And sow sweet fruits of love:
In your sweet hearts well may it prove.

Exeunt.

*Enter the harvest men singing, with women in their hands.
Here they begin to sing, the song doubled.*

>Lo here we come a-reaping, a-reaping,
>To reap our harvest fruit,
>And thus we pass the year so long,
>And never be we mute.

>>*Exit the harvest men.*

>>>THE OLD WIVES TALE.

*He [Prologus] draws a curtain, and discovers Bethsabe with
her maid bathing over a spring: she sings, and David sits
above, viewing her.*

>>*Song.*

>HOT sun, cool fire, tempered with sweet air,
>Black shade, fair nurse, shadow my white hair:
>Shine, sun; burn, fire; breathe, air, and ease me;
>Black shade, fair nurse, shroud me, and please me:
>Shadow, my sweet nurse, keep me from burning,
>Make not my glad cause cause of mourning.
>>Let not my beauty's fire
>>Inflame unstaid desire,
>>Nor pierce any bright eye
>>That wandereth lightly.

>THE LOVE OF KING DAVID AND FAIR BETHSABE. 1599.

ANONYMOUS

*Enter Strumbo, Dorothy, Trumpart, cobbling shoes and sing-
ing.*

>*Trum:* WE cobblers lead a merry life:
>*All:* Dan, dan, dan, dan:
>*Strum:* Void of all envy and of strife:
>*All:* Dan diddle dan.
>*Dor:* Our ease is great, our labour small:
>*All:* Dan, dan, dan, dan.
>*Strum:* And yet our gains be much withall:
>*All:* Dan diddle dan.

Dor: With this art so fine and fair:
All: Dan, dan, dan, dan.
Trum: No occupation may compare:
All: Dan diddle dan.
Strum: For merry pastime and joyful glee:
          Dan, dan, dan, dan.
Dor: Most happy men we cobblers be:
          Dan diddle dan.
Trum: The can stands full of nappy ale:
          Dan, dan, dan, dan:
Strum: In our shop still withouten fail:
          Dan diddle dan.
Dor: This is our meat, this is our food:
          Dan, dan, dan, dan:
Trum: This brings us to a merry mood:
          Dan diddle dan.
Strum: This makes us work for company:
          Dan, dan, dan, dan:
Dor: To pull the tankards cheerfully:
          Dan diddle dan.
Trum: Drink to thy husband, Dorothy,
          Dan, dan, dan, dan:
Dor: Why, then, my Strumbo, there's to thee:
          Dan diddle dan:
Strum: Drink thou the rest, Trumpart, amain:
          Dan, dan, dan, dan.
Dor: When that is gone, we'll fill't again:
          Dan diddle dan.

THE LAMENTABLE TRAGEDY OF LOCRINE, ii. 2. 1595.

ANONYMOUS

YE sacred fires, and powers above,
Forge of desires working love,
Cast down your eye, cast down your eye
Upon a maid in misery.
My sacrifice is lovers blood:
And from eyes salt tears a flood:
All which I spend, all which I spend
For thee, Ascanio, my dear friend:

And though this hour I must feel
The bitter sour of pricking steel,
Yet ill or well, yet ill or well
To thee Ascanio still farewell.

THE MAID'S METAMORPHOSIS, i. 1600.

Enter at one door, Mopso singing.

Mop: TERLITELO, Terlitelo, terlitelee, terlo,
So merrily this shepherds boy
His horn that he can blow,
Early in a morning, late, late in an evening,
And ever sat this little boy,
So merrily piping.

Enter at the other door, Frisco singing.

Fris: Can you blow the little horn?
Well, well, and very well.
And can you blow the little horn,
Amongst the leaves green?

Enter Joculo in the midst singing.

Joc: Fortune my foe, why dost thou frown on me?
And will my fortune never better be:
Wilt thou I say, for ever breed my pain?
And wilt thou not restore my joys again?

THE MAID'S METAMORPHOSIS, ii.

Enter the Fairies, singing and dancing.

By the moon we sport and play,
With the night begins our day:
As we dance the dew doth fall,
Trip it, little urchins all:
Lightly as the little bee,
Two by two, and three by three:
And about go we, and about go we.

THE MAID'S METAMORPHOSIS, ii.

They all dance in a ring, and sing as followeth.

ROUND about, round about, in a fine ring a:
Thus we dance, thus we dance, and thus we sing a.
Trip and go, to and fro, over this green a:
All about, in and out, for our brave Queen a.

We have danced round about, in a fine ring a:
We have danced lustily, and thus we sing a.
All about, in and out, over this green a:
To and fro, trip and go, to our brave Queen a.

THE MAID'S METAMORPHOSIS, ii.

AMIDST the mountain Ida's groves,
Where Paris kept his herd,
Before the other ladies all,
He would have thee preferred.
Pallas for all her painting then,
Her face would seem but pale:
Then Juno would have blushed for shame,
And Venus looked stale.
Eurymine, thy self alone
Shouldst bear the golden ball:
So far would thy most heavenly form
Excell the others all.
O happy Phœbus, happy then,
Most happy should I be:
If fair Eurymine would please,
To join in love with me.

THE MAID'S METAMORPHOSIS, iii. 1.

Gemulo: As little lambs lift up their snowy sides,
          When mounting lark salutes the gray-eyed morn:
Silvio: As from the oaken leaves the honey glides,
          Where nightingales record upon the thorn.
Gemulo: So rise my thoughts.
Silvio: So all my sense cheer
Gemulo: When she surveys my flocks,
Silvio: And she my dear.
Gemulo: Eurymine.

Silvio: Eurymine.
Gemulo: Come forth,
Silvio: Come forth,
Gemulo: Come forth and cheer these plains.

(*And both sing this together, when they have sung it single.*)

Silvio: The wood-man's love,
Gemulo: And lady of the swains.

THE MAID'S METAMORPHOSIS, iv.

ALL hail fair Phœbus, in thy purple throne,
Vouchsafe the regarding of our deep moan.
Hide not, Oh hide not, thy comfortable face,
But pity, but pity a virgin's poor case.

THE MAID'S METAMORPHOSIS, v.

SINCE painful sorrow's date hath end,
And time hath coupled friend with friend:
Rejoice we all, rejoice and sing,
Let all these groves of Phœbus ring.
Hope having won, despair is vanished:
Pleasure revives, and care is banished.
Then trip we all this roundelay,
And still be mindful of the bay.

THE MAID'S METAMORPHOSIS, v.

ANONYMOUS

Enter the Nymphs and Satyrs singing.

SATYRS sing, let sorrow keep her cell,
Let warbling echoes ring,
And sounding music yell
Through hills, through dales, sad grief and care to kill
In him long since, alas, hath grieved his fill.

Sleep no more, but wake and live content,
Thy grief the nymphs deplore,

The sylvan gods lament
To hear, to see thy moan, thy loss thy love:
Thy plaints to tears the flinty rocks do move.

Grieve not then, the Queen of Love is mild,
She sweetly smiles on men,
When reason's most beguiled:
Her looks, her smiles, are kind, are sweet, are fair,
Awake therefore and sleep not still in care.

Love intends to free thee from annoy,
His nymphs Sylvanus sends
To bid thee live in joy,
In hope, in joy, sweet love delights embrace,
Fair love herself will yield thee so much grace.

WILY BEGUILED. 1606.

OLD Tithon must forsake his dear,
The lark doth chant her cheerful lay:
Aurora smiles with merry cheer,
To welcome in a happy day.

The beasts do skip,
The sweet birds sing,
The wood nymphs dance,
The echoes ring.

The hollow cave with joy resounds,
And pleasure everywhere abounds:
The Graces, linking hand in hand,
In love have knit a glorious band.

WILY BEGUILED.

ANONYMOUS

LOVE is a law, a discord of such force,
That 'twixt our sense and reason makes divorce.
Love's a desire that to obtain betime,

We lose an age of tears plucked from our prime.
Love is a thing to which we soon consent,
As soon refuse, but sooner far repent.

Then what must women be that are the cause,
That Love hath life? that lovers feel such laws?
They're like the winds upon Lapanthæ's shore,
That still are changing. Oh then love no more.
A woman's love is like that Syrian flower,
That buds and spreads, and withers in an hour.

THE THRACIAN WONDER, i. 1. 1661.

ART thou gone in haste?
  I'll not forsake thee;
Runnest thou ne'er so fast,
  I'll o'ertake thee:
O'er the dales, o'er the downs,
  Through the green meadows,
From the fields through the towns,
  To the dim shadows.

All along the plain
  To the low fountains,
Up and down again
  From the high mountains:
Echo then, shall again
  Tell her I follow,
And the floods to the woods
Carry my holla, holla, ce, la, ho, ho hu.

THE THRACIAN WONDER, i. 1.

LOVE's a lovely lad,
  His bringing up is Beauty,
Who loves him not is mad;
  For I must pay him duty
  Now I am sad.

Hail to those sweet eyes,
  That shine celestial wonder,
From thence do flames arise
  Burns my poor heart asunder,
    Now it fries.

Cupid sets a crown
  Upon those lovely tresses;
Oh spoil not with a frown
  What he so sweetly dresses.
    I'll sit down.

Whither shall I go
  To escape away from folly?
For now there's love I know,
  Or else 'tis melancholy.
    Heigh, heigho.

Yonder lies the snow,
  But my heart cannot melt it:
Love shoots from his bow,
  And my poor heart hath felt it.
    Heigh, heigho.

THE THRACIAN WONDER, ii. 1.

Enter Ariadna, and Titterus after her singing.

OH stay, Oh turn, Oh pity me,
  That sighs, that sues for love of thee,
Oh lack, I never loved before,
  If you deny, I'll ne'er love more.

No hope, no help, then wretched I
  Must lose, must lack, must pine, and die,
Since you neglect when I implore,
  Farewell hard, I'll ne'er love more.

THE THRACIAN WONDER, iv. 1.

SAMUEL DANIEL
1563-1619

ARE they shadows that we see?
And can shadows pleasure give?
Pleasures only shadows be,
Cast by bodies we conceive,
And are made the things we deem
In those figures which they seem.
But these pleasures vanish fast
Which by shadows are exprest.
Pleasures are not, if they last;
In their passing, is their best.
Glory is most bright and gay
In a flash, and so away.
Feed apace then, greedy eyes,
On the wonder you behold.
Take it sudden as it flies,
Though you take it not to hold:
When your eyes have done their part,
Thought must length it in the heart.

TETHYS' FESTIVAL, OR THE QUEEN'S WAKE. 1610.

The Song.

HAD sorrow ever fitter place
  To act his part,
  Than is my heart,
Where it takes up all the space?
  Where is no vein
  To entertain
A thought that wears another face.
Nor will I sorrow ever have
  Therein to be,
  But only thee,
To whom I full possession gave:
  Thou in thy name
  Must hold the same,
Until thou bring it to the grave.

HYMEN'S TRIUMPH. A PASTORAL TRAGI-COMEDY, i. 1. 1615.

The Song of the First Chorus.

LOVE is a sickness full of woes,
    All remedies refusing:
A plant that with most cutting grows,
    Most barren with best using.
        Why so?
More we enjoy it, more it dies;
If not enjoyed, it sighing cries,
        Hey ho.
Love is a torment of the mind,
    A tempest everlasting;
And Jove hath made it of a kind
    Not well, nor full, nor fasting.
        Why so?
More we enjoy it, more it dies;
If not enjoyed, it sighing cries,
        Hey ho.

HYMEN'S TRIUMPH, i. v.

EYES, hide my love, and do not show
    To any but to her my notes,
Who only doth that cipher know
    Wherein we pass our secret thoughts:
Belie your looks in others' sight,
And wrong yourselves to do her right.

HYMEN'S TRIUMPH, iv. 2.

The Fourth Song of the Chorus.

Question: WERE ever chaste and honest hearts
        Exposed unto such great distresses?
Answer: Yes; they that act the worthiest parts,
        Most commonly have worst successes.
    Great fortunes follow not the best,
    It's virtue that is most distrest.

Then, fortune, why do we admire
    The glory of thy great excesses?

Since by thee what men acquire,
  Thy work and not their worth expresses.
Nor dost thou raise them for their good,
But t'have their ills more understood.

HYMEN'S TRIUMPH, iv. 5.

WILLIAM SHAKESPEARE

1564-1616

The Song.

[*Ver*]

WHEN daisies pied, and violets blue,
And cuckoo-buds of yellow hue:
And lady-smocks all silver white,
Do paint the meadows with delight:
The cuckoo then on every tree,
Mocks married men; for thus sings he,
Cuckoo.
Cuckoo, Cuckoo: O word of fear,
Unpleasing to a married ear.

When shepherds pipe on oaten straws,
And merry larks are ploughmen's clocks:
When turtles tread, and rooks and daws,
And maidens bleach their summer smocks:
The cuckoo then on every tree,
Mocks married men; for thus sings he,
Cuckoo.
Cuckoo, Cuckoo: O word of fear,
Unpleasing to a married ear.

Winter.

WHEN icicles hang by the wall,
And Dick the shepherd blows his nail:

And Tom bears logs into the hall,
And milk comes frozen home in pail:
When blood is nipped, and ways be foul,
Then nightly sings the staring owl,
Tu-whit to-who.
    A merry note,
    While greasy Joan doth keel the pot.

When all aloud the wind doth blow,
And coughing drowns the parson's saw:
And birds sit brooding in the snow,
And Marian's nose looks red and raw:
When roasted crabs hiss in the bowl,
Then nightly sings the staring owl,
Tu-whit to-who.
    A merry note,
    While greasy Joan doth keel the pot.

LOVE'S LABOR'S LOST, v. 1598.

Fairies sing.

You spotted snakes, with double tongue,
Thorny hedge-hogs, be not seen,
Newts, and blindworms, do no wrong,
Come not near our fairy queen.
Philomel, with melody,
Sing in our sweet lullaby,
Lulla, lulla, lullaby, lulla, lulla, lullaby,
Never harm, nor spell, nor charm,
Come our lovely lady nigh.
So, good night, with lullaby.
1 Fairy: Weaving spiders, come not here:
Hence, you long-legged spinners, hence!
Beetles black, approach not near;
Worm, nor snail, do no offence.
Philomel, with melody, &c.
2 Fairy: Hence away: now all is well:
One aloof stand sentinel.

A MIDSUMMER'S NIGHT'S DREAM, ii. 1600.

THE ousel cock, so black of hue,
With orange tawny bill,
The throstle, with his note so true,
The wren with little quill.

The finch, the sparrow, and the lark,
The plainsong cuckoo gray,
Whose note full many a man doth mark,
And dares not answer nay.

A MIDSUMMER'S NIGHT'S DREAM, iii.

A Song the whilst Bassanio comments on the caskets to him-self.

TELL me where is fancy bred,
Or in the heart, or in the head,
How begot, how nourished?
    Reply, reply.
It is engendered in the eyes,
With gazing fed, and fancy dies
In the cradle where it lies.
Let us all ring fancy's knell.
I'll begin it.
Ding, dong, bell.
All: Ding, dong, bell.

THE MERCHANT OF VENICE, iii. 1600.

SIGH no more, ladies, sigh no more,
Men were deceivers ever,
One foot in sea, and one on shore,
To one thing constant never,
Then sigh not so, but let them go,
And be you blithe and bonnie,
Converting all your sounds of woe
Into hey nony nony.

Sing no more ditties, sing no moe,
Of dumps so dull and heavy,
The fraud of men was ever so,
Since summer first was leavy,

Then sigh not so, but let them go,
And be you blithe and bonnie,
Converting all your sounds of woe
Into hey nony nony.

MUCH ADO ABOUT NOTHING, ii. 1600.

PARDON, goddess of the night,
Those that slew thy virgin knight,
For the which with songs of woe,
Round about her tomb they go:
Midnight assist our moan,
Help us to sigh and groan,
Heavily, heavily.
Graves yawn and yield your dead,
Till death be uttered,
Heavily, heavily.

MUCH ADO ABOUT NOTHING, v.

Enter Ophelia playing on a Lute, and her hair down, singing.

How should I your true love know
From another one?
By his cockle hat, and his staff,
And his sandal shoon.

White his shroud as mountain snow,
Larded with sweet flowers,
That bewept to the grave did not go
With true lovers showers.

He is dead and gone, Lady,
He is dead and gone,
At his head a grass green turf,
At his heels a stone.

HAMLET. 1603.

AND will he not come again?
And will he not come again?
No, no, he's gone,
And we cast away moan,
And he never will come again.

His beard as white as snow,
All flaxen was his poll,
　He is dead, he is gone,
　And we cast away moan:
God 'a mercy on his soul.

HAMLET. 1603.

TOMORROW is St. Valentine's day,
　All in the morning betime,
And a maid at your window,
　To be your Valentine:
The young man rose, and donned his clothes,
　And dupped the chamber door,
Let in the maid, that out a maid
　Never departed more.

By Gis, and by saint Charity,
　Away, and fie for shame:
Young men will do't when they come to't,
　By Cock they are to blame.
Quoth she, 'before you tumbled me,
　You promised me to wed.'
'So would I 'a done, by yonder sun,
　If thou hadst not come to my bed.'

HAMLET. 1604.

THEY bore him bare faced on the bier,
And in his grave rain'd many a tear,
Fare you well my Dove.

HAMLET. 1604.

IN youth when I did love, did love,
　Me thought it was very sweet:
To contract O the time for a my behove,
　O me thought a there was nothing a meet.

But age with his stealing steps
　Hath clawed me in his clutch,
And hath shipped me into the land,
　As if I had never been such.

A pickaxe and a spade, a spade,
  For and a shrouding sheet.
O a pit of clay for to be made,
  For such a guest is meet.

HAMLET. 1604.

AND let me the cannikin clink, clink,
  And let me the cannikin clink, clink:
A soldier's a man, a life's but a span,
  Why then let a soldier drink.

OTHELLO, ii. 1622.

THE poor soul sat singing, by a Sycamore tree.
Sing all a green willow:
Her hand on her bosom, her head on her knee,
Sing willow, willow, willow.
The fresh streams ran by her, and murmur'd her moans,
Sing willow, &c.
Her salt tears fell from her, and softened the stones,
Sing willow &c. (*Lay by these*)
Willow, willow. (*Prithee hie thee: he'll come anon*)
Sing all a green willow must be my garland.
Let no body blame him, his scorn I approve.
(*Nay that's not next. Hark, who is't that knocks? Emilia: It's
  the wind*)
I called my love false love; but what said he then?
Sing willow &c.
If I court mo women, you'll couch with mo men.

OTHELLO, iv. 3. 1623.

Enter Ferdinand and Ariel, invisible playing and singing.

Ariel: COME unto these yellow sands,
      And then take hands:
    Curtsied when you have, and kissed
      The wild waves whist:
    Foot it featly here and there,
    And sweet sprites the burden bear.
        Burden dispersedly:
    Hark, hark, bow-wow:
    The watch-dogs bark, bow-wow.

Ariel: Hark, hark, I hear
The strain of strutting chanticleer
Cry cockadidle-dow.

THE TEMPEST, i. 2. 1623.

Ariel: FULL fathom five thy father lies,
Of his bones are coral made:
Those are pearls that were his eyes,
Nothing of him that doth fade
But doth suffer a sea-change
Into something rich and strange:
Sea nymphs hourly ring his knell.
Burden. Ding-dong.
Hark now I hear them, ding-dong bell.

THE TEMPEST, i. 2.

Caliban sings drunkenly.

No more dams I'll make for fish,
Nor fetch in firing, at requiring,
Nor scrape trenchering, nor wash dish.
Ban, Ban, Cacaliban
Has a new master, get a new man.

THE TEMPEST, iii. 2.

Ariel sings, and helps to attire him.

WHERE the bee sucks, there suck I,
In a cowslip's bell I lie,
There I couch when owls do cry,
On the bat's back I do fly
After summer merrily.
Merrily, merrily, shall I live now,
Under the blossom that hangs on the bough.

THE TEMPEST, v. 1.

WHO is Sylvia? what is she?
That all our swains commend her?
Holy, fair, and wise is she,
The heaven such grace did lend her,
That she might admired be.

Is she kind as she is fair?
For beauty lives with kindness:
Love doth to her eyes repair,
To help him of his blindness:
    And being help'd, inhabits there.

Then to Sylvia, let us sing,
That Sylvia is excelling;
She exceeds each mortal thing
Upon the dull earth dwelling.
    To her let us garlands bring.

THE TWO GENTLEMEN OF VERONA, iv. 2. 1623.

FIE on sinful fantasy: Fie on lust, and luxury:
Lust is but a bloody fire, kindled with unchaste desire,
    Fed in heart whose flames aspire,
    As thoughts do blow them higher and higher.
Pinch him (Fairies) mutually: Pinch him for his villainy.
    Pinch him, and burn him, and turn him about,
    Till candles, and star-light, and moonshine be out.

THE MERRY WIVES OF WINDSOR, v. 5. 1623.

Enter Mariana, and Boy singing.

TAKE, oh take those lips away,
    That so sweetly were forsworn,
And those eyes, the break of day,
    Lights that do mislead the morn;
But my kisses bring again, bring again,
Seals of love, but sealed in vain, sealed in vain.

MEASURE FOR MEASURE, iv. 1. 1623.

Enter Amiens, Jaques, and others.

UNDER the greenwood tree,
Who loves to lie with me,
And turn his merry note
Unto the sweet bird's throat:

Come hither, come hither, come hither,
   Here shall he see
   No enemy
But winter and rough weather.

     All together here.

   Who doth ambition shun,
   And loves to live i' the sun:
   Seeking the food he eats,
   And pleased with what he gets:
Come hither, come hither, come hither,
   Here shall he see
   No enemy
But winter and rough weather.

   If it do come to pass,
   That any man turn ass,
   Leaving his wealth and ease,
   A stubborn will to please,
Ducdame, ducdame, ducdame,
   Here shall he see
   Gross fools as he,
And if he will come to me.

     As You Like It, ii. 5. 1623.

Blow, blow, thou winter wind,
Thou art not so unkind
   As man's ingratitude;
Thy tooth is not so keen,
Because thou art not seen,
   Although thy breath be rude.
Heigh ho, sing heigh ho, unto the green holly,
Most friendship is feigning, most loving mere folly:
   Then heigh ho, the holly,
   This life is most jolly.

Freeze, freeze, thou bitter sky,
That dost not bite no nigh
   As benefits forgot:
Though thou the waters warp,
Thy sting is not so sharp

As friend remembered not.
Heigh ho, sing heigh ho, unto the green holly,
All friendship is feigning, most loving mere folly:
    Then heigh ho, the holly,
    This life is most jolly.

As You Like It, ii. 6.

It was a lover and his lass,
    With a hey, and a ho, and a hey nonino,
That o'er the green corn-field did pass,
    In the spring time, the only pretty ring time,
When birds do sing, hey ding a ding, ding.
Sweet lovers love the spring.

Between the acres of the rye,
    With a hey, and a ho, and a hey nonino,
These pretty country folks would lie,
    In spring time, &c.

This carol they began that hour,
    With a hey, and a ho, and a hey nonino,
How that a life was but a flower
    In spring time, &c.

And therefore take the present time,
    With a hey, and a ho, and a hey nonino,
For love is crowned with the prime
    In spring time, &c.

As You Like It, v. 3.

Clown sings.

O MISTRESS mine, where are you roaming?
O stay and hear, your true love's coming,
    That can sing both high and low.
Trip no further, pretty sweeting;
Journeys end in lovers' meeting,
    Every wise man's son doth know.

What is love? 'tis not hereafter,
Present mirth hath present laughter:
    What's to come is still unsure:

In delay there lies no plenty,
Then come kiss me sweet and twenty:
Youth's a stuff will not endure.

TWELFTH NIGHT, ii. 3. 1623.

COME away, come away death,
And in sad cypress let me be laid:
Fly away, fly away breath,
I am slain by a fair cruel maid.
My shroud of white, stuck all with yew,
O prepare it.
My part of death no one so true
Did share it.

Not a flower, not a flower sweet
On my black coffin, let there be strown:
Not a friend, not a friend greet
My poor corpse, where my bones shall be thrown:
A thousand thousand sighs to save,
Lay me O where
Sad true lover never find my grave,
To weep there.

TWELFTH NIGHT, ii. 4.

Clown: I AM gone sir, and anon sir,
I'll be with you again:
In a trice, like to the old Vice,
Your need to sustain.
Who with dagger of lath,
In his rage and his wrath,
Cries ah ha, to the devil:
Like a mad lad,
Pare thy nails dad,
Adieu good man devil.

TWELFTH NIGHT, iv. 2.

WHEN that I was and a little tiny boy,
With hey, ho, the wind and the rain,
A foolish thing was but a toy,
For the rain it raineth every day.

But when I came to man's estate,
  With hey, ho, the wind and the rain,
'Gainst knaves and thieves men shut their gate,
  For the rain it raineth every day.

But when I came, alas! to wive,
  With hey, ho, the wind and the rain,
By swaggering could I never thrive,
  For the rain it raineth every day.

But when I came unto my beds,
  With hey, ho, the wind and the rain,
With toss-pots still had drunken heads,
  For the rain it raineth every day.

A great while ago the world begun,
  With hey, ho, the wind and the rain,
But that's all one, our Play is done,
  And we'll strive to please you every day.

TWELFTH NIGHT, v.

Enter Autolycus singing.

WHEN daffodils begin to peer,
With heigh the doxy over the dale,
Why, then comes in the sweet o' the year,
For the red blood reigns in the winter's pale.

The white sheet bleaching on the hedge,
With heigh the sweet birds, O how they sing:
Doth set my pugging tooth on edge,
For a quart of ale is a dish for a king.

The lark, that tirra-lirra chants,
With heigh the thrush and the jay:
Are summer songs for me and my aunts,
While we lie tumbling in the hay.

I have served Prince Florizel, and in my time wore three pile, but now I am out of service.

BUT shall I go mourn for that (my dear)
    The pale moon shines by night:
And when I wander here and there,
    I then do most go right.
If tinkers may have leave to live,
    And bear the sow-skin budget,
Then my account I well may give,
    And in the stocks avouch it.

THE WINTER'S TALE, iv. 3. 1623.

7. pugging: *thieving.*

JOG on, jog on, the footpath way
And merrily hent the stile-a;
A merry heart goes all the day,
Your sad tires in a mile-a.

THE WINTER'S TALE, iv. 3.

Enter Autolycus singing.

LAWN as white as driven snow,
Cypress black as e'er was crow,
Gloves as sweet as damask roses,
Masks for faces, and for noses:
Bugle-bracelet, necklace-amber,
Perfume for a lady's chamber:
Golden quoifs, and stomachers
For my lads to give their dears;
Pins, and poking-sticks of steel.
What maids lack from head to heel:
    Come buy of me, come; come buy, come buy,
    Buy, lads, or else your lasses cry: Come buy.

THE WINTER'S TALE, iv. 4.

9. poking sticks: *rods for stiffening plaits of ruffs.*

Autolycus: GET you hence, for I must go
          Where it fits not you to know.
Dorcas: Whither?
Mopsa: O whither?
Dorcas: Whither?
Mopsa: It becomes thy oath full well,

	Thou to me thy secrets tell.
Dorcas:	Me too: let me go thither.
Mopsa:	Or thou goest to th' grange, or mill,
Dorcas:	If to either thou dost ill,
Autolycus:	Neither.
Dorcas:	What neither?
Autolycus:	Neither.
Dorcas:	Thou hast sworn my love to be,
Mopsa:	Thou hast sworn it more to me.
	Then whither goest? Say whither?

THE WINTER'S TALE, iv. 4.

WILL you buy any tape, or lace for your cape?
    My dainty duck, my dear-a?
Any silk, any thread, any toys for your head
 Of the new'st, and fin'st, fin'st wear-a.
Come to the pedlar, money's a medlar
That doth utter all men's wear-a.

THE WINTER'S TALE, iv. 4.

Music plays. Enobarbus places them hand in hand.

The Song.

COME thou Monarch of the vine,
Plumpy Bacchus, with pink eyne:
In thy fats our cares be drowned,
With thy grapes our hairs be crowned.
    Cup us till the world go round,
    Cup us till the world go round.

ANTONY AND CLEOPATRA, ii. 7. 1623.

HARK, hark, the lark at Heaven's gate sings,
    And Phœbus 'gins arise,
His steeds to water at those springs
    On chaliced flowers that lies:
And winking Mary-buds begin to ope their golden eyes,
With every thing that pretty is, my Lady sweet arise:
    Arise, arise.

THE TRAGEDY OF CYMBELINE, ii. 3. 1623.

Guiderius: FEAR no more the heat o' the sun,
    Nor the furious winter's rages,
Thou thy worldly task hast done,
    Home art gone, and ta'en thy wages.
Golden lads and girls all must,
As chimney-sweepers, come to dust.

Arviragus: Fear no more the frown o' the great,
    Thou art past the tyrant's stroke,
Care no more to clothe and eat,
    To thee the reed is as the oak:
The sceptre, learning, physic, must
All follow this, and come to dust.

Guiderius: Fear no more the lightning-flash.
Arviragus: Nor the all-dreaded thunder-stone.
Guiderius: Fear not slander, censure rash.
Arviragus: Thou hast finished joy and moan.
Both: All lovers young, all lovers must
Consign to thee, and come to dust.

Guiderius: No exorciser harm thee,
Arviragus: Nor no witchcraft charm thee.
Guiderius: Ghost unlaid forbear thee.
Arviragus: Nothing ill come near thee.
Both: Quiet consummation have,
And renowned be thy grave.

CYMBELINE, iv. 2.

THOMAS CAMPION

1567-1620

A Hymn in Praise of Neptune.

OF Neptune's empire let us sing,
At whose command the waves obey:
To whom the rivers tribute pay,
    Down the high mountains sliding.

To whom the scaly nation yields
Homage for the crystal fields
     Wherein they dwell;
And every sea-god pays a gem,
Yearly out of his watery cell,
To deck great Neptune's diadem.

The tritons dancing in a ring,
Before his palace gates, do make
The water with their echoes quake,
     Like the great thunder sounding:
The sea-nymphs chaunt their accents shrill,
And the sirens taught to kill
     With their sweet voice,
Make every echoing rock reply,
Unto their gentle murmuring noise,
The praise of Neptune's empery.

                FRANCIS DAVISON'S A POETICAL RHAPSODY. 1602.

Now hath Flora robbed her bowers
To befriend this place with flowers:
     Strow about, strow about.
The sky rained never kindlier showers.
Flowers with bridals well agree,
Fresh as brides and bridegrooms be:
     Strow about, strow about;
And mix them with fit melody.
     Earth hath no princelier flowers
Than roses white and roses red,
But they must still be mingled:
And as a rose new plucked from Venus' thorn,
So doth a bride her bridegroom's bed adorn.

Divers divers flowers affect
For some private dear respect:
     Strow about, strow about.
Let every one his own protect;
But he's none of Flora's friend
That will not the rose commend.
     Strow about, strow about!

Let princes princely flowers defend:
    Roses, the garden's pride,
Are flowers for love and flowers for kings,
In courts desired and weddings:
And as a rose in Venus' bosom worn,
So doth a bridegroom his bride's bed adorn.

THE DESCRIPTION OF A MASK PRESENTED BEFORE THE KING'S
MAJESTY AT WHITE HALL IN HONOUR OF THE LORD HAYES
AND HIS BRIDE, 1607.

*Dialogue of two voices, a bass and tenor, sung by a Silvan and
an Hour.*

Tenor. Silvan: TELL me gentle hour of night
            Wherein dost thou most delight?
Bass.   *Hour:* Not in sleep. *Silvan:* Wherein then?
    Hour: In the frolic view of men.
    Silvan: Lovest thou music? *Hour:* O, 'tis sweet.
    Silvan: What's dancing? *Hour:* Ev'n the mirth of
            feet.
    Silvan: Joy you in fairies and in elves?
    Hour: We are of that sort ourselves.
            But Silvan say why do you love
            Only to frequent the grove?
    Silvan: Life is fullest of content
            Where delight is innocent.
    Hour: Pleasure must vary, not be long,
            Come then let's close, and end our song.
  Chorus: Yet ere we vanish from this princely sight,
            Let us bid Phœbus, and his states good-night.

THE DESCRIPTION OF A MASK.

A Song of Three Voices with divers Instruments.

NIGHT as well as brightest day hath her delight,
Let us then with mirth and music deck the night,
    Never did glad day such store
        Of joy to night bequeath.
    Her stars then adore,
        Both in Heaven, and here beneath.

Love and beauty, mirth and music yield true joys,
Though the cynics in their folly count them toys.
　　Raise your spirits ne'er so high,
　　　　They will be apt to fall:
　　None brave thoughts envy,
　　　　Who had e'er brave thought at all.

Joy is the sweet friend of life, the nurse of blood,
Patron of all health, and fountain of all good:
　　Never may joy hence depart,
　　　　But all your thoughts attend,
　　Nought can hurt the heart,
　　　　That retains so sweet a friend.

A RELATION OF THE LATE ROYAL ENTERTAINMENT GIVEN BY THE
RIGHT HONOURABLE THE LORD KNOWLES, AT CAWSOME (CAVER-
SHAM) HOUSE, NEAR READING, TO OUR MOST GRACIOUS QUEEN,
QUEEN ANNE IN HER PROGRESS TOWARD THE BATH. 1613.

Woo her, and win her, he that can;
　　Each woman hath two lovers,
So she must take and leave a man,
　　Till time more grace discovers.
This doth Jove to show that want
　　Makes beauty most respected;
If fair women were more scant,
　　They would be more affected.

Courtship and music suit with love,
　　They both are works of passion;
Happy is he whose words can move,
　　Yet sweet notes help persuasion.
Mix your words with music then,
　　That they the more may enter;
Bold assaults are fit for men,
　　That on strange beauties venture.

THE DESCRIPTION, SPEECHES, AND SONGS OF THE LORDS' MASK
PRESENTED IN THE BANQUETING-HOUSE ON THE MARRIAGE
NIGHT OF THE HIGH AND MIGHTY COUNT PALATINE, AND THE
ROYALLY DESCENDED THE LADY ELIZABETH. 1613.

The third song of three parts, with a chorus of five parts.

> WHILE dancing rests, fit place to music granting,
> Good spells the fates shall breathe, all envy daunting,
> Kind ears with joy enchanting, chanting,

Chorus: *Io, Io Hymen.*

> Like looks, like hearts, like loves linked together,
> So must the fates be pleased, so come they hether,
> To make this joy persever, ever.

Chorus: *Io, Io Hymen.*

> Love decks the Spring, her buds to th' air exposing,
> Such fire here in these bridal breasts reposing
> We leave with charms enclosing, closing.

Chorus: *Io, Io Hymen.*

THE DESCRIPTION OF A MASK. AT THE MARRIAGE OF THE RIGHT HONOURABLE THE EARL OF SOMERSET AND THE RIGHT NOBLE LADY FRANCES HOWARD. 1614.

Straight in the Thames appeared four barges with skippers in them, and withal this song was sung.

> COME ashore, come merry mates,
> With your nimble heels and pates:
> Summon every man his knight,
> Enough honoured is this night.
> Now, let your sea-born Goddess come,
> Quench these lights, and make all dumb.
> Some sleep; others let her call,
> And so good-night to all, good-night to all.

This song is sung while the boats pass away:

> HASTE aboard, haste now away,
> Hymen frowns at your delay:
> Hymen doth long night affect;
> Yield him then his due respect.
> The sea-born Goddess straight will come,
> Quench these lights, and make all dumb.
> Some sleep; others she will call,
> And so good-night to all, good-night to all.

THE DESCRIPTION OF A MASK.

THOMAS CAMPION?

The Dance.

ROBIN is a lovely lad,
No lass a smoother ever had.
Tommy hath a look as bright
As is the rosy morning light.
Tib is dark and brown of hue,
But like her colour firm and true.
Jinny hath a lip to kiss
Wherein a spring of nectar is.
Simkin well his mirth can place
And words to win a woman's grace.
Sib is all in all to me,
There is no queen of love but she.
Let us in a lover's round
Circle all this happy ground.
Softly, softly trip and go,
The lightfoot fairies jet it so.
Forward then and back again,
Here and there and everywhere,
Winding to and winding fro,
Skipping high and louting low.
And like lovers hand in hand
March around and make a stand.

THE AIRS THAT WERE SUNG AND PLAYED AT BROUGHAM CAS-
TLE IN WESTMERLAND, IN THE KING'S ENTERTAINMENT. 1618.

THOMAS NASHE

1567-1601?

*Enter Summer, leaning on Autumn's and Winter's shoulders,
and attended on with a train of satyrs and wood-nymphs,
singing.*

FAIR summer droops, droop men and beasts therefore:
So fair a summer look for never more.
All good things vanish, less than in a day,

Peace, plenty, pleasure, suddenly decay.
   Go not yet away, bright soul of the sad year;
   The earth is hell when thou leav'st to appear.

What, shall those flowers that decked thy garland erst,
Upon thy grave be wastefully dispersed?
O trees, consume your sap in sorrow's source;
Streams, turn to tears your tributary course.
   Go not yet hence, bright soul of the sad year,
   The earth is hell when thou leav'st to appear.

    The Satyrs and Wood-nymphs go out singing.

A PLEASANT COMEDY CALLED SUMMER'S LAST WILL AND TESTAMENT.
1600.

*Enter Ver with his train, overlaid with suits of green moss,
representing short grass, singing.*

   SPRING, the sweet Spring, is the year's pleasant king,
   Then blooms each thing, then maids dance in a ring,
   Cold doth not sting, the pretty birds do sing,
   Cuckoo, jugge, jugge, pu we, to witta woo.

   The palm and may make country houses gay,
   Lambs frisk and play, the shepherds pipe all day,
   And we hear aye birds tune this merry lay,
   Cuckoo, jugge, jugge, pu we, to witta woo.

   The fields breathe sweet, the daisies kiss our feet,
   Young lovers meet, old wives a-sunning sit,
   In every street these tunes our ears do greet,
   Cuckoo, jugge, jugge, pu we, to witta woo.
     Spring, the sweet spring.

     SUMMER'S LAST WILL AND TESTAMENT.

*(Here enter three clowns and three maids, singing this song,
dancing.)*

      TRIP and go, heave and ho,
      Up and down, to and fro,
      From the town to the grove,
      Two and two, let us rove

A-maying, a-playing:
Love hath no gainsaying:
So merrily trip and go.

SUMMER'S LAST WILL AND TESTAMENT.

ADIEU, farewell earth's bliss,
This world uncertain is,
Fond are life's lustful joys,
Death proves them all but toys,
None from his darts can fly,
I am sick, I must die;
       Lord have mercy on us.

Rich men, trust not in wealth,
Gold cannot buy you health,
Physic himself must fade.
All things to end are made,
The plague full swift goes by,
I am sick, I must die;
       Lord have mercy on us.

Beauty is but a flower,
Which wrinkles will devour,
Brightness falls from the air,
Queens have died young and fair,
Dust hath closed Helen's eye.
I am sick, I must die;
       Lord have mercy on us.

Strength stoops unto the grave,
Worms feed on Hector brave,
Swords may not fight with fate,
Earth still holds ope her gate,
Come, come, the bells do cry.
I am sick, I must die;
       Lord have mercy on us.

Wit with his wantonness,
Tasteth death's bitterness,
Hell's executioner

Hath no ears for to hear
What vain art can reply.
I am sick, I must die;
   Lord have mercy on us.

Haste therefore each degree
To welcome destiny:
Heaven is our heritage,
Earth but a player's stage,
Mount we unto the sky.
I am sick, I must die;
   Lord have mercy on us.

SUMMER'S LAST WILL AND TESTAMENT.

(Here the satyrs and wood-nymphs carry him out, singing as he came in.)

AUTUMN hath all the summer's fruitful treasure,
Gone is our sport, fled is our Croydon's pleasure:
Short days, sharp days, long nights come on apace,
Ah who shall hide us from the winter's face?
Cold doth increase, the sickness will not cease,
And here we lie, God knows, with little ease.
 From winter, plague and pestilence, good Lord deliver us.

London doth mourn, Lambeth is quite forlorn,
Trades cry, Woe worth that ever they were born:
The want of term is town and city's harm;
Close chambers we do want to keep us warm.
Long banished must we live from our friends:
This low-built house will bring us to our ends.
 From winter, plague and pestilence, good Lord deliver us.

SUMMER'S LAST WILL AND TESTAMENT.

THOMAS MIDDLETON

1570?-1627

LOVE for such a cherry lip
  Would be glad to pawn his arrows;
Venus here to take a sip
  Would sell her doves and teams of sparrows.
    But they shall not so;
      Hey nonny, nonny no.
    None but I this lip must owe,
      Hey nonny, nonny no.

Did Jove see this wanton eye,
  Ganymede must wait no longer;
Phœbe here one night did lie,
  Would change her face and look much younger.
    But they shall not so;
      Hey nonny, nonny no.
    None but I this lip must owe;
      Hey nonny, nonny no.

BLURT MASTER CONSTABLE, V. 1602.

7. owe: *own.*

HAPPY times we live to see,
Whose master is Simplicity:
This is the age where blessings flow,
In joy we reap, in peace we sow;
We do good deeds without delay,
We promise and we keep our day;
We love for virtue, not for wealth,
We drink no healths but all for health;
We sing, we dance, we pipe, we play,
Our work's continual holiday;
We live in poor contented sort,
Yet neither beg nor come at court.

A COURTLY MASQUE; THE WORLD TOST AT TENNIS. 1620.

WEEP eyes, break heart!
My love and I must part.
Cruel fates true love do soonest sever;
O, I shall see thee never, never, never.
O, happy is the maid whose life takes end
Ere it knows parent's frown or loss of friend.
Weep eyes, break heart!
My love and I must part.

A CHASTE MAID IN CHEAPSIDE, v. 1630.

IN a maiden-time professed,
Then we say that life is best;
Tasting once the married life,
Then we only praise the wife.
There's but one state more to try,
Which makes women laugh or cry—
Widow, widow: of these three
The middle's best, and that give me.

THE WITCH, ii. 2. MS. undated.

A Charm Song about a Vessel.

BLACK spirits and white, red spirits and gray,
Mingle, mingle, mingle, you that mingle may.
    Titty, Tiffin, keep it stiff in;
    Firedrake, Puckey, make it lucky;
    Liard, Robin, you must bob in.
Round, around, around, about, about.
All ill come running in, all good keep out.

1 Witch:	Here's the blood of a bat.
Hecate:	Put in that, O put in that.
2 Witch:	Here's libbard's bane.
Hecate:	Put in again.
1 Witch:	The juice of toad, the oil of adder;
2 Witch:	Those will make the younker madder.
Hecate:	Put in, there's all, and rid the stench.
Firestone:	Nay, here's three ounces of the red-haired wench.
All:	Round, around, around, about, about.

THE WITCH, v. 2.

Song by Latrocinio and the other Thieves.

How round the world goes, and every thing that's in it;
The tides of gold and silver ebb and flow in a minute:
From the usurer to his sons, there a current swiftly runs;
From the sons to queans in chief, from the gallant to the
    thief;
From the thief unto his host, from the host to husbandmen;
From the country to the court; and so it comes to us again.
How round the world goes, and every thing that's in it.
The tides of gold and silver ebb and flow in a minute.

THE WIDOW, iii. 1. 1652.

Song in parts by Thieves.

GIVE me fortune, give me health,
Give me freedom, I'll get wealth.
Who complains his fate's amiss,
When he has the wide world his?
He that has the Devil in fee,
Can have but all, and so have we.
Give us fortune, give us health,
Give us freedom, we'll get wealth.
    In every hamlet, town and city,
    He has lands that was born witty.

THE WIDOW, iv. 2.

*Enter a company of Gipsies, men and women, with booties of
hens, and ducks, etc., singing.*

Captain: COME, my dainty doxies,
    My dells, my dells most dear;
    We have neither house nor land,
    Yet never want good cheer.
All: We never want good cheer.
Captain: We take no care for candle rents.
2 Gipsy: We lie. *3 Gipsy:* We snort.
Captain: We sport in tents.
    Then rouse betimes and steal our dinners.
    Our store is never taken

Without pigs, hens, or bacon,
And that's good meat for sinners:
    At wakes and fairs we cozen
    Poor country folks by dozen;
If one have money, he disburses;
Whilst some tell fortunes, some pick purses;
    Rather than be out of use,
    We'll steal garters, hose or shoes,
Boots, or spurs with gingling rowels,
Shirts or napkins, smocks or towels.
    Come live with us, come live with us,
All you that love your eases;
        He that's a gipsy
        May be drunk or tipsy
    At any hour he pleases.
All: We laugh, we quaff, we roar, we scuffle
We cheat, we drab, we filch, we shuffle.

MORE DISSEMBLERS BESIDES WOMEN, iv. 1. 1657.

THOMAS DEKKER

1570?-1632

The First Three Man's Song.

O, THE month of May, the merry month of May,
So frolic, so gay, and so green, so green, so green:
O, and then did I unto my true love say,
Sweet Peg, thou shalt be my Summer's Queen.

Now the nightingale, the pretty nightingale,
The sweetest singer in all the forest's quire,
Entreats thee, sweet Peggy, to hear thy true love's tale,
Lo, yonder she sitteth, her breast against a brier.

But O, I spy the cuckoo, the cuckoo, the cuckoo,
See where she sitteth, come away, my joy:
Come away, I prithee, I do not like the cuckoo
Should sing where my Peggy and I kiss and toy.

O, the month of May, the merry month of May,
So frolic, so gay, and so green, so green, so green:
And then did I unto my true love say,
Sweet Peg, thou shalt be my Summer's Queen.

THE SHOEMAKER'S HOLIDAY, OR THE GENTLE CRAFT. 1600.

The Second Three Man's Song.

COLD's the wind, and wet's the rain,
    Saint Hugh be our good speed:
Ill is the weather that bringeth no gain,
    Nor helps good hearts in need.

Troll the bowl, the jolly nut-brown bowl,
    And here, kind mate, to thee:
Let's sing a dirge for Saint Hugh's soul,
    And down it merrily.

Down-a-down, hey, down-a-down,
    Hey derry derry down-a-down,
    Close with the tenor, boy:
Ho! well done, to me let come,
    Ring compass, gentle joy.

Troll the bowl, the nut-brown bowl,
    And here kind, &c. (*as often as there be men to drink*).

At last, when all have drunk, this verse.

Cold's the wind, and wet's the rain,
    Saint Hugh be our good speed:
Ill is the weather that bringeth no gain,
    Nor helps good hearts in need.

THE SHOEMAKER'S HOLIDAY.

FORTUNE smiles, cry holyday!
Dimples on her cheeks do dwell.
Fortune frowns, cry well-a-day!
Her love is heaven, her hate is hell.
Since heaven and hell obey her power,

Tremble when her eyes do lower,
Since heaven and hell her power obey,
When she smiles cry holyday!
 Holyday with joy we cry,
 And bend, and bend, and merrily
 Sing hymns to Fortune's deity,
 Sing hymns to Fortune's deity.
All: Let us sing merrily, merrily, merrily,
 With our song let heaven resound,
 Fortune's hands our heads have crowned,
 Let us sing merrily, merrily, merrily.

THE PLEASANT COMEDY OF OLD FORTUNATUS. 1600.

Priest: VIRTUE's branches wither, Virtue pines,
 O pity, pity, and alack the time!
 Vice doth flourish, Vice in glory shines,
 Her gilded boughs above the cedar climb.
 Vice hath golden cheeks, O pity, pity,
 She in every land doth monarchize.
 Virtue is exiled from every city,
 Virtue is a fool, Vice only wise.
 O pity, pity, Virtue weeping dies.
 Vice laughs to see her faint (alack the time)
 This sinks; with painted wings the other flies,
 Alack that best should fall, and bad should climb,
 O pity, pity, pity, mourn, not sing,
 Vice is a saint, Virtue an underling.
 Vice doth flourish, Vice in glory shines,
 Virtue's branches wither, Virtue pines.

OLD FORTUNATUS.

 VIRTUE stand aside: the fool is caught,
 Laugh to see him, laugh aloud to wake him,
 Folly's nets are wide, and neatly wrought,
 Mock his horns, and laugh to see Vice take him.
Quire: Ha, ha, ha, ha, ha, laugh, laugh in scorn,
 Who's the fool? The fool, he wears a horn.

 Virtue stand aside, mock him, mock him, mock him,
 Laugh aloud to see him, call him fool.

Error gave him suck, now sorrows rock him,
Send the riotous beast to madness' school.
Quire: Ha, ha, ha, ha, ha, laugh, laugh in scorn,
Who's the fool? The fool, he wears a horn.

Virtue stand aside: your school he hates.
Laugh aloud to see him, mock, mock, mock him.
Vanity and hell keep open gates,
He's in, and a new nurse, Despair, must rock him.
Quire: Ha, ha, ha, ha, ha, laugh, laugh in scorn,
Who's the fool? The fool, he wears a horn.

OLD FORTUNATUS.

ART thou poor yet hast thou golden slumbers?
O, sweet content!
Art thou rich, yet is thy mind perplexed?
O, punishment!
Dost thou laugh to see how fools are vexed
To add to golden numbers golden numbers?
O, sweet content, O, sweet, &c.

Work apace, apace, apace, apace:
Honest labour bears a lovely face,
Then hey noney, noney, hey noney, noney.

Canst drink the waters of the crisped spring?
O, sweet content!
Swim'st thou in wealth, yet sink'st in thine own tears?
O, punishment!
Then he that patiently want's burden bears,
No burden bears, but is a king, a king.
O, sweet content, &c.
Work apace, apace, &c.

THE PLEASANT COMEDY OF PATIENT GRISSILL. 1603.

GOLDEN slumbers kiss your eyes,
Smiles awake you when you rise:
Sleep, pretty wantons, do not cry,
And I will sing a lullaby,
Rock them, rock them, lullaby.

Care is heavy, therefore sleep you,
You are care, and care must keep you:
Sleep, pretty wantons, do not cry,
And I will sing a lullaby,
Rock them, rock them, lullaby.

PATIENT GRISSILL.

BEAUTY arise, show forth thy glorious shining,
Thine eyes feed love, for them he standeth pining,
Honour and youth attend to do their duty
To thee, (their only sovereign) Beauty.
Beauty, arise, whilst we, thy servants, sing
Io to Hymen, wedlock's jocund king.
　Io to Hymen, Io, Io, sing,
　　Of wedlock, love, and youth, is Hymen king.

Beauty arise, Beauty arise, thy glorious lights display,
Whilst we sing Io, glad to see this day.
　Io, Io, to Hymen, Io, Io, sing,
　　Of wedlock, love, and youth, is Hymen king.

PATIENT GRISSILL.

　　OARS, Oars, Oars, Oars:
　　To London hey, to London hey:
　　Hoist up sails and lets away,
　　　For the safest bay
　　For us to land is London shores.
　　Oars, Oars, Oars, Oars:
　　Quickly shall we get to land,
　　If you, if you, if you,
　　Lend us but half a hand.
　　O lend us half a hand.

WESTWARD HO, v. i. 1607.

BRAVE iron! brave hammer! from your sound
The art of music has her ground;
On the anvil thou keep'st time,
Thy knick-a-knock is a smith's best chime.

Yet thwick-a-thwack,
Thwick, thwack-a-thwack, thwack,
Make our brawny sinews crack,
Then pit-a-pat, pat, pit-a-pat, pat,
Till thickest bars be beaten flat.

We shoe the horses of the sun,
Harness the dragons of the moon,
Forge Cupid's quiver, bow, and arrows,
And our dame's coach that's drawn with sparrows.
    Till thwick-a-thwack, &c.

Jove's roaring cannons, and his rammers
We beat out with our Lemnian hammers;
Mars his gauntlet, helm, and spear,
And Gorgon shield, are all made here.
    Till thwick-a-thwack, &c.

The grate which (shut) the day outbars,
Those golden studs which nail the stars,
The globe's case, and the axle-tree,
Who can hammer these but we?
    Till thwick-a-thwack, &c.

A warming-pan to heat earth's bed,
Lying i' th' frozen zone half-dead;
Hob-nails to serve the man i' th' moon,
And sparrowbills to clout Pan's shoon,
    Whose work but ours?
    Till thwick-a-thwack, &c.

Venus' kettles, pots, and pans
We make, or else she brawls and bans;
Tongs, shovels, andirons have their places,
Else she scratches all our faces.
    Till thwick-a-thwack, &c.

LONDON'S TEMPE, OR THE FIELD OF HAPPINESS. [1629?]

28. sparrowbills: *clout-nails for soles of shoes.*

FANCIES are but streams
    Of vain pleasure.
They who by their dreams
    True joys measure,
Feasting, starve; laughing, weep;
Playing, smart; whilst in sleep
    Fools with shadows smiling,
        Wake and find
        Hopes like wind,
    Idle hopes beguiling.
Thoughts fly away, Time hath passed them;
Wake, now awake! see and taste them.

THE SUN'S DARLING, i. 1. 1656.

HAYMAKERS, rakers, reapers, and mowers,
    Wait on your Summer-queen;
Dress up with musk-rose her eglantine bowers,
    Daffodils strew the green;
        Sing, dance, and play,
        'Tis holiday;
    The sun does bravely shine
    On our ears of corn.
        Rich as a pearl
        Comes every girl,
    This is mine, this is mine, this is mine;
Let us die, ere away they be borne.

Bow to the Sun, to our queen, and that fair one
    Come to behold our sports:
Each bonny lass here is counted a rare one,
    As those in princes' courts.
        These and we
        With country glee,
    Will teach the woods to resound,
    And the hills with echoes hollow:
        Skipping lambs
        Their bleating dams,
    'Mongst kids shall trip it round;
For joy thus our wenches we follow.

Wind, jolly huntsmen, your neat bugles shrilly,
    Hounds make a lusty cry;
Spring up, you falconers, the partridges freely,
    Then let your brave hawks fly.
        Horses amain,
        Over ridge, over plain,
The dogs have the stag in chase:
'Tis a sport to content a king.
        So ho ho! through the skies
        How the proud bird flies,
And sousing kills with a grace,
Now the deer falls, hark, how they ring.

THE SUN'S DARLING, iii.

35. sousing: *swooping with speed.*

CAST away care, he that loves sorrow
Lengthens not a day, nor can buy to-morrow:
    Money is trash; and he that will spend it,
    Let him drink merrily, Fortune will send it.
Merrily, merrily, merrily, oh, ho!
Play it off stiffly, we may not part so.

Wine is a charm, it heats the blood too,
Cowards it will arm, if the wine be good too;
    Quickens the wit, and makes the back able,
    Scorns to submit to the watch or constable.
Merrily, &c.

Pots fly about, give us more liquor,
Brothers of a rout, our brains will flow quicker;
    Empty the cask, score up, we care not;
    Fill all the pots again, drink on, and spare not.
Merrily, &c.

THE SUN'S DARLING, iv.

THOMAS HEYWOOD

1570?-1641

*Enter with music (before Diana) six satyrs, after them all
their nymphs, garlands on their heads, and javelins in their
hands, their bows and quivers. The satyrs sing.*

HAIL, beauteous Dian, queen of shades,
That dwells beneath these shadowy glades,
Mistress of all those beauteous maids
   That are by her allowed.
Virginity we all profess,
Abjure the worldly vain excess,
And will to Dian yield no less
   Than we to her have vowed.
The shepherds, satyrs, nymphs, and fauns
For thee will trip it o'er the lawns.

Come, to the forest let us go,
And trip it like the barren doe,
The fauns and satyrs still do so,
   And freely thus they may do.
The fairies dance and satyrs sing,
And on the grass tread many a ring,
And to their caves their venison bring,
   And we will do as they do.
The shepherd, satyrs, nymphs, and fauns
For thee will trip it o'er the lawns.

Our food is honey from the bees,
And mellow fruits that drop from trees,
In chase we climb the high degrees
   Of every steepy mountain,
And when the weary day is past,
We at the evening hie us fast,
And after this, our field repast,
   We drink the pleasant fountain.
The shepherds, satyrs, nymphs, and fauns
For thee will trip it o'er the lawns.

THE GOLDEN AGE, ii. 1. 1611.

Enter Ceres and Proserpine attired like the Moon, with a company of swains and country wenches: They sing.

WITH fair Ceres, Queen of Grain,
The reaped fields we roam, roam, roam,
Each country peasant, nymph, and swain
Sing their harvest home, home, home;
    Whilst the Queen of Plenty hallows
    Growing fields as well as fallows.

Echo, double all our lays,
Make the champians sound, sound, sound
To the Queen of harvest's praise,
That sows and reaps our ground, ground, ground.
    Ceres, Queen of Plenty, hallows
    Growing fields as well as fallows.

(Exeunt singing)

Tempests hence, hence winds and hails,
Tares, cockles, rotten showers, showers, showers,
Our song shall keep time with our flails,
When Ceres sings, none lowers, lowers, lowers.
    She it is whose God-hood hallows
    Growing fields as well as fallows.

THE SILVER AGE, iii. 1613.

8. champians: *champaigns; level, open country.*

PACK, clouds, away, and welcome, day,
With night we banish sorrow.
Sweet air, blow soft; mount, lark, aloft
To give my love good morrow:
Wings from the wind, to please her mind,
Notes from the lark I'll borrow;
Bird, prune thy wing, nightingale, sing,
To give my love good morrow.
    To give my love good morrow,
    Notes from them all I'll borrow.

Wake from thy nest, robin redbreast,
Sing, birds, in every furrow,

And from each bill, let music shrill
Give my fair love good morrow.
Black-bird and thrush, in every bush,
Stare, linnet, and cock-sparrow,
You pretty elves, amongst yourselves,
Sing my fair love good morrow.
  To give my love good morrow,
  Sing, birds, in every furrow.

THE RAPE OF LUCRECE. 1630.

16. stare: *starling*.

COME list and hark,
  The bell doth toll
For some but new
  Departing soul.
And was not that
  Some ominous fowl,
The bat, the night-
  Crow or screech owl?
To these I hear
  The wild-wolf howl
In this black night
  That seems to scowl.
All these my black-
  Book shall enroll
For hark, still, still
  The bell doth toll
For some but now
  Departing soul.

THE RAPE OF LUCRECE.

WE that have known no greater state
Than this we live in, praise our fate:
For courtly silks in cares are spent,
When country's russet breeds content.
The power of scepters we admire;
But sheep-hooks for our use desire.
Simple and low is our condition;
For here with us is no ambition.

We with the sun our flocks unfold,
Whose rising makes their fleeces gold.
"Our music from the birds we borrow;   *These last two*
They bidding us, we them, good morrow."   *lines twice.*

A PASTORAL DRAMA CALLED AMPHRISA OR THE FORSAKEN
SHEPHERDESS. 1637.

THOMAS HEYWOOD?

YE little birds that sit and sing
Amidst the shady valleys,
And see how Phillis sweetly walks
Within her garden-alleys;
Go, pretty birds, about her bower,
Sing, pretty birds, she may not lower,
Ah, me! methinks I see her frown,
   Ye pretty wantons, warble.

Go, tell her through your chirping bills,
As you by me are bidden,
To her is only known my love,
Which from the world is hidden:
Go, pretty birds and tell her so,
See that your notes strain not too low,
For still, methinks, I see her frown,
   Ye pretty wantons, warble.

Go, tune your voices' harmony,
And sing, I am her lover;
Strain loud and sweet, that every note
With sweet content may move her:
And she that hath the sweetest voice,
Tell her I will not change my choice,
Yet still, methinks, I see her frown,
   Ye pretty wantons, warble.

Oh, fly! make haste! see, see, she falls
Into a pretty slumber,
Sing round about her rosy bed,
That waking, she may wonder.

Say to her, 'tis her lover true
That sendeth love to you, to you:
And when you hear her kind reply,
    Return with pleasant warblings.

THE FAIR MAID OF THE EXCHANGE. 1607.

PHŒBUS, unto thee we sing,
O thou great Idalian king:
Thou the God of Physic art,
Of Poetry and Archery;
We sing unto thee with a heart,
Devoted to thy deity:
All bright glory crown thy head,
Thou sovereign of all piety,
Whose golden beams and rays are shed
As well upon the poor as rich,
For thou alike regardest each;
Phœbus unto thee we sing,
O thou great Idalian king.

LOVE'S MISTRESS, iii. 1. 1636.

BEN JONSON

1572-1637

SLOW, slow, fresh fount, keep time with my salt tears;
    Yet slower, yet; O faintly, gentle springs;
List to the heavy part the music bears,
    Woe weeps out her division when she sings:
        "Droop herbs and flowers;
        Fall grief in showers,
        Our beauties are not ours:"
        O, I could still,
Like melting snow upon some craggy hill,
        Drop, drop, drop, drop,
Since nature's pride is now a withered daffodil.

CYNTHIA'S REVELS, i. 2. 1601.

O THAT joy so soon should waste!
   Or so sweet a bliss
     As a kiss
Might not for ever last!
   So sugared, so melting, so soft, so delicious,
     The dew that lies on roses,
     When the morn itself discloses,
       Is not so precious.
   O rather than I would it smother,
   Were I to taste such another;
     It should be my wishing
     That I might die kissing.

CYNTHIA'S REVELS, iv. 3.

THOU more than most sweet glove,
Unto my more sweet love,
Suffer me to store with kisses
This empty lodging that now misses
   The pure rosy hand that ware thee,
   Whiter than the kid that bare thee.
     Thou are soft, but that was softer;
     Cupid's self hath kissed it ofter
     Than e'er he did his mother's doves,
     Supposing her the queen of loves,
      That was thy mistress, best of gloves.

CYNTHIA'S REVELS, iv. 3.

QUEEN and huntress, chaste and fair,
Now the sun is laid to sleep,
Seated in thy silver chair,
State in wonted manner keep:
   Hesperus entreats thy light,
   Goddess excellently bright.

Earth, let not thy envious shade
Dare itself to interpose;
Cynthia's shining orb was made
Heaven to clear, when day did close:
   Bless us then with wished sight,
   Goddess excellently bright.

Lay thy bow of pearl apart,
And thy crystal shining quiver;
Give unto the flying hart
Space to breathe, how short soever:
  Thou that mak'st a day of night,
  Goddess excellently bright.

CYNTHIA'S REVELS, V. 1.

IF I freely may discover,
What would please me in my lover:
  I would have her fair, and witty,
  Savouring more of court than city;
  A little proud, but full of pity;
  Light and humourous in her toying,
  Oft building hopes, and soon destroying,
  Long, but sweet in the enjoying;
Neither too easy nor too hard:
All extremes I would have barred.

She should be allowed her passions,
So they were but used as fashions;
  Sometimes froward, and then frowning,
  Sometimes sickish, and then swowning,
  Every fit with change still crowning.
  Purely jealous, I would have her,
  Then only constant when I crave her;
  'Tis a virtue should not save her.
Thus, nor her delicates would cloy me,
Neither her peevishness annoy me.

THE POETASTER, ii. 2. 1602.

LOVE is blind, and a wanton;
In the whole world, there is scant one
    Such another:
    No, not his mother.
He hath plucked her doves and sparrows,
To feather his sharp arrows,
    And alone prevaileth,
    Whilst sick Venus waileth.

But if Cypris once recover
The wag, it shall behove her
    To look better to him,
    Or she will undo him.

               THE POETASTER, iv. 3.

WAKE, our mirth begins to die,
Quicken it with tunes and wine,
Raise your notes; you're out: fie, fie!
This drowsiness is an ill sign.
We banish him the quire of gods,
    That droops again:
    Then all are men,
For here's not one but nods.

               THE POETASTER, iv. 5.

Her.:   THEN, in a free and lofty strain
         Our broken tunes we thus repair;
Crisp.: And we answer them again,
         Running division on the panting air;
Ambo: To celebrate this feast of sense,
         As free from scandal as offence.
Her.:   Here is beauty for the eye;
Crisp.:   For the ear sweet melody;
Her.:   Ambrosiac odours for the smell
Crisp.: Delicious nectar for the taste;
Ambo: For the touch a lady's waist,
         Which doth all the rest excel.

               THE POETASTER, iv. 5.

FOOLS, they are the only nation
Worth men's envy or admiration;
Free from care or sorrow-taking,
Themselves and others merry making:
All they speak or do is sterling.
Your fool, he is your great man's darling,
And your ladies' sport and pleasure;
Tongue and bable are his treasure.
His very face begetteth laughter,

And he speaks truth, free from slaughter;
He's the grace of every feast,
And sometimes the chiefest guest:
Hath his trencher and his stool,
When wit shall wait upon the fool.
    O, who would not be
        He, he, he?

             . VOLPONE, OR THE FOX, i. 2. 1607.

COME, my Celia, let us prove,
While we can, the sports of love,
Time will not be ours for ever,
He, at length, our good will sever;
Spend not then his gifts in vain.
Suns that set may rise again;
But if once we lose this light,
'Tis with us perpetual night.
Why should we defer our joys?
Fame and rumour are but toys.
Cannot we delude the eyes
Of a few poor household spies?
Or his easier ears beguile,
Thus removed by our wile?
'Tis no sin love's fruits to steal;
But the sweet thefts to reveal:
To be taken, to be seen,
These have crimes accounted been.

                   VOLPONE, iii. 7.

Song.

So Beauty on the waters stood,
When Love had severed earth from flood!
So when he parted air from fire,
He did with concord all inspire!
And then a motion he them taught,
That elder than himself was thought.
Which thought was yet the child of earth,
For Love is elder than his birth.

8. his: *its*.

Song. By a treble voice.

IF all these Cupids, now, were blind
    As is their wanton brother;
Or play should put it in their mind
    To shoot at one another:
What pretty battle they would make
If they their objects should mistake
    And each one wound his mother!

which was seconded by another treble thus:

IT was no policy of court,
    Allbe the place were charmed,
To let in earnest, or in sport,
    So many loves in, armed.
For say, the Dames should, with their eyes,
Upon the hearts here mean surprise,
    Were not the men like harmed?

to which a tenor answered

YES, were the Loves or false or straying;
Or Beauties not their beauty weighing:
But here, no such deceipt is mixed,
Their flames are pure, their eyes are fixed:
They do not war, with different darts,
But strike a music of like hearts.

*After which songs, they danced Galliards and Corantos and
with those excellent graces that the music, appointed to celebrate them, showed that it could be silent no longer: but by
the first tenor admired them thus:*

Song.

HAD those, that dwell in error foul,
And hold that women have no soul,
But seen these move, they would have then
Said, Women were the souls of men.
So they do move each heart and eye
With the world's soul, true harmony.

THE MASQUE OF BEAUTY. [1609?]

The Satyrs fell suddenly into this catch.

> Buzz, quoth the Blue-Fly,
> Hum, quoth the Bee:
> Buzz and hum, they cry,
> And so do we.
> In his ear, in his nose,
> Thus, do you see?
> He eat the dormouse,
> Else it was he.

OBERON, THE FAIRY PRINCE. A MASQUE OF PRINCE HENRY'S. 1616.

STILL to be neat, still to be drest,
As you were going to a feast;
Still to be powdered, still perfumed:
·Lady, it is to be presumed,
Though art's hid causes are not found,
All is not sweet, all is not sound.

Give me a look, give me a face,
That makes simplicity a grace;
Robes loosely flowing, hair as free:
Such sweet neglect more taketh me
Than all the adulteries of art.
They strike mine eyes, but not my heart

EPICŒNE, OR THE SILENT WOMAN, i. 1. 1616.

Chorus.

SPRING all the graces of the age,
And all the Loves of time;
Bring all the pleasures of the stage,
And relishes of rime:
Add all the softnesses of courts,
The looks, the laughters, and the sports:
And mingle all their sweets and salts,
That none may say the Triumph halts.

NEPTUNE'S TRIUMPH FOR THE RETURN OF ALBION. 1624.

Proteus, Portunus, Saron, go up to the Ladies with this Song.

Pro.:   COME, noble nymphs, and do not hide
     The joys for which you so provide.
Sar.:   If not to mingle with the men,
     What do you here? Go home again.
Por.:   Your dressings do confess,
     By what we see, so curious parts
     Of Pallas and Arachne's arts,
        That you could mean no less.
Pro.:   Why do you wear the silk-worm's toils;
     Or glory in the shellfish' spoils?
     Or strive to show the grains of ore,
     That you have gathered on the shore,
        Whereof to make a stock
     To graft the greener emerald on
     Or any better-watered stone?
Sar.:   Or ruby of the rock?
Pro.:   Why do you smell of ambergrise,
     Of which was formed Neptune's niece,
     The Queen of Love, unless you can,
     Like sea-born Venus, love a man?
Sar.:   Try, put yourselves unto 't.
Chorus: Your looks, your smiles, and thoughts that meet,
     Ambrosian hands, and silver feet,
       Do promise you will do 't.

NEPTUNE'S TRIUMPH.

SEE the chariot at hand here of Love
    Wherein my Lady rideth!
Each that draws is a swan or a dove,
    And well the car Love guideth.
As she goes, all hearts do duty
    Unto her beauty;
And enamoured do wish, so they might
    But enjoy such a sight,
That they still were to run by her side,
Through swords, through seas, whither she would ride.

Do but look on her eyes! they do light—
    All that Love's world compriseth!

Do but look on her hair! it is bright
  As Love's star when it riseth!
Do but mark, her forehead's smoother
  Than words that soothe her!
And from her arched brows such a grace
  Sheds itself through the face,
As alone there triumphs to the life
All the gain, all the good of the elements' strife!

Have you seen but a bright lily grow,
  Before rude hands have touched it?
Have you marked but the fall of the snow,
  Before the soil hath smutched it?
Have you felt the wool o' the beaver?
  Or swan's down, ever?
Or have smelt o' the bud o' the brier?
  Or the nard i' the fire?
Or have tasted the bag o' the bee?
O, so white! O, so soft! O, so sweet is she!

> Stanzas 2 and 3 from THE DEVIL IS AN ASS, ii. 6. 1631.
> Stanza 1 from UNDERWOODS in the 1641 folio.

THE faery beam upon you,
The stars to glister on you;
  A moon of light,
  In the noon of night,
Till the fire-drake hath o'ergone you.

The wheel of fortune guide you,
The boy with the bow beside you,
  Run aye in the way,
  Till the bird of day,
And the luckier lot betide you.

> A MASQUE OF THE GYPSIES METAMORPHOSED. 1640.

THOUGH I am young and cannot tell
Either what Death or Love is well,
Yet I have heard they both bear darts,
And both do aim at human hearts;
And then again, I have been told,

Love wounds with heat, as Death with cold;
So that I fear they do but bring
Extremes to touch, and mean one thing.

As in a ruin, we it call
One thing to be blown up, or fall;
Or to our end, like way may have
By a flash of lightning, or a wave:
So Love's inflamed shaft, or brand,
May kill as soon as Death's cold hand;
Except Love's fires the virtue have
To fright the frost out of the grave.

THE SAD SHEPHERD, i. 5. 1640.

Song 4.

AN eye of looking back were well,
   Or any murmur that would tell
   Your thoughts, how you were sent,
     And went
To walk with Pleasure, not to dwell.
These, these are hours by Virtue spared
Herself, she being her own reward:
   But she will have you know
     That though
Her sports be soft, her life is hard:
   You must return unto the Hill
     And there advance
With labour, and inhabit still
    That height and crown,
From whence you ever may look down
    Upon triumphed chance.
She, she it is in darkness shines,
'Tis she that still herself refines.
    By her own light to every eye:
More seen, more known when vice stands by.
   And though a stranger here on earth,
   In Heaven she hath her right of birth:
    There, there is Virtue's seat,
    Strive to keep her your own,

'Tis only she can make you great,
Though place here makes you known.

PLEASURE RECONCILED TO VIRTUE. 1640.

Hymn I.

1.   OF Pan we sing, the best of singers, Pan
        That taught us swains how first to tune our lays,
        And on the pipe more airs than Phœbus can.
Chorus: Hear, O you groves, and hills resound his praise.

2.   Of Pan we sing, the best of leaders, Pan
        That leads the Naiads and the Dryads forth;
        And to their dances more than Hermes can.
Chorus: Hear, O you groves, and hills resound his worth.

3.   Of Pan we sing, the best of hunters, Pan
        That drives the hart to seek unused ways,
        And in the chase more than Silvanus can.
Chorus: Hear, O you groves, and hills resound his praise.

4.   Of Pan we sing, the best of shepherds, Pan,
        That keeps our flocks and us, and both leads forth
        To better pastures than great Pales can.
Chorus: Hear, O you groves, and hills resound his worth.
        And while his powers and praises thus we sing,
        The valleys let rebound, and all the rivers ring.

PAN'S ANNIVERSARY; OR, THE SHEPHERDS HOLIDAY. 1640.

Hymn III.

IF yet, if yet
Pan's orgies you will further fit,
See where the silver-footed fays do sit,
    The nymphs of wood and water;
    Each tree's and fountain's daughter,
Go take them forth, it will be good
To see some wave it like a wood,
And others wind it like a flood;

In springs,
And rings,
Till the applause it brings,
Wakes Echo from her seat,
The closes to repeat.
(*Echo:* The closes to repeat.)
Echo the truest oracle on ground,
Though nothing but a sound.
(*Echo:* Though nothing but a sound.)
Beloved of Pan, the valley's queen.
(*Echo:* The valley's queen)
And often heard, though never seen.
(*Echo:* Though never seen.)

PAN'S ANNIVERSARY.

ANONYMOUS

Philomusus sings.

How can he sing whose voice is hoarse with care?
How can he play whose heart strings broken are?
How can he keep his rest that ne'er found rest?
How can he keep his time whom time ne'er blest?
Only he can in sorrow bear a part,
With untaught hand and with untunèd heart.
Fond arts farewell, that swallowed have my youth.
Adieu vain muses that have wrought my ruth.
Repent fond sire that train'dst thy hapless son
In learning's lore, since bounteous alms are done.
Cease, cease harsh tongue, untuned music rest:
Entomb thy sorrows in thy hollow breast.

THE RETURN FROM PARNASSUS, V. I. 1606.

ANONYMOUS

SISTER, awake, close not your eyes,
The day her light discloses;
And bright the morning doth arise
Out of her bed of roses.

See the clear sun, the world's bright eye,
    In at our window peeping;
Lo, how he blusheth to espy
    Us idle wenches sleeping.
Therefore awake, make haste I say,
    And let us without staying
All in our gowns of green so gay
    Into the park a maying.

    EVERY WOMAN IN HER HUMOR. 1609. (See Notes.)

My love can sing no other song,
But still complains I did her wrong.
Believe her not; it was not so,
I did but kiss her and let her go.

And now she swears I did—But what?
Nay, nay, I must not tell you that.
And yet I will, it is so sweet
As "te-he, ta-ha" when lovers meet.

But women's words they are heedless
To tell you more it is needless.
I ran and caught her by the arm,
And then I kissed her; this was no harm.

But she, alas, is angry still,
Which showeth but a woman's will.
She bites the lip and cries "fie, fie."
And kissing sweetly away she doth fly.

Yet sure her looks bewrays content,
And cunningly her brawls are meant,
As lovers use to play and sport
When time and leisure is too too short.

    EVERY WOMAN IN HER HUMOR. (See Notes.)

Enter the Masque and the Song.

CHANT birds in every bush,
The blackbird and the thrush,
The chirping nightingale,

The mavis and wagtail,
The linet and the lark,
Oh how they begin, hark, hark.

EVERY WOMAN IN HER HUMOR.

JOHN MARSTON

1575?-1634

O Love, how strangely sweet
  Are thy weak passions,
That love and joy should meet
  In self same fashions.
O who can tell
  The cause why this should move?
But only this:
  No reason ask of Love.

THE DUTCH COURTEZAN, V. I. 1605.

JOHN MARSTON?

The Players Song.

THE nut-brown ale, the nut-brown ale,
Puts down all drink when it is stale,
The toast, the nutmeg, and the ginger
Will make a sighing man a singer.
Ale gives a buffet in the head,
But ginger under-props the brain:
When ale would strike a strong man dead,
Then nutmeg tempers it again.
The nut-brown ale, the nut-brown ale,
Puts down all drink when it is stale.

HISTRIOMASTIX, OR THE PLAYER WHIPT, i. I. 1610.

Enter harvest-folks with a bowl: after them, Peace leading in Plenty. Plutus with ingots of gold. Ceres with sheaves: Bacchus with grapes.

The Harvest Folks Song.

HOLIDAY, O blessed morn,
This day plenty hath been born,
Plenty is the child of Peace;
To her birth the Gods do press,
Full crown'd mazers Bacchus brings,
With liquor which from grapes he wrings:
Holiday, O blessed morn,
This day Plenty hath been born,
Holiday let's loudly cry,
For joy of her nativity.
Ceres with a bounteous hand
Doth at Plenty's elbow stand:
Binding mixèd coronets
Of wheat which on her head she sets.
Holiday, O blessed morn,
This day Plenty hath been born,
Holiday lets loudly cry,
For joy of her nativity.

HISTRIOMASTIX, i. 1.

ANONYMOUS

THE hour of sweety night decays apace,
And now warm beds are better than this place.
All time is long that is unwilling spent,
But hours are minutes when they yield content:
The gathered flowers we love that breathe sweet scent,
But loathe them, their sweet odours being spent.
It is a life is never ill
To lie and sleep in roses still.

The rarer pleasure is it is more sweet,
And friends are kindest when they seldom meet.
Who would not hear the nightingale still sing,

Or who grew ever weary of the spring?
The day must have her night, the spring her fall,
All is divided, none is lord of all:
>   It were a most delightful thing
>   To live in a perpetual spring.

THE MONTEBANK'S MASQUE. MS. Acted 1618.

SAMUEL ROWLEY?

?-1624

A table set out covered with black: two waxen tapers: the King's picture at one end, a crucifix at the other, Onælia walking discontentedly weeping to the crucifix, her maid with her.

Quest.: OH, sorrow, sorrow, say where dost thou dwell?
Ans.:   In the lowest room of hell.
Quest.: Art thou born of human race?
Ans.:   No, no, I have a fury's face.
Quest.: Art thou in city, town, or court?
Ans.:   I to every place resort.
Quest.: Oh, why into the world is sorrow sent?
Ans.:   Men afflicted best repent.
Quest.: What does thou feed on?
Ans.:   Broken sleep.
Quest.: What takest thou pleasure in?
Ans.:   To weep.
          To sigh, to sob, to pine, to groan,
          To wring my hands, to sit alone.
Quest.: Oh when, oh when shall sorrow quiet have?
Ans.:   Never, never, never, never,
          Never till she finds a grave.

THE NOBLE SOLDIER OR A CONTRACT BROKEN, JUSTLY
REVENGED, i. 1. 1634.

TRIP it, gipsies, trip it fine,
>   Show tricks and lofty capers;
At threading-needles we repine,
>   And leaping over rapiers.

Pindy-pandy rascal toys,
   We scorn cutting purses;
Though we live by making noise,
   For cheating none can curse us.

Over high ways, over low,
   And over stones and gravel,
Though we trip it on the toe,
   And thus for silver travel;
Though our dances waste our backs,
   At night fat capons mend them;
Eggs well brewed in buttered sack,
   Our wenches say befriend them.

Oh that all the world were mad,
   Then should we have fine dancing;
Hobby-horses would be had,
   And brave girls keep a-prancing;
Beggars would on cock-horse ride,
   And boobies fall a-roaring;
And cuckolds, though no horns be spied,
   Be one another goring.

Welcome, poet to our ging!
   Make rhymes, we'll give thee reason,
Canary bees thy brains shall sting,
   Mull-sack did ne'er speak treason.
Peter-see-me shall wash thy nowl,
   And Malaga glasses fox thee;
If, poet, thou toss not bowl for bowl,
   Thou shalt not kiss a doxy.

               THE SPANISH GYPSY, iii. 1653.

25. ging: *gang, company.* 29. Peter-see-me: *Pedro Ximenes, a Spanish wine;* nowl: *noll, head.* 30. fox: *befuddle.*

COME, follow your leader, follow;
Our convoy be Mars and Apollo,
The van comes brave up here;
Answer As hotly comes the rear.
Omnes: Our knackers are the fifes and drums,
     Sa, Sa, the gipsies' army comes!

Horsemen we need not fear,
There's none but footmen here;
The horse sure charge without;
Or if they wheel about,

Omnes: Our knackers are the shot that fly,
Pit-a-pat rattling in the sky.

If once the great ordnance play,
That's laughing, yet run not away,
But stand the push of pike,
Scorn can but basely strike;

Omnes: Then let our armies join and sing,
And pit-a-pat make our knackers ring.

Arm, arm! what bands are those?
They cannot be sure our foes;
We'll not draw up our force,
Nor muster any horse;

Omnes: For since they pleased to view our sight,
Let's this way, this way, give delight.

A council of war let's call,
Look either to stand or fall;
If our weak army stands,
Thank all these noble hands;

Omnes: Whose gates of love being open thrown,
We enter, and then the town's our own.

THE SPANISH GYPSY, iii.

5. knackers: *castanets.*

JOHN WEBSTER

1580?-1634

CALL for the robin-redbreast and the wren,
Since o'er shady groves they hover,
And with leaves and flowers do cover
The friendless bodies of unburied men.
Call unto his funeral dole

The ant, the field-mouse, and the mole,
To rear him hillocks that shall keep him warm,
And (when gay tombs are robbed) sustain no harm;
But keep the wolf far thence; that's foe to men,
For with his nails he'll dig them up again.

THE WHITE DEVIL. 1612.

HARK, now everything is still,
The screech-owl and the whistler shrill,
Call upon our dame aloud,
And bid her quickly don her shroud:
Much you had of land and rent,
Your length in clay's now competent.
A long war disturbed your mind;
Here your perfect peace is signed.
Of what is't fools make such vain keeping?
Sin their conception, their birth weeping:
Their life a general mist of error,
Their death a hideous storm of terror.
Strew your hair with powders sweet,
Don clean linen, bathe your feet,
And (the foul fiend more to check)
A crucifix let bless your neck,
'Tis now full tide, 'tween night and day,
End your groan, and come away.

THE DUCHESS OF MALFI, iv. 2. 1623.

DABRIDGECOURT BELCHIER

1580?-1621

WALKING in a shadowed grove,
Near silver streams fair gliding,
Where trees in ranks did grace those banks,
And nymphs had their abiding;
Here as I stayed I saw a maid,
A beauteous lovely creature,
With angel's face and goddess' grace,
Of such exceeding feature.

Her looks did so astonish me,
And set my heart a-quaking,
Like stag that gazed was I amazed,
And in a stranger taking;
Yet roused myself to see this elf,
And lo! a tree did hide me,
Where I unseen beheld this queen
Awhile, ere she espied me.

Her voice was sweet melodiously,
She sung in perfect measure;
And thus she said with trickling tears:
"Alas, my joy, and treasure,
I'll be thy wife, or lose my life.
There's no man else shall have me,
If God say so: I will say no,
Although a thousand crave me.

"Oh! stay not long, but come, my dear,
And knit our marriage knot;
Each hour a day, each month a year,
Thou knowest I think, God wot.
Delay not then, like worldly men,
Good works till withered age;
'Bove other things, the King of kings
Blessed a lawful marriage.

"Thou art my choice, I constant am,
I mean to die unspotted;
With thee I'll live, for thee I love,
And keep my name unblotted.
A virtuous life in maid and wife,
The Spirit of God commends it;
Accursed he for ever be,
That seeks with shame to offend it."

With that she rose like nimble roe,
The tender grass scarce bending,
And left me there perplexed with fear
At this her sonnet's ending.
I thought to move this dame of love,

But she was gone already;
Wherefore I pray that those that stay
May find their loves as steady.

HANS BEER-POT, HIS INVISIBLE COMEDY OF SEE ME,
AND SEE ME NOT. 1618.

PHILIP MASSINGER

1583-1640

A Sad Song. Athenais in sackcloth. Her hair loose.

WHY art thou slow, thou rest of trouble, Death,
    To stop a wretch's breath,
That calls on thee, and offers her sad heart
    A prey unto thy dart?
I am nor young nor fair; be, therefore, bold:
    Sorrow hath made me old,
Deformed, and wrinkled; all that I can crave
    Is quiet in my grave.
Such as live happy, hold long life a jewel,
    But to me thou art cruel:
If thou end not my tedious misery,
    And I soon cease to be.
Strike, and strike home, then; pity unto me,
    In one short hour's delay, is tyranny.

THE EMPEROR OF THE EAST, v. iii. 1632.

Enter the two Boys, one with his lute, the other like Pallas.

A Song in praise of Soldiers, especially being victorious.

Song by Pallas.

THOUGH we contemplate to express
The glory of your happiness,
That by your powerful arm have been
So true a victor, that no sin
Could ever taint you with a blame
To lessen your deserved fame;

Or though we contend to set
Your worth in the full height, or get
Celestial singers (crowned with bays,
With flourishes to dress your praise)
You know your conquest, but your story
Lives in your triumphant glory.

THE PICTURE, ii. 2. 1630.

Music above. A song of pleasure.

THE blushing rose and purple flower,
  Let grow too long are soonest blasted.
Dainty fruits, though sweet, will sour
  And rot in ripeness, left untasted.
Yet here is one more sweet than these,
The more you taste, the more she'll please.

Beauty, though inclosed with ice,
  Is a shadow chaste as rare;
Then how much those sweets entice
  That have issue full as fair.
Earth cannot yield from all her powers
One equal, for Dame Venus' bowers.

THE PICTURE, iii. 5.

PHILIP MASSINGER?

TURN, turn thy beauteous face away,
How pale and sickly looks the day,
  In emulation of thy brighter beams!
Oh envious light, fly, fly, begone,
Come, night, and piece two breasts as one.
  When what love does we will repeat in dreams.
  Yet, thy eyes open, who can day hence fright?
  Let but their lids fall, and it will be night.

LOVE'S CURE, OR THE MARTIAL MAID, iii. 2. 1647.

MASSINGER AND FIELD

FIE, cease to wonder,
Though you hear Orpheus with his ivory lute
Move trees and rocks,
Charm bulls, bears, and men more savage to be mute,
Weak, foolish singer, here is one,
Would have transformed thyself—to stone.

THE FATAL DOWRY. 1632.

THOMAS TOMKIS

SING sweetly, that our notes may cause
The heavenly orbs themselves to pause:
And at our music stand as still
As at Jove's amorous will.
So now release them as before,
Th' have waited long enough—no more.

ALBUMAZAR, i. 3. 1615.

FRANCIS BEAUMONT

1584-1616

COME, Sleep, and with thy sweet deceiving,
Lock me in delight awhile;
Let some pleasing dreams beguile
All my fancies; that from thence
I may feel an influence,
All my powers of care bereaving.

Though but a shadow, but a sliding,
Let me know some little joy.
We that suffer long annoy
Are contented with a thought,
Through an idle fancy wrought:
O, let my joys have some abiding.

THE WOMAN HATER, iii. 1. 1607.

SHAKE off your heavy trance,
And leap into a dance,
Such as no mortals use to tread,
Fit only for Apollo
To play to, for the moon to lead,
And all the stars to follow.

THE MASQUE OF THE INNER TEMPLE AND GRAY'S INN. [1613?].

YE should stay longer if we durst:
Away! Alas that he that first
Gave Time wild wings to fly away,
Hath now no power to make him stay.
But though these games must needs be played,
I would this pair, when they are laid,
And not a creature nigh them,
Could catch his scythe, as he doth pass,
And cut his wings, and break his glass,
And keep him ever by them.

THE MASQUE OF THE INNER TEMPLE AND GRAY'S INN.

PEACE and silence be the guide
To the man and to the bride!
If there be a joy yet new
In marriage, let it fall on you,
That all the world may wonder.
If we should stay, we should do worse,
And turn our blessing to a curse
By keeping you asunder.

THE MASQUE OF THE INNER TEMPLE AND GRAY'S INN.

'TIS mirth that fills the veins with blood,
More than wine, or sleep, or food.
Let each man keep his heart at ease,
No man dies of that disease.
He that would his body keep
From diseases, must not weep;
But whoever laughs and sings,
Never he his body brings
Into fevers, gouts, or rheums,

Or lingeringly his lungs consumes;
Or meets with aches in the bone,
Or catarrhs, or griping stone:
But contented lives for aye,
The more he laughs, the more he may.

THE KNIGHT OF THE BURNING PESTLE, ii. 1. 1613.

Jasper: TELL me, dearest, what is Love?
Luce: 'Tis a lightning from above,
'Tis an arrow, 'tis a fire,
'Tis a boy they call desire,
'Tis a smile
Doth beguile
Jasper: The poor hearts of men that prove.
Tell me more, are women true?
Luce: Some love change, and so do you.
Jasper: Are they fair, and never kind?
Luce: Yes, when men turn with the wind.
Jasper: Are they froward?
Luce: Ever toward
Those that love, to love anew.

THE KNIGHT OF THE BURNING PESTLE, iii. 1.

COME you whose loves are dead,
And whiles I sing,
Weep, and wring
Every hand, and every head
Bind with cypress and sad yew;
Ribbons black and candles blue
For him that was of men most true.

Come with heavy mourning,
And on his grave
Let him have
Sacrifice of sighs and groaning;
Let him have fair flowers enow,
White and purple, green and yellow,
For him that was of men most true.

THE KNIGHT OF THE BURNING PESTLE, iv. 1.

BETTER music ne'er was known,
Than a choir of hearts in one.
Let each other that hath been
Troubled with the gall or spleen,
Learn of us to keep his brow
Smooth and plain as ours are now.
Sing though before the hour of dying
He shall rise, and then be crying,
Heyho! 'Tis naught but mirth
That keeps the body from the earth.

THE KNIGHT OF THE BURNING PESTLE, v. 1.

FRANCIS BEAUMONT AND JOHN FLETCHER

LOVERS, rejoice! your pains shall be rewarded,
The god of love himself grieves at your crying;
No more shall frozen honour be regarded,
Nor the coy faces of a maid denying.
No more shall virgins sigh, and say "We dare not,
For men are false, and what they do they care not."
All shall be well again; then do not grieve;
Men shall be true, and women shall believe.

Lovers, rejoice! what you shall say henceforth,
When you have caught your sweethearts in your arms,
It shall be accounted oracle and worth;
No more faint-hearted girls shall dream of harms,
And cry they are too young; the god hath said,
Fifteen shall make a mother of a maid:
Then, wise men, pull your roses yet unblown:
Love hates the too-ripe fruit that falls alone.

CUPID'S REVENGE, i. 1. 1615.

CYNTHIA, to thy power and thee
        We obey.
Joy to this great company,
        And no day

Come to steal this night away,
Till the rites of love are ended,
And the lusty bridegroom say,
"Welcome, light, of all befriended."

Pace out, you watery powers below;
    Let your feet,
Like the galleys when they row,
    Even beat.
Let your unknown measures, set
To the still winds, tell to all
That gods are come, immortal, great,
To honour this great nuptial.

THE MAID'S TRAGEDY, i. 1. 1619.

LAY a garland on my hearse of the dismal yew,
Maidens, willow branches bear, say I died true.
My love was false, but I was firm from my hour of birth,
Upon my buried body lay lightly, gently, earth.

THE MAID'S TRAGEDY, ii. 1622.

I COULD never have the power
To love one above an hour,
But my head would prompt mine eye
On some other man to fly.
Venus, fix mine eyes fast,
Or, if not, give me all that I shall see at last.

THE MAID'S TRAGEDY, ii. 2. 1622.

JOHN FORD

1586-1640?

FLY hence, shadows, that do keep
Watchful sorrows charmed in sleep;
Though the eyes be overtaken,
Yet the heart doth ever waken
Thoughts, chained up in busy snares

Of continual woes and cares:
Love and griefs are so exprest
As they rather sigh than rest.
Fly hence, shadows, that do keep
Watchful sorrows charmed in sleep.

THE LOVER'S MELANCHOLY, v. 1. 1629.

Soft Music. A song.

CAN you paint a thought? or number
Every fancy in a slumber?
Can you count soft minutes roving
From a dial's point by moving?
Can you grasp a sigh? or lastly,
Rob a virgin's honour chastely?
    No, O no; yet you may
        Sooner do both that and this,
        This and that, and never miss,
    Than by any praise display
        Beauty's beauty, such a glory
        As beyond all fate, all story,
            All arms, all arts,
            All loves, all hearts,
    Greater than those, or they,
    Do, shall, and must obey.

THE BROKEN HEART, iii. 1. 1633.

COMFORTS lasting, loves increasing,
Like soft hours never ceasing;
Plenty's pleasure, peace complying
Without jars, or tongues envỳing;
Hearts by holy union wedded,
More than theirs by custom bedded;
Fruitful issues; life so graced,
Not by age to be defaced;
Budding as the year ensu'th,
Every spring another youth:
All what thought can add beside,
Crown this bridegroom and this bride.

THE BROKEN HEART, iii. 1.

(Soft sad music. A Song.)

Oh no more, no more, too late
Sighs are spent; the burning tapers
Of a life as chaste as Fate,
Pure as are unwritten papers,
    Are burnt out: no heat, no light
    Now remains, 'tis ever night.
Love is dead, let lovers eyes,
    Lock'd in endless dreams,
    Th' extremes of all extremes,
Ope no more, for now Love dies,
    Now Love dies, implying
Love's martyrs must be ever, ever dying.

THE BROKEN HEART, iv. 1.

All: Glories, pleasures, pomps, delights, and ease,
          Can but please
      Outward senses, when the mind
Is not untroubled, or by peace refined.
1.   Crowns may flourish and decay,
     Beauties shine, but fade away.
2.   Youth may revel, yet it must
     Lie down in a bed of dust:
3.   Earthly honours flow and waste,
     Time alone doth change and last.
All: Sorrows mingled with contents, prepare
         Rest for care;
     Love only reigns in death; though Art
Can find no comfort for a broken heart.

THE BROKEN HEART, v. 2.

NATHANIEL FIELD

1587-1633

A Boy sings this to the tun'd music.

THEY that for worldly wealth do wed,
That buy and sell the marriage-bed,
That come not warmed with the true fire,
Resolved to keep this vow entire:
    Too soon find discontent,
    Too soon shall they repent.
But Hymen, these are no such lovers,
Which thy burning torch discovers:
Though they live, then, many a year,
Let each day as new appear
    As this first; and delights
    Make of all bridal nights.
Io, Hymen! give consent;
Blessed are the marriages that ne'er repent.

A WOMAN IS A WEATHERCOCK, ii. 1. 1612.

RISE, lady mistress, rise:
The night hath tedious been,
No sleep hath fallen into my eyes,
Nor slumbers made me sin.
Is not she a saint, then, say,
Thought of whom keeps sin away?

Rise, madam, rise and give me light,
Whom darkness still will cover,
And ignorance darker than night,
Till thou smile on thy lover.
All want day till thy beauty rise,
For the gray morn breaks from thine eyes.

AMENDS FOR LADIES, iv. 1. 1618.

WILLIAM BROWNE

1590-1650?

STEER hither, steer your winged pines,
 All beaten mariners,
Here lie Love's undiscovered mines,
 A prey to passengers;
Perfumes far sweeter than the best
Which make the Phœnix' urn and nest.
  Fear not your ships,
 Nor any to oppose you save our lips,
  But come on shore,
Where no joy dies till love hath gotten more.

Chorus.

 But come on shore
Where no joy dies till love hath gotten more.

For swelling waves, our panting breasts
 Where never storms arise
Exchange; and be awhile our guests:
 For stars gaze on our eyes.
The compass love shall hourly sing,
And as he goes about the ring,
  He will not miss
To tell each point he nameth with a kiss.

Chorus.

 Then come on shore,
Where no joy dies till love hath gotten more.

MS. THE INNER TEMPLE MASQUE, PRESENTED BY THE
GENTLEMEN THERE. January 13, 1614 [O.S.].

The Song in the Wood.

WHAT sing the sweet birds in each grove?
    Nought but love.
What sound our echoes day and night?
    All delight.
What doth each wind breathe us that fleets?
    Endless sweets.

Chorus.

Is there a place on earth this isle excells,
Or any nymphs more happy live than we.
When all our songs, our sounds, and breathings be
That here all love, delight, and sweetness dwells.

THE INNER TEMPLE MASQUE.

BARTEN HOLIDAY

Fl. 1618

TOBACCO'S a musician,
And in a pipe delighteth;
    It descends in a close,
    Through the organ of the nose,
With a relish that inviteth.
    This makes me sing So ho, ho, So ho, ho boys,
    Ho boys sound I loudly:
        Earth ne'er did breed
        Such a jovial weed
    Whereof to boast so proudly.

Tobacco is a lawyer,
His pipes do love long cases:
    When our brain it enters,
    Our feet do make indentures,
Which we seal with stamping paces.
    This makes me sing, etc.,

Tobacco's a physician
Good both for sound and sickly:
    Tis a hot perfume
    That expells cold rheum,
And makes it flow down quickly.
    This makes me sing, etc.,

Tobacco is a traveller
Come from the Indies hither;
    It pass'd sea and land
    Ere it came to my hand,
And scap'd the wind and weather.
    This makes me sing, etc.,

Tobacco is a critic,
That still old paper turneth;
    Whose labour, and care
    Is as smoke in the air,
That ascends from a rag when it burneth.
    This makes me sing, etc.,

Tobacco's an Ignis fatuus,
A fat and fiery vapour;
    That leads men about
    Till the fire be out
Consuming like a taper.
    This makes me sing, etc.

TECHNOGAMIA OR THE MARRIAGE OF THE ARTS, ii. 2. 1618.

THE black jack,
The merry black jack,
As it is tost on high-a
        Grows,
        Flows,
Till at last they fall to blows,
And make their noddles cry-a.

The brown bowl,
The merry brown bowl,

As it goes round about-a
    Fill,
    Still,
Let the world say what it will
And drink your drink all out-a.

The deep can,
The merry deep can,
As thou dost freely quaff-a.
    Sing,
    Fling,
Be as merry as a king
And sound a lusty laugh-a.

TECHNOGAMIA, iii. 5.

1. black jack: *leathern tankard.*

ANONYMOUS

A Song in parts.

WHILST we sing the doleful knell
Of this princess' passing-bell,
Let the woods and valleys ring
Echoes to our sorrowing;
And the tenor of their song,
Be ding dong, ding, dong, dong,
    Ding dong, dong,
        Ding, dong.

Nature now shall boast no more
Of the riches of her store,
Since in this her chiefest prize,
All the stock of beauty dies;
Then, what cruel heart can long
Forbear to sing this sad ding dong?
    This sad ding dong,
        Ding dong.

Fauns and sylvans of the woods,
Nymphs that haunt the crystal floods,
Savage beasts more milder then
The unrelenting hearts of men,
Be partakers of our moan,
And with us sing ding dong, ding dong,
  Ding dong, dong,
    Ding dong.

SWETNAM, THE WOMAN HATER, ARRAIGNED BY WOMEN,
iv. 2. 1620.

19. then: *than.*

WILLIAM SAMPSON

1590?-1636?

Enter Joshua, reeling with Jacks.

WHEN from the wars I do return,
And at a cup of good ale mourn,
I'll tell how towns without fire we did burn,
  And is not that a wonder?

I'll tell how that my general
Entered the breach, and scaled the wall,
And made the foremost battery of all,
  And is not that a wonder?

How that we went to take a fort,
And took it too in war-like sort,
I'll swear that a lie is a true report,
  And is not that a wonder?

How that we soldiers have true pay,
And clothes, and victuals every day,
And never a captain ran away,
  And is not that a wonder?

THE VOW BREAKER, OR THE FAIR MAID OF CLIFTON. 1636.

THOMAS GOFFE

1591-1629

DROP golden showers, gentle sleep;
And all the angels of the night,
Which do us in protection keep,
Make this queen dream of delight.
Morpheus, be kind a little, and be
Death's now true image, for 'twill prove
To this poor queen that then thou art he.
Her grave is made i' th' bed of love:
Thus with sweet sweets can Heaven mix gall,
And marriage turn to funeral.

THE COURAGEOUS TURK, OR AMURATH THE FIRST, ii. 2. 1632.

Nurse sings: LULLABY, lullaby baby,
      Great Argos joy,
    The King of Greece thou art born to be,
      In despite of Troy.
    Rest ever wait upon thy head,
      Sleep close thine eyes,
    The blessed guard tend on thy bed
        Of deities.
    O how his brow will beseem a crown!
    How these locks will shine!
    Like the rays of the sun on the ground,
    These locks of thine.
    The nurse of Heaven still send thee milk,
    May'st thou suck a queen.
    Thy drink Jove's nectar, and clothes of silk,
    A god mayst thou seem.
    Cupid sit on this rosean cheek,
        On these ruby lips.
    May thy mind like a lamb be meek,
    In the vale which trips.
    Lullaby, lullaby baby.

THE TRAGEDY OF ORESTES, iii. 1. 1633.

T. G.

They sing.

GRIEVE not, fond man, nor let one tear
Steal from thy eyes, she'll hear
No more of Cupid's shafts; they fly
For wounding her, so let them die.
For why shouldst thou nourish such flames as burn
Thy easy breast, and have not like return.

Chorus: Love forces love, as flames expire,
     If not increased by gentle fire.

Let then her frigid coolness move
Thee to withdraw thy purer love;
And since she is resolved to show
She will not love, do thou so too;
For why should beauty so far charm thy eyes,
That if she frown, thou'lt prove her sacrifice.

Chorus: Love forces love, as flames expire,
     If not increased by gentle fire.

THE CARELESS SHEPHERDESS, i. 1. 1656.

Sylvia discovered in her bower singing.

COME, shepherds, come, impale your brows
With garlands of the choicest flowers
        The time allows.
Come, nymphs, decked in your dangling hair
And unto Sylvia's shady bowers
        With haste repair;
Where you shall see chaste turtles play,
And nightingales make lasting May,
As if old Time his youthful mind
To one delightful season had confined.

On, shepherds, on! we'll sacrifice
    Those spotless lambs we prize
At highest rate, for Pan doth keep

From harm our scattering sheep:
   And hath deserved
   For to be served
With those ye do esteem the best
Amongst the flock, as fittest for his feast.

Come, virgins, bring your garlands here,
   And hang them everywhere:
Then let his altars be o'erspread
   With roses fresh and red.
     Burn gums and spice,
     Rich sacrifice,
The gods so bounteous are, ye know
Ye mortals cannot pay them what ye owe.

THE CARELESS SHEPHERDESS, ii. 1.

   SIGH, shepherds, sigh,
Spend all your breath in groans,
   Lay your sweeter music by,
Harken only to the drones.
Henceforth no other garlands view
But what are made of dismal yew.
   Tis fit all nature now should mourn
   And every tree to cypress turn.

    Those nymphs are gone
   Whose looks in awe did keep
    The wolf and fox, who alone
More than Pales blest our sheep.
Their sweetest grass the lambs did find
Where their bright eyes, not Phœbus, shined.
   In every place where they did come
   They made a new Elysium.

Wretched swains, ye now can have
No Paradise but in the grave.
Chorus: Die, then die, since they are fled,
   The only life is to be dead.

THE CARELESS SHEPHERDESS, v. 13.

4. drones: *bagpipes.* 12. Pales: *god of flocks and shepherds.*

FRANCIS QUARLES

1592-1644

How blest are they that waste their weary hours
In solemn groves and solitary bowers,
Where neither eye nor ear
Can see, or hear,
The frantic mirth,
And false delights of frolic earth;
Where they may sit and pant,
And breathe their pursy souls;
Where neither grief consumes, nor griping want
Afflicts, nor sullen care controls.
Away false joys, ye murder where ye kiss:
There is no heaven to that, no life to this.

THE VIRGIN WIDOW, iii. 1. 1649.

WILLIAM CAVENDISH, DUKE OF NEWCASTLE

1592-1676

THINE eyes to me like suns appear
    Or brighter stars, their light
Which makes it summer all the year,
    Or else a day of night:
But truly I do think they are
But eyes, and neither sun nor star.

Thy brow is as the milky way,
    Whereon the gods might trace;
Thy lips ambrosia I dare say
    Or nectar of thy face:
But to speak truly I do vow
They are but woman's lips and brow.

Thy cheek it is a mingled bath
    Of lilies and of roses;

But here there's no man power hath
   To gather love's fresh posies:
Believe it, here the flowers that bud
Are but a woman's flesh and blood.

Thy nose a promontory fair,
   Thy neck a neck of land;
At nature's gifts that are so rare
   All men amazed do stand:
But to the clearer judgment those
Are but a woman's neck and nose.

For lines in passion I can die
   As is the lover's guise,
And dabble too in poetry
   Whilst love possessed, then wise
As greatest statesmen, or as those
That know love best, yet live in prose.

THE VARIETY, iv. 1. 1649.

I'D have her merry, laugh, and smile,
   And then look grave and sad;
In every humour but a while,
   Make love as 'tis, that's mad.

I'd have your dress of several shapes,
   Like Proteus carved, not he;
In humour a she coy jackanapes,
   Then a grave monkey be.

Discourse of all that comes to sense,
   But speak none, yet still speak;
No matter here is no offence,
   But to speak matter weak.

With thy soft voice sing me asleep,
   Then startle me awake,
With love's notes-passion make me weep,
   Then merry for thy sake.

THE VARIETY, iv. 1.

THOMAS MAY

1595-1650

Not he that knows how to acquire
  But to enjoy, is blest.
Nor does our happiness consist
  In motion, but in rest.

The gods pass man in bliss, because
  They toil not for more height;
But can enjoy, and in their own
  Eternal rest delight.

Then, Princes, do not toil, nor care;
  Enjoy what you possess.
Which whilst you do, you equalize
  The gods in happiness.

THE TRAGEDY OF CLEOPATRA QUEEN OF EGYPT, i. 1639.

Dear, do not your fair beauty wrong
In thinking still you are too young.
The rose and lilies in your cheek
Flourish, and no more ripening seek.
Your cherry lip, red, soft, and sweet,
Proclaims such fruit for taste is meet;
Then lose no time, for love hath wings,
And flies away from aged things.

THE OLD COUPLE, iii. 1658.

JAMES SHIRLEY

1596-1666

Music. Enter Shepherds and Shepherdesses with garlands.

Woodmen, shepherds, come away,
This is Pan's great holiday;
  Throw off cares;

With your heaven-aspiring airs
    Help us to sing,
While valleys with your echoes ring.

Nymphs that dwell within these groves
Leave your arbours, bring your loves;
    Gather posies,
Crown your golden hair with roses;
    As you pass,
Foot like fairies on the grass.

Joy crown our bowers! Philomel,
Leave of Tereus' rape to tell.
    Let trees dance,
As they at Thracian lyre did once;
    Mountains play,
This is the shepherds' holiday.

Dance.

THE SCHOOL OF COMPLIMENT, v. 1631.

MELANCHOLY, hence! go get
Some piece of earth to be thy seat;
Here the air and nimble fire
Would shoot up to meet desire;
Sullen humour, leave the blood,
Mix not with the purer flood,
But let pleasure swelling there
Make a springtide of the year.

THE CHANGES, OR LOVE IN A MAZE, iv. 1632.

IF Love his arrows shoot so fast,
Soon his feathered stock will waste:
But I mistake in thinking so,
Love's arrows in his quiver grow;
How can he want artillery?
That appears too true in me:
Two shafts feed upon my breast,
Oh make it quiver for the rest.
Kill me with love, thou angry son

Of Cytherea, or let one,
One sharp golden arrow fly
To wound her heart for whom I die.
Cupid, if thou beest a child,
Be no god, or be more mild.

THE CHANGES, v.

Love, a thousand sweets distilling,
And with nectar bosoms filling,
Charm all eyes that none may find us,
Be above, before, behind us;
And, while we thy pleasures taste,
Enforce time itself to stay,
And by forelock hold him fast
Lest occasion slip away.

THE WITTY FAIR ONE, iv. 1633.

1. Come away, away, away,
   See the dawning of the day,
   Risen from the murmuring streams;
   Some stars show with sickly beams,
   What stock of flame they are allowed,
   Each retiring to a cloud,
   Bid your active sports adieu,
   The morning else will blush for you.

2. Ye feather-footed hours run
   To dress the chariot of the sun;
   Harness the steeds, it quickly will
   Be time to mount the eastern hill.

3. The lights grow pale with modest fears,
   Lest you offend those sacred ears,
   And eyes, that lent you all this grace;
   Retire, retire, to your own place.

4. And as you move from that blest pair,
   Let each heart kneel, and think a prayer,
   That all, that can make up the glory,
   Of good and great may fill their story.

THE TRIUMPH OF PEACE. 1633.

I NEITHER will lend nor borrow,
Old age will be here to-morrow;
'Tis pleasure we are made for,
When death comes all is paid for:
    No matter what's the bill of fare,
    I'll take my cup, I'll take no care.

Be wise, and say you had warning,
To laugh is better than learning;
To wear no clothes, not neat is;
But hunger is good where meat is:
    Give me wine, give me a wench,
    And let her parrot talk in French.

It is a match worth the making,
To keep the merry-thought waking;
A song is better than fasting,
And sorrow's not worth the tasting:
    Then keep your brain light as you can,
    An ounce of care will kill a man.

      St. Patrick for Ireland. The First Part, v. 1640.

CEASE warring thoughts, and let his brain
No more discord entertain,
But be smooth and calm again.

Ye crystal rivers that are nigh,
As your streams are passing by,
Teach your murmurs harmony.

Ye winds that wait upon the spring,
And perfumes to flowers do bring,
Let your amorous whispers here
Breathe soft music to his ear.

Ye warbling nightingales repair
From every wood, to charm this air,
And with the wonders of your breast,
Each striving to excel the rest.
    When it is time to wake him, close your parts,
    And drop down from the trees with broken hearts.

      The Triumph of Beauty. 1646.

BEAUTY, and the various graces
That adorn the sweetest faces,
Here take their glorious throne; may he
That is the god of archery
Never aim one angry dart,
But soft, and gentle as your heart,
Court it with flame, and rich perfume,
To light and sweeten, not consume.

THE SISTERS, iii. 1652.

YOU virgins, that did late despair
    To keep your wealth from cruel men,
Tie up in silk your careless hair:
    Soft peace is come again.

Now lovers' eyes may gently shoot
    A flame that will not kill;
The drum was angry, but the lute
    Shall whisper what you will.

Sing Io, Io! for his sake
    That hath restored your drooping heads:
With choice of sweetest flowers make
    A garden where he treads;

Whilst we whole groves of laurel bring,
    A petty triumph to his brow,
Who is the master of our spring
    And all the bloom we owe.

THE IMPOSTURE, i. 1652.

16. owe: *own*.

Nuns discovered singing.

O FLY my soul, what hangs upon
        Thy drooping wings,
        And weighs them down
With love of gaudy mortal things?
The sun is now i' the east; each shade,
        As he does rise,
        Is shorter made,

That earth may lessen to our eyes:
Oh be not careless then and play
        Until the star of peace
Hide all his beams in dark recess;
Poor pilgrims needs must lose their way,
When all the shadows do increase.

(Soft music, after the song)

THE IMPOSTURE, ii.

Song within.

Strephon: COME, my Daphne, come away,
        We do waste the crystal day;
        'Tis Strephon calls.
Daphne: What says my love?
Strephon: Come, follow to the myrtle grove,
        Where Venus shall prepare
        New chaplets for thy hair.
Daphne: Were I shut up within a tree,
        I'd rend my bark to follow thee.
Strephon: My shepherdess, make haste,
        The minutes slide too fast.
Daphne: In those cooler shades will I,
        Blind as Cupid, kiss thine eye.
Strephon: In thy bosom then I'll stay;
        In such warm snow who would not lose his way.
Chorus: We'll laugh and leave the world behind;
        And gods themselves that see
        Shall envy thee and me,
                But never find
        Such joys, when they embrace a deity.

THE CARDINAL, v. 1652.

*Enter Cupid, Folly, Madness: the Host joins with them in a
dance. Song.*

THOUGH little be the god of love,
Yet his arrows mighty are,
And his victories above
What the valiant reach by war.
Nor are his limits with the sky;

O'er the milky way he'll fly
And sometimes wound a deity.
Apollo once the Python slew,
But a keener arrow flew
From Daphne's eye, and made a wound
For which the god no balsam found.
One smile of Venus, too, did more
On Mars than armies could before.
If a warm fit thus pull him down,
How will she ague-shake him with a frown.
Thus Love can fiery spirits tame,
And, when he please, cold rocks inflame.

CUPID AND DEATH. A MASQUE. 1653.

VICTORIOUS men of earth, no more
  Proclaim how wide your empires are;
Though you bind in every shore
  And your triumphs reach as far
    As night or day,
  Yet you, proud monarchs, must obey
And mingle with forgotten ashes when
Death calls ye to the crowd of common men.

Devouring Famine, Plague, and War,
  Each able to undo mankind,
Death's servile emissaries are;
  Nor to these alone confined,
    He hath at will
  More quaint and subtle ways to kill;
A smile or kiss, as he will use the art,
Shall have the cunning skill to break a heart.

CUPID AND DEATH.

Arismena sings.

Now fie on love, it ill befits,
  Or man and woman know it,
Love was not meant for people in their wits,
  And they that fondly show it
Betray their too much feathered brains,
And shall have only Bedlam for their pains.

To love is to distract my sleep,
   And waking, to wear fetters;
To love is but to go to school to weep;
   I'll leave it for my betters.
If single love be such a curse,
To marry is to make it ten times worse.

    FROM THE CARELESS SHEPHERDESS BY T. G., ii. 3. 1656.

Graculus sings.

I AM in love and cannot woo,
Heigho! Heigho! what shall I do;
I gape and sigh and sometimes weep
For Phillis that my heart doth keep.

I love her hair and forehead high,
Then am I taken with her eye,
Her cheek I do commend for gay
But then her nose hangs in my way.

Her lips I praise but then steps in
Her white and pretty dimpled chin,
But there her neck I do behold
Fit to be hung with chains of gold.

Her breasts are soft as any down
Beneath which lies her Maiden Town,
So strong and fortified within
In vain I hope to take it in.

   FROM THE CARELESS SHEPHERDESS BY T. G., iii. 10. 1656.

THE glories of our blood and state
   Are shadows, not substantial things;
There is no armour against Fate;
   Death lays his icy hand on kings:
      Sceptre and crown
      Must tumble down,
And in the dust be equal made
With the poor crooked scythe and spade.

Some men with swords may reap the field,
  And plant fresh laurels where they kill;
But their strong nerves at last must yield;
  They tame but one another still:
        Early or late,
        They stoop to fate,
And must give up their murmuring breath,
When they, pale captives, creep to death.

The garlands wither on your brow,
  Then boast no more your mighty deeds;
Upon Death's purple altar now,
  See where the victor-victim bleeds:
        Your heads must come
        To the cold tomb;
Only the actions of the just
Smell sweet and blossom in their dust.

THE CONTENTION OF AJAX AND ULYSSES. 1659.

JOHN FLETCHER

1597-1625

They rise and sing in praise of Pan.

SING his praises that doth keep
  Our flocks from harm,
Pan, the father of our sheep;
  And arm in arm
Tread we softly in a round,
Whilst the hollow neighbouring ground
Fills the music with her sound.

Pan, O great god Pan, to thee
  Thus do we sing:
Thou that keep'st us chaste and free
  As the young spring;
Ever be thy honour spoke,
From that place the morn is broke,
To that place day doth unyoke.

THE FAITHFUL SHEPHERDESS, i. 1. [1609-10?]

COME, shepherds, come,
Come away without delay,
Whilst the gentle time doth stay.
Green woods are dumb,
And will never tell to any
Those dear kisses, and those many
Sweet embraces, that are given;
Dainty pleasures, that would even
Raise in coldest age a fire,
And give virgin-blood desire.
          Then if ever,
          Now or never,
          Come and have it:
          Think not I
          Dare deny,
          If you crave it.

THE FAITHFUL SHEPHERDESS, i. I.

Do not fear to put thy feet
Naked in the river sweet,
Think not leech, or newt, or toad,
Will bite thy foot, when thou hast trod;
Nor let the water rising high,
As thou wad'st in, make thee cry
And sob; but ever live with me,
And not a wave shall trouble thee.

THE FAITHFUL SHEPHERDESS, iii. I.

They all sing.

ALL ye woods, and trees, and bowers,
All ye virtues and ye powers
That inhabit in the lakes,
In the pleasant springs or brakes,
          Move your feet
          To our sound,
          Whilst we greet
          All this ground
With his honour and his name
That defends our flocks from blame.

He is great, and he is just,
He is ever good, and must
Thus be honoured. Daffadillies,
Roses, pinks, and loved lilies
    Let us fling,
    Whilst we sing,
    Ever holy,
    Ever holy,
Ever honoured, ever young,
Thus great Pan is ever sung.

THE FAITHFUL SHEPHERDESS, v. 1.

The Drinking Song.

DRINK to-day, and drown all sorrow,
You shall perhaps not do it to-morrow.
Best, while you have it, use your breath;
There is no drinking after death.

Wine works the heart up, wakes the wit,
There is no cure 'gainst age but it.
It helps the head-ache, cough, and tisic,
And is for all diseases physic.

Then let us swill, boys, for our health;
Who drinks well, loves the commonwealth.
And he that will to bed go sober
Falls with the leaf still in October.

THE BLOODY BROTHER, ii. 2. 1639.

TAKE, Oh take those lips away
    That so sweetly were forsworn,
And those eyes, like break of day,
    Lights that do mislead the morn,
But my kisses bring again,
    Seals of love, though sealed in vain.

Hide, Oh hide those hills of snow,
    Which thy frozen bosom bears,

On whose tops, the pinks that grow
Are of those that April wears.
But first set my poor heart free.
Bound in those icey chains by thee.

THE BLOODY BROTHER, v. 2.

AWAY, delights, go seek some other dwelling,
For I must die.
Farewell, false love, thy tongue is ever telling
Lie after lie.
For ever let me rest now from thy smarts;
Alas, for pity, go,
And fire their hearts
That have been hard to thee, mine was not so.

Never again deluding love shall know me,
For I will die;
And all those griefs that think to overgrow me,
Shall be as I:
For ever will I sleep, while poor maids cry
"Alas, for pity, stay,
And let us die
With thee; men cannot mock us in the clay."

THE CAPTAIN, iii. 4. 1647.

Now the lusty spring is seen;
Golden yellow, gaudy blue,
Daintily invite the view.
Everywhere on every green,
Roses blushing as they blow,
And enticing men to pull,
Lilies whiter than the snow,
Woodbines of sweet honey full:
All love's emblems, and all cry,
"Ladies, if not plucked, we die."

Yet the lusty spring hath stayed;
Blushing red and purest white,
Daintily to love invite

Every woman, every maid.
Cheeries kissing as they grow,
  And inviting men to taste,
Apples, even ripe below,
Winding gently to the waist:
    All love's emblems, and all cry,
    "Ladies, if not plucked, we die."

           THE TRAGEDY OF VALENTINIAN, ii. 4. 1647.

HEAR, ye ladies that despise
  What the mighty Love has done;
Fear examples, and be wise:
  Fair Calisto was a nun;
Leda, sailing on the stream
  To deceive the hopes of man,
Love accounting but a dream,
  Doted on a silver swan;
    Danaë, in a brazen tower,
    Where no love was, loved a shower.

Hear, ye ladies that are coy,
  What the mighty Love can do;
Fear the fierceness of the boy:
  The chaste moon he makes to woo;
Vesta, kindling holy fires,
  Circled round about with spies,
Never dreaming loose desires,
  Doting at the altar dies;
    Ilion, in a short hour, higher
    He can build, and once more fire.

              VALENTINIAN, ii. 4.

Music and Song.

CARE-charming Sleep, thou easer of all woes,
Brother to Death, sweetly thyself dispose
On this afflicted prince; fall like a cloud
In gentle showers; give nothing that is loud,
Or painful to his slumbers; easy, sweet,
And as a purling stream, thou son of Night,

Pass by his troubled senses; sing his pain,
Like hollow murmuring wind or silver rain;
Into this prince gently, oh, gently slide,
And kiss him into slumbers like a bride.

VALENTINIAN, v. 2.

God Lyæus, ever young,
Ever honoured, ever sung;
Stained with blood of lusty grapes,
In a thousand lusty shapes,
Dance upon the mazer's brim,
In the crimson liquor swim;
From thy plenteous hand divine,
Let a river run with wine:
   God of youth, let this day here
   Enter neither care nor fear.

VALENTINIAN, v. 8.

ORPHEUS I am, come from the deeps below,
To thee, fond man, the plagues of love to show:
To the fair fields where loves eternal dwell
There's none that come, but first they pass through hell:
  Hark, and beware! unless thou hast loved ever,
  Beloved again, thou shalt see those joys never.

Hark how they groan that died despairing,
    Oh, take heed, then:
Hark how they howl for over-daring!
    All these were men.

   They that be fools, and die for fame,
     They lose their name;
   And they that bleed,
    Hark how they speed.

Now in cold frosts, now scorching fires
They sit, and curse their lost desires;
Nor shall these souls be free from pains and fears,
Till women waft them over in their tears.

THE MAD LOVER, iv. 1. 1647.

Orpheus: CHARON, O Charon,
    Thou wafter of the souls to bliss or bane!
Charon: Who calls the ferry-man of Hell?
Orpheus: Come near,
    And say who lives in joy, and who in fear.
Charon: Those that die well, eternal joys shall follow;
    Those that die ill, their own foul fate shall swal-
        low.
Orpheus: Shall thy black bark those guilty spirits stow
    That kill themselves for love?
Charon: O no, no,
    My cordage cracks when such great sins are near,
    No wind blows fair, nor I myself can steer.
Orpheus: What lovers pass and in Elysium reign?
Charon: Those gentle loves that are beloved again.
Orpheus: This soldier loves, and fain would die to win,
    Shall he go on?
Charon: No, 'tis too foul a sin.
    He must not come aboard; I dare not row,
    Storms of despair and guilty blood will blow.
Orpheus: Shall time release him, say?
Charon: No, no, no, no,
    Nor time nor death can alter us, nor prayer;
    My boat is destiny, and who then dare
    But those appointed come aboard? Love still
    And love by reason, mortal, not by will.
Orpheus: And when thy mistress shall close up thine eyes,
Charon: Then come aboard and pass,
Orpheus: Till when, be wise.
Charon: Till when, be wise.

                THE MAD LOVER, iv. 1.

Enter Calis and her train with lights, singing.

    OH, fair sweet goddess, queen of loves,
    Soft and gentle as thy doves,
    Humble-eyed, and ever ruing
    Those poor hearts, their loves pursuing:
    O, thou mother of delights,
    Crowner of all happy nights,
    Star of dear content and pleasure,

Of mutual loves the endless treasure,
Accept this sacrifice we bring,
Thou continual youth and spring;
Grant this lady her desires,
And every hour we'll crown thy fires.

THE MAD LOVER, v. i.

ARM, arm, arm, arm! the scouts are all come in;
Keep your ranks close, and now your honours win.
Behold from yonder hill the foe appears,
Bows, bills, glaives, arrows, shields, and spears,
Like a dark wood he comes, or tempest pouring;
Oh, view the wings of horse the meadows scouring,
The van-guard marches bravely. Hark, the drums,—*Dub,*
    Dub!
They meet, they meet, now the battle comes:
    See how the arrows fly,
    That darken all the sky,
    Hark how the trumpets sound,
    Hark how the hills rebound,—*Tara, tara, tara.*
Hark how the horses charge! in, boys, boys, in—*Tara, tara.*
The battle totters; now the wounds begin:
    Oh, how they cry,
    Oh, how they die.
Room for the valiant Memnon, armed with thunder,
  See how he breaks the ranks asunder.
They fly, they fly, Eumenes has the chase,
And brave Polybius makes good his place.
    To the plains, to the woods,
    To the rocks, to the floods,
    They fly for succour. Follow, follow, follow. *Hey,*
    hey!
    Brave Diocles is dead,
    And all his soldiers fled;
    The battle's won, and lost,
    That many a life hath cost.

THE MAD LOVER, v. i.

4. glaives: *swords.*

A Song.

RISE from the shades below,
All you that prove
· The helps of looser love;
Rise and bestow
Upon this cup whatever may compel
By powerful charm and unresisted spell,
A heart unwarmed to melt in love's desires.
Distil into this liquor all your fires,
Heats, longings, tears,
But keep back frozen fears,
That she may know, that has all power defied,
Art is a power that will not be denied.

The Answer.

I OBEY, I obey,
And am come to view the day,
Brought along all may compell,
All the earth has, and our Hell.
Here's a little, little flower,
This will make her sweat an hour,
Then unto such flames arise,
A thousand joys will not suffice.
Here's the powder of the Moon,
With which she caught Endymion;
The powerful tears that Venus cried
When the boy Adonis died.
Here's Medea's charm with which
Jason's heart she did bewitch;
Omphale this spell put in,
When she made the Libyan spin.
This dull root plucked from Lethe flood,
Purges all pure thoughts, and good.
    These I stir thus, round, round, round,
    Whilst our light feet beat the ground.

THE HUMOUROUS LIEUTENANT, iv. 3. 1647.

O, FAIR sweet face, O, eyes, celestial bright,
Twin stars in heaven, that now adorn the night;
O, fruitful lips, where cherries ever grow,
And damask cheeks, where all sweet beauties blow;
· O, thou, from head to foot divinely fair,
Cupid's most cunning net's made of that hair;
And, as he weaves himself for curious eyes,
"O me, O me, I'm caught myself," he cries:
Sweet rest about thee, sweet and golden sleep,
Soft peaceful thoughts your hourly watches keep,
Whilst I in wonder sing this sacrifice,
To beauty sacred, and those angel eyes.

WOMEN PLEASED, iii. 4. 1647.

LOOK out bright eyes, and bless the air:
Even in shadows you are fair.
Shut-up beauty is like fire,
That breaks out clearer still and higher.
Though your body be confined,
And soft love a prisoner bound,
Yet the beauty of your mind
Neither check, nor chain hath found.
    Look out nobly then, and dare
    Even the fetters that you wear.

THE FALSE ONE, i. 2. 1647.

Nilus' Song.

MAKE room for my rich waters' fall,
    And bless my flood;
Nilus comes flowing, to you all
    Increase and good.
Now the plants and flowers shall spring,
And the merry ploughman sing:
In my hidden waves I bring
Bread, and wine, and every thing.
Let the damsels sing me in,
Sing aloud that I may rise:
Your holy feasts and hours begin,

And each hand bring a sacrifice.
   Now my wanton pearls I show,
That to ladies' fair necks grow;
   Now my gold,
And treasures that can ne'er be told,
Shall bless this land, by my rich flow;
   And after this, to crown your eyes,
   My hidden holy head[s] arise.

THE FALSE ONE, iii. 4.

Song at the Wedding. An Epithalamion.

COME away, bring on the bride
And place her by her lover's side:
You fair troop of maids attend her,
Pure and holy thoughts befriend her.
Blush, and wish, you virgins all,
Many such fair nights may fall.

Chorus.

Hymen, fill the house with joy;
All thy sacred fires employ;
Bless the bed with holy love:
Now, fair orb of beauty, move.

THE LITTLE FRENCH LAWYER, i. 1. 1647.

Song in the Woods.

THIS way, this way come, and hear,
You that hold these pleasures dear,
Fill your ears with our sweet sound,
Whilst we melt the frozen ground.
This way come; make haste, oh, fair,
Let your clear eyes gild the air;
Come, and bless us with your sight,
This way, this way, seek delight.

THE LITTLE FRENCH LAWYER, iv. 1.

Cast our caps and cares away:
This is beggars' holiday.
At the crowning of our king,
Thus we ever dance and sing.
In the world look out and see,
Where so happy a prince as he?
Where the nation live[s] so free,
And so merry as do we?
Be it peace, or be it war,
Here at liberty we are,
And enjoy our ease and rest;
To the field we are not pressed;
Nor are called into the town
To be troubled with the gown.
Hang all officers, we cry,
And the magistrate too, by.
When the subsidy's increased,
We are not a penny sessed;
Nor will any go to law
With the beggar for a straw.
All which happiness, he brags,
He doth owe unto his rags.

THE BEGGARS BUSH, ii. 1. 1647.

Song by the Novice.

Adieu, fond love; farewell, you wanton powers,
    I am free again;
Thou dull disease of blood, and idle hours,
    Bewitching pain,
Fly to the fools that sigh away their time.
My nobler love to heaven doth climb,
And there behold beauty still young
That time can ne'er corrupt nor death destroy;
Immortal sweetness by fair angels sung,
And honoured by eternity and joy.
There lives my love, thither my hopes aspire;
Fond love declines, this heavenly grows higher.

THE LOVER'S PROGRESS, iii. 1. 1647.

'TIS late and cold; stir up the fire;
Sit close, and draw the table nigher;
Be merry, and drink wine that's old,
A hearty medicine 'gainst a cold.
Your bed of wanton down's the best,
Where you shall tumble to your rest;
I could wish you wenches too,
But I am dead, and cannot do.
Call for the best the house may ring,
Sack, white, and claret, let them bring,
And drink apace, while breath you have,
You'll find but cold drink in the grave:
Plover, partridge, for your dinner,
And a capon for the sinner,
You shall find ready when you're up,
And your horse shall have his sup:
　　Welcome, welcome shall fly round,
　　And I shall smile, though under ground.

THE LOVER'S PROGRESS, iii. 1.

　　OH, turn thy bow,
　　Thy power we feel and know,
　　Fair Cupid, turn away thy bow:
　　They be those golden arrows,
　　Bring ladies all their sorrows,
　　And till there be more truth in men,
　　Never shoot at maid again.

THE NICE VALOUR, OR THE PASSIONATE MAD MAN, ii. 1. 1647.

HENCE, all you vain delights,
As short as are the nights
　　Wherein you spend your folly,
There's nought in this life sweet,
If man were wise to see't,
　　But only melancholy,
　　Oh, sweetest melancholy.
Welcome, folded arms, and fixed eyes,
A sigh that piercing mortifies,
A look that's fastened to the ground,
A tongue chained up without a sound.

Fountain-heads, and pathless groves,
Places which pale passion loves:
Moonlight walks, when all the fowls
Are warmly housed, save bats and owls;
  A midnight bell, a parting groan,
  These are the sounds we feed upon;
Then stretch our bones in a still gloomy valley,
Nothing's so dainty sweet as lovely melancholy.

THE NICE VALOUR, iii. 1.

COME follow me, you country lasses,
And you shall see such sport as passes:
You shall dance and I will sing;
Pedro, he shall rub the string;
Each shall have a loose-bodied gown
Of green, and laugh till you lie down.
    Come follow me, come follow, &c.

You shall have crowns of roses, daisies,
Buds where the honey-maker gazes;
You shall taste the golden thighs,
Such as in wax-chamber lies:
What fruit please you, taste, freely pull,
Till you have all your bellies full.
    Come follow me, &c.

THE MAID IN THE MILL, ii. 1. 1647.

Lute and Song.

DEAREST, do not you delay me,
  Since, thou knowest, I must be gone;
Wind and tide 'tis thought doth stay me,
  But 'tis wind that must be blown
    From that breath, whose native smell
    Indian odours far excel.

Oh, then speak, thou fairest fair.
  Kill not him that vows to serve thee;
But perfume this neighbouring air,

Else dull silence sure will starve me:
   'Tis a word that's quickly spoken,
Which being restrained, a heart is broken.

THE SPANISH CURATE, ii. 4. 1679.

LET the bells ring, and let the boys sing,
   The young lasses skip and play,
Let the cups go round, till round goes the ground,
   Our learned old vicar will stay.

Let the pig turn merrily, merrily, ah,
   And let the fat goose swim,
For verily, verily, verily, ah,
   Our vicar this day shall be trim.

The stewed cock shall crow, cock-a-loodle-loo,
   A loud cock-a-loodle shall he crow;
The duck and the drake shall swim in a lake
   Of onions and claret below.

Our wives shall be neat, to bring in our meat;
   To thee our most noble adviser,
Our pains shall be great, and bottles shall sweat,
   And we ourselves will be wiser.

We'll labour and swink, we'll kiss and we'll drink,
   And tithes shall come thicker and thicker;
We'll fall to our plough, and get children enow,
   And thou shalt be learned old vicar.

THE SPANISH CURATE, iii. 2.

A sad Song.

WEEP no more, nor sigh, nor groan,
Sorrow calls no time that's gone:
Violets plucked, the sweetest rain
Makes not fresh nor grow again;
Trim thy locks, look cheerfully;
Fate's hid ends eyes cannot see.

Joys as winged dreams fly fast,
Why should sadness longer last.
Grief is but a wound to woe;
Gentlest fair, mourn, mourn no moe.

THE QUEEN OF CORINTH, iii. 2. 1679.

JOHN FLETCHER?

ORPHEUS with his lute made trees,
And the mountain-tops that freeze,
  Bow themselves when he did sing:
To his music plants and flowers
Ever sprung, as sun and showers
  There had made a lasting spring.

Everything that heard him play,
Even the billows of the sea,
  Hung their heads, and then lay by.
In sweet music is such art,
Killing care and grief of heart
  Fall asleep, or hearing die.

KING HENRY VIII, iii. 1. 1623.

ROSES, their sharp spines being gone,
Not royal in their smells alone,
  But in their hue;
Maiden pinks, of odour faint,
Daisies smell-less, yet most quaint,
  And sweet thyme true;

Primrose, firstborn child of Ver,
Merry springtime's harbinger,
  With harebells dim;
Oxlips, in their cradles growing,
Marigolds, on deathbeds blowing,
  Larks'-heel trim.

All dear Nature's children sweet,
Lie 'fore bride and bridegroom's feet,   *Strew*
   Blessing their sense.   *Flowers.*
Not an angel of the air,
Bird melodious, or bird fair,
   Is absent hence.

The crow, the slanderous cuckoo, nor
The boding raven, nor chough hoar,
   Nor chattering pie,
May on our bride-house perch or sing,
Or with them any discord bring,
   But from it fly.

> THE TWO NOBLE KINSMEN, i. 1. 1634.

URNS and odours, bring away,
Vapours, sighs, darken the day;
Our dole more deadly looks than dying;
Balms, and gums, and heavy cheers,
Sacred vials filled with tears,
And clamors through the wild air flying:

Come all sad and solemn shows,
That are quick-eyed pleasures foes;
We convent nought else but woes.
      We convent, etc.

> THE TWO NOBLE KINSMEN, i. 5.

THOMAS CAREW

1598?-1639?

The Song in Parts.

Q. FROM whence was first this Fury hurled,
This Jealousy into the world?
From Hell? *A.* No, there doth reign
Eternal hatred with disdain.

But she the daughter is of Love,
Sister of Beauty. *Q.* Then above
She must derive, from the third sphere,
Her heavenly off-spring? *A.* Neither there,
From those immortal flames could she
Draw her cold frozen pedigree.
Q. If not in Heaven, nor Hell, where then
Had she her birth? *A.* In the hearts of men.
Beauty and Fear did her create
Younger than Love, elder than Hate,
Sister to both, by Beauty's side
To Love, by Fear to Hate, allied.
Despair her issue is, whose race
Of fruitful mischiefs drowns the space
Of the wide earth in a swoll'n flood
Of wrath, revenge, spite, rage and blood.
Q. Oh! how can such a spurious line
Proceed from parents so divine?
A. As streams which from their crystal spring
Do sweet and clear their waters bring;
Yet mingling with the brackish main,
Nor taste, nor colour they retain.
Q. Yet rivers 'twixt their banks do flow
Still fresh; can jealousy do so?
A. Yes, while she keeps the steadfast ground
Of hope and fear, her equal bound;
Hope, sprung from favour, worth, or chance,
Towards the fair object doth advance:
Whilst Fear as watchful sentinel
Doth the invading foe repel;
And Jealousy thus mixed doth prove
The season and the salt of Love.
But when Fear takes a larger scope,
Stifling the child of Reason, Hope;
Then sitting on the usurped throne,
She, like a tyrant, rules alone,
As the wild ocean unconfined,
And rages as the Northern wind.

THOMAS KILLIGREW'S THE SECOND PART OF CICILIA
AND CLORINDA OR LOVE IN ARMS, v. 2. 1663.

HENRY SHIRLEY

?-1627

WHAT are earthly honours
But sin's glorious banners?
Let not golden gifts delight thee,
Let not death nor torments fright thee
From thy place thy Captain gives thee;
When thou faintest he relieves thee.
Hark how the lark
Is to the morning singing,
Hark how the bells are ringing,
It is for joy that thou to Heaven art flying:
This is not life; true life is got by dying.

THE MARTYRED SOLDIER, iii. 1638.

RICHARD BROME

?-1652

You say my love is but a man.
    But I can find more odds
'Twixt him and others that I can
    Find between him and gods.
        He has in's eye
        Such majesty,
    His shape is so divine
That were I owner of the world
    He only should be mine.

THE NORTHERN LASS, ii. 3. 1632.

*Music. The masquers enter. All in willow garlands, four men,
four women. Before the dance, Constance sings this song.*

NOR Love nor Fate dare I accuse,
For that my love did me refuse;
But oh! mine own unworthiness,
That durst presume so mickle bliss.

It was too much for me to love
A man, so like the gods above;
An angel's shape, a saint-like voice,
Are too divine for human choice.

Oh had I wisely given my heart
For to have loved him but in part;
Sought only to enjoy his face,
Or any one peculiar grace
    Of foot, of hand, of lip, or eye,
I might have lived where now I die:
But I, presuming all to choose,
Am now condemnèd all to lose.

THE NORTHERN LASS, ii. 6.

A BONNY, bonny bird I had,
    A bird that was my marrow;
A bird whose pastime made me glad,
    And Philip, 'twas my sparrow.
A pretty play-fere; chirp it would,
    And hop, and fly to fist,
Keep cut, as 'twere a usurer's gold,
    And bill me when I list.
        "Philip, Philip, Philip" it cries,
        But he is fled, and my joy dies.

But were my Philip come again,
    I would not change my Love
For Juno's bird with gaudy train,
    Nor yet for Venus' dove.
Nay, would my Philip come again,
    I would not change my state,
For his great name sake's wealth of Spain,
    To be another's mate.
        "Philip, Philip, Philip" it cries,
        But he is fled, and my joy dies.

THE NORTHERN LASS, iii. 2.

2. marrow: *companion.* 5. play-fere: *playmate.* 7. keep cut: *be coy.*

PEACE, wayward barne, O cease thy moan;
Thy far more wayward daddy's gone,
And never will recalled be
By cries of either thee, or me.
    For should we cry
    Until we die,
We should not scant his cruelty.
    Ballow, Ballow, etc.

He needs might in himself foresee
What thou successively might'st be;
And could he then (though me forego)
His infant leave, ere he did know
    How like the dad
    Would be the lad,
In time, to make fond maidens glad?
    Ballow, Ballow, etc.

THE NORTHERN LASS, iv. 4.

1. barne: *bairn, child.*

COME, come, away: the spring
(By every bird that can but sing,
Or chirp a note) doth now invite
Us forth to taste of his delight,
In field, in grove, on hill, in dale;
But above all the nightingale,
Who in her sweetness strives t'outdo
The loudness of the hoarse cuckoo.
    "Cuckoo," cries he; "Jug, jug, jug," sings she;
    From bush to bush, from tree to tree,
    Why in one place then tarry we?

Come away; why do we stay?
We have no debt or rent to pay.
No bargains or accounts to make;
Nor land or lease to let or take:
Or if we had, should that remore us
When all the world's our own before us,
And where we pass, and make resort,
It is our kingdom and our court?

"Cuckoo," cries he, "Jug, jug, jug," sings she;
From bush to bush, from tree to tree,
Why in one place then tarry we?

A JOVIAL CREW, OR THE MERRY BEGGARS, i. 1652.

16. remore: *hinder.*

The Catch Sung. And they drink about. The singers are all graybeards.

A ROUND, a round, a round, boys, a round,
Let mirth fly aloft, and sorrow be drowned.
Old sack, and old songs, and a merry old crew
Can charm away cares when the ground looks blue.

A JOVIAL CREW, iv. 1.

ROBERT COX

Fl. 1625-1650

Enter the Huntsmen, with three Country Wenches. As they come in they sing this song.

COME, you young men, come along
With your music, dance and song;
Bring your lasses in your hands,
For 'tis that which Love commands:
  Then to the maypole come away,
  For it is now a holiday.

It is the choice time of the year,
For the violets now appear;
Now the rose receives its birth,
And pretty primrose decks the earth:
  Then to the maypole come away,
  For it is now a holiday.

Here each batchelor may chose
One that will not faith abuse;
Nor repay with coy disdain,

Love, that should be loved again:
    Then to the maypole come away,
    For it is now a holiday.

And when you well reckoned have
What kisses you your sweethearts gave,
Take them all again, and more;
It will never make them poor:
    Then to the maypole come away,
    For it is now a holiday.

When you thus have spent the time,
Till the day be past its prime,
To your beds repair at night,
And dream there of your days delight:
    Then to the maypole come away,
    For it is now a holiday.

ACTÆON AND DIANA. N. D.

PETER HAUSTED

?-1645

A Dialogue betwixt Venus, Thetis, and Phœbus, sung by two
trebles and a bass.

Venus: DROWSY Phœbus, come away,
        And let out the longed-for day,
        Leave thy Thetis' silver breast,
        And ope the casements of the east.
          'Tis Venus calls: away, away,
          The waking mortals long for day.
Thetis: And let them long; 'tis just and right
        To shut them in eternal night,
        Whose deeds deserve no day. Lie still,
          Arise not yet, lie still, my Sun;
          My night begins when thou art gone.
Venus: I'll woo thee with a kiss to come away.
Thetis: And I with forty for to stay.
Venus: I'll give to thee the fair Adonis' spear,

	So thou wilt rise.
Thetis:	And I, to keep thee here,
	Will give a wreath of pearl as fair
	As ever sea-nymph yet did wear.
	'Tis Thetis woos thee stay, O stay, O stay.
Venus:	'Tis Venus woos thee rise, O come away!
Phœbus:	To which of these shall I mine ear incline?
Venus:	Unto the upper world repair.
Thetis:	O no, I'll bind him in my flowing hair.
Phœbus:	But see fond mortals how they gaze
	On that same petty blaze!
	Thetis, adieu, I am no longer thine;
	I must away, for if I stay,
	My deity's quite undone,
	They will forget t'adore the rising sun.

THE RIVAL FRIENDS. INTRODUCTION. 1632.

HAVE pity, Grief; I cannot pay
    The tribute which I owe thee, tears;
        Alas those fountains are grown dry,
        And 'tis in vain to hope supply
From others' eyes; for each man bears
    Enough about him of his own
    To spend his stock of tears upon.

Woo then the heavens, gentle Love,
    To melt a cloud for my relief,
        Or woo the deep, or woo the grave;
        Woo what thou wilt, so I may have
Wherewith to pay my debt, for Grief
    Has vowed, unless I quickly pay,
    To take both life and love away.

THE RIVAL FRIENDS, i. 3.

CUPID, if a God thou art,
Transfix this monster's stubborn heart.
But if all thy shafts be flown,
And thy quiver empty grown,
Here be ladies that have eyes

Can furnish thee with new supplies.
   Yet, wingèd archer, do not shoot at all;
   Tis pity that he should so nobly fall.

THE RIVAL FRIENDS, i. 8.

The Song, sung by two Trebles.

1st Treble: BUT why
      Do the wing'd minutes fly
        So fast away?
   Stop your course, ye hasty hours,
   And sollicit all the powers
      To let you stay.
   For the earth could ne'er show forth
   An object of a greater worth.

2nd Treble: But why
      Do the wing'd minutes fly
        So fast away?
1st Treble: It is because that they which follow
   Crowd on to have a sight as well as they;
2nd Treble: Hark how the ghosts of passed moments groan
      'Cause they are gone;
    And rail at Fate
    And curse the date
   Of their short lives expired so soon.

Chorus: Then stop your course, you hasty hours,
   And solicit all the powers
      To let you stay,
   For the earth could ne'er show forth
   An object of a greater worth.

THE RIVAL FRIENDS, iii. 8.

HAVE you a desire to see
The glorious Heaven's epitome?
Or an abstract of the spring?
Adonis' garden? or a thing
   Fuller of wonder: Nature's shop displayed,
   Hung with the choicest pieces she has made?
      Here behold it open laid.

Or else would you bless your eyes
With a type of paradise?
Or behold how poets feign
Jove to sit amidst his train?
 Or see (what made Actæon rue)
 Diana 'mongst her virgin crew?
  Lift up your eyes and view.

THE RIVAL FRIENDS, iv. 15.

ROBERT DAVENPORT

Fl. 1623

MATILDA, now go take thy bed
In the dark dwellings of the dead;

And rise in the great waking day,
Sweet as incense, fresh as May.

Rest thou, chaste soul, fixed in thy proper sphere,
Amongst Heaven's fair ones; all are fair ones there.

Chorus: Rest there, chaste soul, whilst we here troubled say
 "Time gives us griefs, Death takes our joys away."

KING JOHN AND MATILDA, v. 1. 1655.

ROBERT GOMERSALL

1602-1646?

How I laugh at their fond wish
 Whose desire
 Aims no higher
Than the baits of Midas' dish?
What is gold but yellow dirt?
 Which th'unkind
 Heavens refined
When they made us love our hurt.

Would to heaven that I might steep
    My faint eyes
    In the wise,
In the gentle dews of sleep!
Whose effects do pose us so,
    That we deem
    It does seem
Both Death's brother and his foe.
This does always with us keep,
    And being dead
    That's not fled:
Death is but a longer sleep.

THE TRAGEDY OF LODOVICK SFORZA DUKE OF MILAN,
iv. 1. 1628.

13. pose: *confuse.*

WILLIAM STRODE

1602-1645

ONCE Venus' cheeks, that shamed the morn,
    Their hue let fall;
Her lips, that winter had out-borne,
    In June looked pale.
Her heat grew cold, her nectar dry;
No juice she had but in her eye,
The wonted fire and flames to mortify.
When was this so dismal sight?
When Adonis bade good-night.

THE FLOATING ISLAND, iv. 14. 1655.

An Attendant sings in a bass.

COME heavy souls oppressèd with the weight
Of crimes, or pangs, or want of your delight,
    Come down in Lethe's sleepy lake,
      Whatever makes you ache.
      Drink health from poisoned bowls,
Breathe out your cares together with your souls.

Cool Death's a salve
Which all may have,
There's no distinction in the grave;
Lay down your loads before death's iron door,
Sigh, and sigh out, groan once, and groan no more.

THE FLOATING ISLAND, v. 7.

WILLIAM HEMING

1602–1632?

The Song by Nuns.

COME, blest virgins, come and bring
To this goddess offering;
Offer to her kisses, such
As make good better by the touch;
Where her eyes let fall a tear,
Another Paradise springs there;
It's preposterous cruelty
To sacrifice a deity.
If a true path should be trod,
To her sacrifice a god.

THE FATAL CONTRACT, iii. 2. 1653.

JASPER MAYNE

1604–1672

The first Song, sung by Two Amazons.

TIME is a feathered thing;
And whilst I praise
The sparklings of thy looks and call them rays,
Takes wing;
Leaving behind him as he flies

An unperceived dimness in thine eyes.
His minutes whilst th' are told,
Do make us old;
And every sand of his fleet glass,
Increasing age as it doth pass,
Insensibly sows wrinkles there
Where flowers and roses do appear.
Whilst we do speak, our fire
Doth into ice expire.
Flames turn to frost;
And ere we can
Know how our crow turns swan,
Or how a silver snow
Springs there where jet did grow,
Our fading spring is in dull winter lost.

Since, then, the night hath hurled
Darkness, love's shade,
Over its enemy the day, and made
The world
Just such a blind and shapeless thing
As 'twas before light did from darkness spring;
Let us employ its treasure,
And make shade pleasure;
Let's number out the hours by blisses,
And count the minutes by our kisses.
Let the heavens new motions feel
And by our embraces wheel.
And whilst we try the way
By which love doth convey
Soul into soul,
And mingling so
Makes them such raptures know
As makes them entranced lie
In mutual ecstasy:
Let the harmonious spheres in music roll.

THE AMOROUS WAR, iv. 5. 1648.

WILLIAM HABINGTON

1605-1654

FINE young folly, though you were
That fair beauty I did swear,
   Yet you ne'er could reach my heart.
For we courtiers learn at school,
Only with your sex to fool,
   You're not worth the serious part.

When I sigh and kiss your hand,
Cross my arms and wondering stand,
   Holding parley with your eye,
Then dilate on my desires,
Swear the sun ne'er shot such fires,
   All is but a handsome lie.

When I eye your curl or lace,
Gentle soul, you think your face
   Straight some murder doth commit;
And your virtue doth begin
To grow scrupulous of my sin,
   When I talk to show my wit.

Therefore, madam, wear no cloud,
Nor to check my love grow proud,
   For in sooth I much do doubt,
'Tis the powder in your hair,
Not your breath, perfumes the air,
   And your clothes that set you out.

Yet though truth has this confessed,
And I vow I love in jest,
   When I next begin to court
And protest an amorous flame,
You will swear I in earnest am:
   Bedlam! this is pretty sport.

THE QUEEN OF ARRAGON, iv. 1. 1640.

THOMAS NABBES

1605-1641?

FLOW, flow delight,
And pleasures swell to height.
Drown every eye with joyful tears,
    And fill the ears
With sounds harmonious as the spheres.
Let every sense be ravished quite
With a large fulness of delight.

Chorus.

Join all ye instruments of pleasure;
And from th'abundance of your treasure
Choose out one t'enrich the bower,
And make the mistress of this paramour.

MICROCOSMUS. A MORAL MASQUE, iii. 1637.

BEAUTY, no more the subject be
Of wanton art to flatter thee:
Or in dull figures call thee Spring,
Lily or Rose, or other thing;
All which beneath thee are, and grow
Into contempt when thou dost show
The unmatched beauty of thy brow.

Chorus.

Behold a sphere of virgins move,
None mongst them less than Queen of Love.
And yet their Queen so far excels
Beauty and she are only parallels.

HANIBAL AND SCIPIO, ii. 5. 1637.

*After the dance, is heard the chirping of birds; and whilest the
following song is singing, the scene again changeth into a
pleasant arbour, in which the Spring in a green robe wrought
over with flowers presents herself.*

SEE, see a metamorphosis,
The late gray field now verdant is.

The sun with warm beams glads the earth,
    And to the springing flowers
He gives a new and lively birth
    By th'aid of gentle showers.
The lambs no longer bleat for cold,
Nor cry for succor from the old:
But frisk and play with confidence
Like emblems of true innocence.

Chorus.

The cheerful birds their voices strain,
The cuckoo's hoarse for want of rain.
The nightingale doth sweetly sing,
To welcome in the joyful Spring.

           THE SPRING'S GLORY. MORALIZED IN A MASK. 1638.

The Song within.

WHAT a dainty life the milkmaid leads,
When over the flowery meads
She dabbles in the dew
And sings to her cow,
    And feels not the pain
    Of love or disdain.
She sleeps in the night, though she toils in the day,
And merrily passeth her time away.

           TOTENHAM COURT, i. 3. 1638.

THOMAS RANDOLPH

1605-1635

SLAVES are they that heap up mountains,
    Still desiring more and more,
Still let's carouse in Bacchus' fountains,
    Never dreaming to be poor.

Give us then a cup of liquor,
    Fill it up unto the brim;
For then methinks my wits grow quicker,
    When my brains in liquor swim.

ARISTIPPUS OR THE JOVIAL PHILOSOPHER. 1630.

WE care not for money, riches or wealth;
Old sack is our money, old sack is our health.
        Then let's flock hither
        Like birds of a feather,
To drink, to fling,
To laugh and sing,
            Conferring our notes together,
            Conferring our notes together.
Come, let us laugh, let us drink, let us sing;
The winter with us is as good as the spring.
        We care not a feather
        For wind or for weather,
But night and day
We sport and play,
            Conferring our notes together,
            Conferring our notes together.

ARISTIPPUS OR THE JOVIAL PHILOSOPHER.

SIR WILLIAM KILLIGREW

1606-1695

CHLORIS, we see the offended gods
At first do show and shake their rods,
That they may rather threat, then strike,
So we forego what they dislike.
These faulty streams shall flow no more
Above their banks, as heretofore:
Nor swelling tempest from my breast
Henceforth thy virgin cares molest.
All shall be fashioned to thy will,
So thou wilt let me love thee still:
My lips shall not a word let go,

That may offend to tell thee so:
But to dissemble, or deny
That I do love thee were a lie
Would stain my soul; 'twill prove a spot,
To look as if I loved thee not.

SELINDRA, ii. 1666.

SIR WILLIAM DAVENANT

1606-1668

A Song between two Boys.

1. THIS lady, ripe, and calm, and fresh,
    As Eastern summers are,
Must now forsake both time and flesh,
    T' add light to some small star.

2. Whilst yet alive, each star decayed
    She may relieve with light;
But death leads beauty to a shade
    More cold, more dark than night.

1. The saucy faith of man doth blind
    His pride, 'till it conduce
To destine all his abject kind
    For some eternal use.

2. But ask not bodies (doomed to die)
    To what abode they go;
Since knowledge is but sorrow's spy,
    It is not safe to know.

THE JUST ITALIAN, v. 1. 1630.

Boy: WEEP no more for what is past,
    For time in motion makes such haste
He hath no leisure to descry
    Those errors which he passeth by.

If we consider accident,
  And how repugnant unto sense
It pays desert with bad event,
  We shall disparage Providence.

THE CRUEL BROTHER, V. I. 1630.

My lodging it is on the cold ground,
  And very hard is my fare,
But that which troubles me most is
  The unkindness of my dear;
Yet still I cry: O turn, love,
  And I prithee, love, turn to me,
For thou art the man that I long for,
  And alack! what remedy.

I'll crown thee with a garland of straw then,
  And I'll marry thee with a rush ring,
My frozen hopes shall thaw then,
  And merrily we will sing.
O turn to me, my dear love,
  And prithee, love, turn to me,
For thou art the man that alone canst
  Procure my liberty.

But if thou wilt harden thy heart still,
  And be deaf to my pitiful moan,
Then I must endure the smart still,
  And tumble in straw alone.
Yet still I cry: O turn, love,
  And I prithee, love, turn to me,
For thou art the man that alone art
  The cause of my misery.

THE RIVALS, V. 1668.

The Song in recitativo and in parts.

THE bread is all baked,
The embers are raked;
'Tis midnight now by chanticleer's first crowing.
Let's kindly carouse
Whilst 'top of the house

The cats fall out in the heat of their wooing.
    Time, whilst the hour-glass does run out,
    This flowing glass shall go about.
Stay, stay, the nurse is waked, the child does cry,
No song so ancient is as lulla-by.
The cradle's rocked, the child is hushed again,
Then hey for the maids, and ho for the men.
    Now everyone advance his glass;
    Then all at once together clash;
      Experienced lovers know
      This clashing does but show
That, as in music, so in love must be
Some discord to make up a harmony.
Sing, sing! When crickets sing why should not we?
    The crickets were merry before us;
They sung us thanks ere we made them a fire.
    They taught us to sing in a chorus:
The chimney is their church, the oven their quire.
Once more the cock cries cock-a-doodle-doo.
The owl cries o'er the barn, to-whit-to-whoo!
Benighted travellers now lose their way
    Whom Will-of-the-wisp bewitches:
About and about he leads them astray
    Through bogs, through hedges, and ditches.
Hark! hark! the cloister bell is rung!
Alas! the midnight dirge is sung.
      Let 'em ring,
      Let 'em sing,
Whilst we spend the night in love and in laughter.
      When night is gone,
      O then too soon
The discords, and cares of the day come after.
Come, boys! a health, a health, a double health
To those who 'scape from care by shunning wealth.
      Dispatch it away
      Before it be day.
Twill quickly grow early when it is late:
      A health to thee,
      To him, to me,
To all who beauty love and business hate.

THE MAN'S THE MASTER, iii. 1669.

Orna: RUN to Love's lottery! Run, maids, and rejoice:
  When, drawing your chance, you meet your own
    choice;
  And boast that your luck you help with design,
  By praying cross-legged to Old Bishop Valentine.
  Hark, hark! a prize is drawn, and trumpets sound!
      Tan, ta, ra, ra, ra!
      Tan, ta, ra, ra, ra!

  Hark, maids! more lots are drawn! prizes abound.
  Dub! dub a, dub a, dub! the drum now beats!
  And, dub a, dub a, dub, echo repeats.
  As if at night the god of war had made
  Love's queen a skirmish for a serenade.
    Haste, haste, fair maids, and come away!
    The priest attends, your bridegrooms stay.
  Roses and pinks will be strewn where you go;
  Whilst I walk in shades of willow, willow.
    When I am dead let him that did slay me
    Be but so good as kindly to lay me
    There where neglected lovers mourn,
    Where lamps and hallowed tapers burn,
    Where clerks in quires sad dirges sing,
    Where sweetly bells at burials ring.
      My rose of youth is gone
      Withered as soon as blown!
      Lovers go ring my knell!
      Beauty and love farewell!
      And lest virgins forsaken
      Should, perhaps, be mistaken
  In seeking my grave, alas! let them know
  I lie near a shade of willow, willow.

     THE UNFORTUNATE LOVERS, iii. 1. 1673.

  'TIS, in good truth, a most wonderful thing
    (I am e'en ashamed to relate it)
  That love so many vexations should bring
    And yet few have the wit to hate it.

Love's weather in maids should seldom hold fair:
    Like April's mine shall quickly alter;
I'll give him to-night a lock of my hair,
    To whom next day I'll send a halter.

I cannot abide these malapert males,
    Pirates of love, who know no duty;
Yet love with a storm can take down their sails
    And they must strike to Admiral Beauty.

Farewell to that maid who will be undone,
    Who in markets of men (where plenty
Is cried up and down) will die even for one.
    I will live to make fools of twenty.

                    THE UNFORTUNATE LOVERS, iv. 1.

Viola sings the Song.

    WAKE all the dead! what ho! what ho!
How soundly they sleep whose pillows lie low!
They mind not poor lovers who walk above
On the decks of the world in storms of love.
    No whisper now nor glance can pass
    Through wickets or through panes of glass;
For our windows and doors are shut and barred.
Lie close in the church, and in the churchyard.
        In every grave make room, make room!
    The world's at an end, and we come, we come.

    The state is now love's foe, love's foe;
Has seized on his arms, his quiver and bow;
Has pinioned his wings, and fettered his feet,
Because he made way for lovers to meet.
    But, O sad chance, his judge was old;
    Hearts cruel grow, when blood grows cold.
No man being young his process would draw.
O heavens, that love should be subject to law!
        Lovers go woo the dead, the dead!
    Lie two in a grave, and to bed, to bed!

                    THE LAW AGAINST LOVERS, iii. 1. 1673.

ANONYMOUS

Night's First Song.

In wet and cloudy mists I slowly rise,
  As with mine own dull weight opprest,
To close with sleep the jealous lover's eyes,
  And give forsaken virgins rest.

Th' advent'rous merchant and the mariner,
  Whom storms all day vex in the deep,
Begin to trust the winds when I appear,
  And lose their dangers in their sleep.

The studious that consume their brains and sight
  In search where doubtful knowledge lies,
Grow weary of their fruitless use of light,
  And with my shades do ease their eyes.

Th' ambitious toiling statesman that prepares
  Great mischiefs ere the day begins,
Not measures day by hours, but by his cares;
  And night must intermit his sins.

Then why, when my slow chariot used to climb,
  Did old mistaking sages weep?
As if my empire did usurp their time,
  And hours were lost when spent in sleep?

I come to ease their labours and prevent
  That weariness which would destroy;
The profit of their toils are still misspent
  Till rest enables to enjoy.

LUMINALIA, OR THE FESTIVAL OF LIGHT. PERSONATED
IN A MASQUE AT COURT BY THE QUEEN'S MAJESTY
AND HER LADIES. 1637.

ANONYMOUS

The Seasons' Song.

Spring.

THOSE flowers your infancy did crown,
Spring doth again to you resign,
Which now are yours, no more her own;
The primrose and sweet eglantine,
The daisy, pink, and violet blue,
All which received their scents from you.
May blossoms now shall never fade,
You have May everlasting made.

Chorus.

All hearts rejoice which now behold
Again the happy Age of Gold.
For Time to us hath brought far more
True joys than feign'd were heretofore.
Three Royal blossoms to us he doth bring,
Whose looks and sweetness make eternal Spring.

May cherries plasht up to the wall,
The dewberry that in valleys grows,
Kept in your lips, shall never fall;
The lady grass and the musk rose
Which were your mantle swathing-band
You make yet flourish freshly, and
Sweet fennel, for court flatterers fit,
Lives under you, you above it.

Winter.

Cold winter brings to crown your age
(Many happy years are told)
The myrtle, savory, and sage,
The semper viva, never old;
To crown your high victorious brows
Green laurel garlands, arbute boughs,
With palms and olives, whose increase
Are emblems of your lasting peace.

Nor is old winter yet at all
Less frolic than the wanton Spring:
The robin redbreasts in the hall
Picking up crumbs at Christmas sing.
When winds blow cold, and ways be foul,
In barns and sheep-cotes sits the owl,
Whose note the husbandman delights
Whenas she hoots in frosty nights.

CORONA MINERVÆ, OR A MASQUE PRESENTED BEFORE PRINCE
CHARLES HIS HIGHNESS, THE DUKE OF YORK HIS BROTHER,
AND THE LADY MARY HIS SISTER THE 27TH OF FEBRUARY, AT
THE COLLEGE OF THE MUSEUM MINERVÆ. 1635.

ROBERT CHAMBERLAIN

1607-1660

BE not so cruel, fairest Boy,
But unstring thy golden bow,
In love we must expect no joy,
Nothing there but sorrows flow;
If thy flaming arrow did
But touch, yet it still appears
We must for ever after bid
Farewell joys, and welcome tears:
Tell us, then tell us where doth grow
The herb that cures the wounded eye,
Else we must cry "Alas and woe,
There's no such herb that grows," and die.

THE SWAGGERING DAMSEL, ii. 1640.

FAREWELL this company,
If you love sadness,
For melancholy is
Nothing but madness;
Hang up proud costly clothes,
Pedlars and pack-toys;
Let's make the hogs-heads weep,
Claret and sack, boys.

THE SWAGGERING DAMSEL, iv.

SIR ASTON COKAYNE

1608-1684

THE spheres are dull and do not make
Such music as mine ears will take.
The slighted birds may cease to sing,
Their chirpings do not grace the Spring:
The Nightingale is sad in vain,
I care not to hear her complain:
    While I have ears and you a tongue,
     I shall think all things else go wrong.

The poets feign'd that Orpheus could
Make stones to follow where he would;
They feign'd indeed, but (had they known
Your voice) a truth they might have shown.
All instruments most sadly go
Because your tongue excels them so:
    While I have ears, and you a tongue,
     I shall think all things else go wrong.

                  THE OBSTINATE LADY, v. 1. 1657.

2. take: *captivate.*

JOHN MILTON

1608-1674

SWEET Echo, sweetest nymph, that liv'st unseen
      Within thy airy shell
By slow Meander's margent green,
And in the violet-embroidered vale
    Where the love-lorn nightingale
Nightly to thee her sad song mourneth well:
Can'st thou not tell me of a gentle pair
    That likest thy Narcissus are?
      Oh if thou have
Hid them in some flowery cave,
    Tell me but where,

Sweet queen of parley, daughter of the sphere,
So may'st thou be translated to the skies,
And give resounding grace to all heaven's harmonies.

COMUS. 1637.

SABRINA fair,
   Listen, where thou art sitting
Under the glassy, cool, translucent wave,
   In twisted braids of lilies knitting
The loose train of thy amber-dropping hair;
     Listen for dear honour's sake,
     Goddess of the silver lake,
      Listen, and save.

COMUS.

Sabrina rises, attended by Water-nymphs, and sings.

BY the rushy-fringèd bank,
Where grows the willow and the osier dank,
   My sliding chariot stays,
Thick-set with agate, and the azurn sheen
Of turkis blue and emerald green,
   That in the channel strays;
Whilst from off the waters fleet
Thus I set my printless feet
O'er the cowslip's velvet head,
   That bends not as I tread.
Gentle swain, at thy request
   I am here.

COMUS.

5. turkis: *turquoise.*

II Song.

O'ER the smooth enamelled green
Where no print of step hath been,
   Follow me as I sing
   And touch the warbled string.
Under the shady roof
Of branching elm star-proof,
   Follow me,

I will bring you where she sits
Clad in splendour as befits
    Her deity.
Such a rural queen
All Arcadia hath not seen.

THE ARCADES. 1645.

III Song.

NYMPHS and shepherds, dance no more
    By sandy Ladon's lilied banks;
On old Lycæus or Cyllene hoar,
    Trip no more in twilight ranks;
Though Erymanth your loss deplore,
    A better soil shall give ye thanks.
From the stony Mænalus
Bring your flocks and live with us;
Here ye shall have better grace,
To serve the Lady of this place.
Though Syrinx your Pan's mistress were,
Yet Syrinx well might wait on her.
Such a rural queen
All Arcadia hath not seen.

THE ARCADES.

ANONYMOUS

The Song.

Shepherd.   Lucinda.

Sh: DID not you once, Lucinda, vow
            You would have none but me?
Lu: Aye, but my mother tells me now
            I must love wealth, not thee.
Sh: 'Tis not my fault my sheep are lean,
            Or that they are so few.
Lu: Nor mine. I cannot love so mean,
            So poor a thing as you.

Sh: Cruel, thy love is in thy power,
        Fortune is not in mine.
Lu: But shepherd, think how great my dower
        Is in respect of thine.
Sh: Ah me! *Lu:* Ah me! *Sh:* Mock you my grief?
Lu: I pity thy hard fate.
Sh: Pity for love is poor relief,
        I'd rather choose thy hate.
Lu: But I must love thee. *Sh:* No. *Lu:* Believe,
        I'll seal it with a kiss,
    And give thee no more cause to grieve
        Than what thou findst in this.
Sh: Lu: Be witness then you powers above,
        And by these holy bands,
    Let it appear that truest love
        Grows not from wealth or lands.

THE KING AND QUEEN'S ENTERTAINMENT AT RICHMOND AFTER THEIR DEPARTURE FROM OXFORD; IN A MASQUE PRESENTED BY THE MOST ILLUSTRIOUS PRINCE, PRINCE CHARLES, September 12, 1636. 1636.

SIR JOHN SUCKLING

1609-1642

WHY so pale and wan, fond lover?
    Prithee why so pale?
Will, when looking well can't move her,
    Looking ill prevail?
    Prithee why so pale?

Why so dull and mute, young sinner?
    Prithee why so mute?
Will, when speaking well can't win her,
    Saying nothing do't?
    Prithee why so mute?

Quit, quit, for shame; this will not move,
    This cannot take her;

If of herself she will not love,
    Nothing can make her,
    The Devil take her.

                 AGLAURA, iv. 1. 1638.

No, no, fair heretic, it needs must be
    But an ill love in me,
    And worse for thee.

For were it in my power
To love thee now this hour,
    More than I did the last;

'Twould then so fall,
I might not love at all;

Love that can flow, and can admit increase,
Admits as well an ebb, and may grow less.

True love is still the same; the torrid zones,
    And those more frigid ones,
    It must not know:

For love, grown cold or hot,
Is lust or friendship, not
    The thing we have;

For that's a flame would die,
Held down, or up too high:

  Then think I love more than I can express,
  And would love more, could I but love thee less.

                 AGLAURA, iv. 1.

    COME let the state stay,
    And drink away,
    There is no business above it.
    It warms the cold brain,

It makes us speak in high strain,
He's a fool that does not approve it.
The Macedon youth
Left behind him this truth,
That nothing is done with much thinking,
He drunk and fought,
Till he had what he sought;
The world was his own by good drinking.

THE DISCONTENTED COLONEL, ii. [1640?].

JOSEPH RUTTER

Fl. 1635.

SHALL I because my Love is gone,
    Accuse those golden darts
Which to a blessed union
    Struck our two loving hearts,
Since Fortune, and not Love hath caused my moan?

No, her pure image I shall prize,
    Imprinted in my breast,
More than the fairest Mistress eyes
    That ever swain possest,
Which in eternal bonds my fancy ties.

Come then your sharpest griefs, and try
    If you can pierce my heart,
But use, if you would have me die,
    The best you can of Art,
To wound a breast so arm'd with constancy.

THE SHEPHERDS HOLIDAY, i. 1. 1635.

Sylvia. Delia.

Q: TELL me what you think on earth
    The greatest bliss?
A: Riches, honor, and high birth.

Q: Ah, what is this?
          If Love be banishèd the heart,
          The joy of Nature, not of Art?

Q: What's honor worth, or high descent?
              Or ample wealth,
          If cares do breed us discontent,
              Or want of health?
A: It is the order of the Fates
          That these should wait on highest states.

Cho: Love only does our souls refine,
              And by his skill
          Turns human things into divine,
              And guides our will.
          Then let us of his praises sing,
          Of love, that sweetens everything.

THE SHEPHERDS HOLIDAY, iii. 1.

Venus and the Graces sing.

COME, lovely boy unto my court,
    And leave these uncouth woods, and all,
    That feed thy fancy with love's gall,
But keep away the honey and the sport.

Chorus of Graces: Come unto me,
                        And with variety
Thou shalt be fed; which Nature loves, and I.

There is no music in a voice
    That is but one, and still the same.
    Inconstancy is but a name
To fright poor lovers from a better choice.

Chorus: Come then to me, etc.

Orpheus that on Eurydice
    Spent all his love, on others scorn,
    Now on the banks of Hebrus torn
Finds the reward of foolish constancy.

Chorus: Come then to me, etc.

And sigh no more for one love lost,
  I have a thousand Cupids here
  Shall recompense with better cheer
Thy misspent labours and thy bitter cost.

Chorus: Come then to me, etc.

THE SHEPHERDS HOLIDAY, iii. 3.

HYMEN, god of marriage-bed,
Be thou ever honoured:
Thou, whose torch's purer light
Death's sad tapers did affright,
And instead of funeral fires
Kindled lovers' chaste desires:
      May their love
      Ever prove
True and constant; let not age
Know their youthful heat t'assuage.

Maids, prepare the genial bed:
Then come, night, and hide that red
Which her cheeks, his heart does burn;
Till the envious day return,
And the lusty bridegroom say,
"I have chased her fears away,
      And instead
      Of virginhead,
Given her a greater good,
Perfection and womanhood."

THE SHEPHERDS HOLIDAY, iv. 4.

The Boy sings.

'TWAS not his person nor his parts,
  Though ne'er so famed that won me,
He loved, he said, which I believed;
  And that faith has undone me.

His virtues were alike to all,
  Nor were they more to me,

I honored them, but loved the man,
  Because that he was he.

Who since he has his love foregone,
  And is himself no more,
I love him not as he is now
  But as he was before.

THE SECOND PART OF THE CID, iii. 7. 1640.

WILLIAM CARTWRIGHT

1611-1643

The Slaves' song within.

A POX on our gaoler, and on his fat jowl.
There's liberty lies in the bottom o' th' bowl.
A fig for whatever the rascal can do,
Our dungeon is deep, but our cup's so too.
Then drink we a round in despite of our foes,
And make our hard irons cry clink in the close.

THE ROYAL SLAVE, i. 1. 1639.

Boy sings.

COME, my sweet, whiles every strain
  Calls our souls into the ear,
Where they greedy list'ning fain
  Would turn into the sound they hear;
      Lest, in desire
      To fill the quire,
      Themselves they tie
      To harmony,
Let's kiss and call them back again.

Now let's orderly convey
  Our souls into each other's breast,
Where interchangèd let them stay
  Slumb'ring in a melting rest.

Then with new fire
Let them retire,
And still present
Sweet fresh content
Youthful as the early day.

Then let us a tumult make,
    Shuffling so our souls that we,
Careless who did give or take,
    May not know in whom they be;
        Then let each smother
        And stifle the other,
        Till we expire
        In gentle fire
Scorning the forgetful lake.

THE ROYAL SLAVE, ii. 3.

1.   Now, now the sun is fled
      Down into Tethys' bed,
      Ceasing his solemn course awhile.
2.   What then?
      'Tis not to sleep, but he
      Merry all night as we;
Gods can be mad sometimes, as well as men.

Cho: Then laugh we and quaff we until our red noses
     Grow red and contest with our chaplets of roses.

1.   If he be fled, whence may
      We have a second day,
      That shall not set 'till we command?
2.   Here see
      A day that does arise
      Like his, but with more eyes,
And warms us with a better fire than he.

Cho: Then laugh we, etc.

1. 2. Thus when we chase the night
      With these true floods of light,
This Lesbian wine, which with its sparkling streams,

Darting diviner graces,
Casts glories round our faces,
And dulls the tapers with majestic beams.

Cho: Then laugh we, etc.

THE ROYAL SLAVE, iii. 1.

The Ode sung by Eumela.

To carve our loves in myrtle rinds,
And tell our secrets to the woods,
To send our sighs by faithful winds,
And trust our tears unto the floods,
　　To call where no man hears,
　　And think that rocks have ears:

To walk, and rest, to live, and die,
And yet not know whence, how, or why;
To have our hopes with fears still checkt,
To credit doubts, and truth suspect,
　　This, this is that we may
　　A lover's absence say.
Follies without are cares within;
Where eyes do fail, there souls begin.

THE LADY ERRANT, i. 4. 1651.

The Ode.

WAKE my Adonis, do not die;
　One life's enough for thee and I.
Where are thy words? thy wiles?
Thy loves, thy frowns, thy smiles?
Alas in vain I call;
　One death hath snatched them all:
Yet death's not deadly in that face,
Death in those looks itself hath grace.

　'Twas this, 'twas this I feared
　When thy pale ghost appeared;
This I presaged when thundering Jove

Tore the best myrtle in my grove;
When my sick rose-buds lost their smell,
And from my temples untouched fell,
   And 'twas for some such thing
   My dove did hang her wing.

Whither art thou my Deity gone?
Venus in Venus there is none.
In vain a goddess now am I
Only to grieve, and not to die.
     But I will love my grief,
     Make tears my tears relief;
     And sorrow shall to me
     A new Adonis be.

And this no fate can rob me of, while I
A goddess am to grieve, and not to die.

THE LADY ERRANT, iii. 4.

SEAL up her eyes, O Sleep, but flow
Mild as her manners, to and fro;
Slide soft into her, that yet she
May receive no wound from thee.
And ye present her thoughts, O dreams,
With hushing winds and purling streams,
Whiles hovering silence sits without,
Careful to keep disturbance out.
Thus seize her, Sleep, thus her again resign,
So what was Heaven's gift, we'll reckon thine.

THE SIEGE, OR LOVE'S CONVERT, ii. 5. 1651.

NATHANIEL RICHARDS

1612?-1654?

Two spirits dreadfully enter and (to the treble violin and lute) sing a song of despair during which Lepida sits weeping.

1st Spirit: HELPLESS wretch, despair, despair,
2nd Spirit: Fool to live, why drawst thou air?
1st Spirit: Friends all are dead, thou hast none.
2nd Spirit: Those that seem'd, like chaff are blown.
1st Spirit: Then die, O die,
             Die, O die.
2nd Spirit: Tis better die than live disgrac'd,
             Joys and glories all defaced.
1st Spirit: Thy pride of eyes,
                 Thy pride of eyes,
             Which world of hearts have fired,
             Gone is their glory now no more desired.
2nd Spirit: Then die, O die,
1st Spirit: Die, O die,
             Die to be free, live exempt
             And scorn the base world's base contempt.
             Come live with us, live with us,
             Live with us, with spirits dwell,
             Life is a lake of woe, continual hell.

THE TRAGEDY OF MESSALINA, V. I. 1640.

JASPER FISHER

Fl. 1639

Chorus of five Bards-Laureate, four voices and a harper, attired.

At the Spring   Flat, acute;
Birds do sing;   And salute
Now with high,   The sun, born
Then low cry: Every morn.

All: He's no bard that cannot sing
The praises of the flowery Spring.

Flora queen	And to spread
All in green,	Cruel red
Doth delight	With a blue
To paint white,	Colour true.

All: He's no bard that cannot sing
The praises of the flowery Spring.

Woods renew	With his pipe
Hunter's hue.	Care doth wipe,
Shepherds gray	Till he dream
Crowned with bay,	By the stream.

All: He's no bard that cannot sing
The praises of the flowery Spring.

Faithful loves,	Country swains
Turtle doves,	On the plains
Sit and bill	Run and leap,
On a hill.	Turn and skip.

All: He's no bard that cannot sing
The praises of the flowery Spring.

Pan doth play	With caps red
Care away.	On their head
Fairies small	Dance around
Two foot tall,	On the ground.

All: He's no bard that cannot sing
The praises of the flowery Spring.

Phillis bright	Rocks doth move
Clothed in white,	With her love,
With neck fair,	And makes mild,
Yellow hair,	Tigers wild.

All: He's no bard that cannot sing
The praises of the flowery Spring.

FUIMUS TROES. THE TRUE TROJANS, i. 5. 1633.

HENRY GLAPTHORNE

Fl. 1639

GREAT Pan, to thee we do confine
This fleece of wool. This bowl of wine
To father Bacchus. Ceres dear,
This garland of the wheaten ear
Accept. Silvanus, we present
These fruits to thee thy bounty sent.
And you maids, from whose each eye
Wingèd shafts of love do fly,
Do not shame to let your feet
In a country measure meet
With these youths, whose active parts
Will play the thieves, and steal your hearts.

Dance.

ARGALUS AND PARTHENIA, ii. 2. 1639.

1. confine: *devote.*

LEWIS SHARPE

Fl. 1640

Boy: TELL me, Jove, should she disdain,
Whether were it greater pain,
Silent in thy flames to die,
Or say I love, and she deny.

Flames suppressed do higher grow;
Should she scorn when she does know
Thy affection, thou shalt prove
A glorious martyrdom for love.

Better to Love's mercy bow,
She may burn as well as thou:
On then timorous heart proceed,
For wounds are death that inward bleed.

THE NOBLE STRANGER, ii. 1640.

CHARM, O charm, thou god of sleep,
Her fair eyes, that waking mourn;
Frightful visions from her keep,
Such as are by sorrows borne:
But let all the sweets that may
Wait on rest, her thoughts obey.

Fly, Oh fly, thou god of love,
To that breast thy dart did wound,
Draw thy shaft, the smart remove,
Let her wonted joys be found:
Raise up pleasure to a flood,
Never ebbing; new joys bud.

THE NOBLE STRANGER, V.

JOHN TATHAM

Fl. 1640

I WILL follow through yon grove,
Where I soon shall meet my love;
Then with sweet embraces we
Will clip, and cull, and none shall see.
A willow garland I will make,
And sweetly wear it for his sake.
Then through the thickets, woods and plains
I will hide me from the swains.

LOVE CROWNS THE END. 1640.

HENRY BURNELL

Fl. 1641

LOVE'S far more powerful than a king,
And wiser than most statesmen are:
For it commands him, and doth spring
In them strange thoughts; in both much care
(Beside th' affairs o' th' Commonwealth)

To crouch and to obey. Nay more;
It makes them lose all joy and health,
And not be the men they were before;
Until wise love, all powerful love,
The gracious physician prove.

LANDGARTHA, ii. 1641.

SIR JOHN DENHAM

1615-1669

SOMNUS, the humble God, that dwells
In cottages and smokey cells,
Hates gilded roofs and beds of down;
And though he fears no Prince's frown
Flies from the circlet of a crown.

Come, I say, thou powerful God,
And thy leaden charming rod,
Dipped in the Lethean lake,
O'er his wakeful temples shake,
Lest he should sleep and never wake.

Nature, alas! why art thou so
Obligèd to thy greatest foe?
Sleep that is thy best repast,
Yet of death it bears a taste,
And both are the same thing at last.

THE SOPHY, v. 1642.

ABRAHAM COWLEY

1618-1667

THE merry waves dance up and down, and play,
    Sport is granted to the sea.
Birds are the choristers of th' empty air,
    Sport is never wanting there.

The ground doth smile at the Spring's flowery birth,
    Sport is granted to the earth.
The fire its cheering flame on high doth rear,
    Sport is never wanting there.
If all the elements, the earth, the sea,
    Air and fire so merry be;
Why is man's mirth so seldom and so small,
    Who is compounded of them all?

LOVE'S RIDDLE. A PASTORAL COMEDY WRITTEN AT THE
TIME OF HIS BEING KING'S SCHOLAR IN WESTMINSTER
SCHOOL, i. 1. 1638.

IT is a punishment to love,
And not to love a punishment doth prove;
    But of all pains there's no such pain
As 'tis to love, and not be loved again.

Till sixteen, parents we obey;
After sixteen, men steal our hearts away:
    How wretched are we women grown,
Whose wills, whose minds, whose hearts are ne'er our own?

LOVE'S RIDDLE, iv. 1.

ROGER BOYLE, EARL OF ORRERY

1621-1679

SINCE you will needs my heart possess,
'Tis just to you I first confess
    The faults to which 'tis given;
It is to change much more inclined
Than women, or the sea or wind,
    Or aught that's under heaven.

Nor will I hide from you this truth,
It has been from its very youth
    A most egregious ranger;
And since from me it often fled,
With whom it was both born and bred,
    'Twill scarce stay with a stranger.

The black, the fair, the gay, the sad,
Which made me often fear 'twas mad,
   With one kind look could win it;
So naturally it loves to range,
That it has left success for change,
   And what's worse, glories in it.

Often when I am laid to rest,
'Twould make me act like one possessed,
   For still 'twill keep a pother;
And though you only I esteem,
Yet it will make me in a dream
   Court and enjoy another.

And now if you are not afraid,
After these truths that I have said,
   To take this arrant rover;
Be not displeased, if I protest
I think the heart within your breast
   Will prove just such another.

         MR. ANTHONY. A COMEDY, iv. 1690.

WHY was I doomed by fate to prove
Absence is Hell to faithful love;
Is it thereby at my return
To make my joys the brighter burn?
If so, that needless care decline,
I want no foil to set off mine.
Or else does fortune think my joy
Not qualified would soon destroy?
Alas! absence is such an ill
It will not qualify but kill.
I ask of Fortune and of Fate
But not to change my present state.
In all things else I shall but find
The one is cruel, t'other blind.

         ALTEMIRA, i. 1. 1702.

12. But: *only*.

RICHARD FLECKNOE

?-1678?

*Filena's Song of the Commutation of Love's and
Death's Darts.*

LOVE and Death o' th' way once meeting,
Having passed a friendly greeting,
Sleep their weary eye-lids closing,
Lay them down themselves reposing.
Love, whom divers cares molested,
Could not sleep, but while Death rested,
All in haste away he posts him,
But his haste full dearly costs him;
For it chanced that going to sleeping
Both did give their darts in keeping
Unto Night, who, Error's mother,
Blindly knowing not one from t'other,
Gave Love Death's, and ne'er perceived it,
Whilst as blindly Love received it;
Since which time their darts confounding,
Love now kills instead of wounding:
Death, our hearts with sweetness filling,
Gently wounds instead of killing.

LOVE'S KINGDOM, 1664.

THOMAS THOMPSON

Sung by Plot-thrift and Cozen.

WHAT need we use many beseeches
Or trouble our brain with long speeches?
  If we love, 'tis enough;
  Hang poetical stuff,
As the rule of honesty teaches.

  Chorus: If we love, 'tis enough
       Hang poetical stuff,
    As the rule of honesty teaches.

Why should we standing whining like fools,
Or woo by Platonical rules?
  If they love, we'll repay't;
  If not, let 'em say't.
What need they the help of the Schools.

   Chorus: If they love etc.

But this must be won by romances;
And that, by verse and fine dances;
  A third does delight
  In a song yet at night.
You must crack a string which she fancies.

   Chorus: A third does delight etc.

This must be extolled to the sky;
That you can get, do but flatter and lie.
  But that lady's for me
  That loves fine and free,
As real and ready as I.

   Chorus: But that lady's for me
      That loves fine and free,
    As real and ready as I.

           THE ENGLISH ROGUE, ii. 3. 1668.

COME let us be frolic and call for our tipple,
Our pockets we'll empty and our veins we will fill.
For sack we'll not lack, nor will we be gripple
But carouse in despite of the two toppèd hill.

Chorus: Parnassus shall pass us
     Nor will we enquire
     For the font of the Muses,
     'Tis sack we desire.

Let the Frenchman delight in his white wine and red;
His *vin de Paris* is but pitiful geer.
'Tis the brave Spanish liquor that brings us to bed,
It charms all our senses and frees us from fear.

Chorus: We'll banish the Rhenish,
      White Metheglin and brown,
      'Tis sack we do love,
      So let it go down.

THE ENGLISH ROGUE, iii. 2.

3. gripple: *niggardly.*

O SWEET Diana, virtuous queen,
That dost affect the meadows green!
By heaven's edict the guide of night,
And dost in fresh leaved woods delight!
Like to the nymphs, so suffer me
To consecrate myself to thee.

Thou that for lust didst transform
Actæon to a hart, so charm
With virtuous spells each virgin's heart
That men may never them divert
From purity; or else pray make
Them other hearts for virgins' sake.

THE LIFE OF MOTHER SHIPTON, iv. 4. N. D.

ANONYMOUS

Ditty: SUBMIT, bunch of grapes,
      To the strong barley-ear,
      The weak vine no longer
      The laurel shall wear.
Budget: Sack, and all drinks else,
      Desist from the strife;
      Ale's th' only *aqua vitæ*
      And liquor of life.
All together: Then come, my boon fellows,
      Let's drink it around;
      It keeps us from th' grave,
      Though it lays us o' th' ground.
Budget: Ale's a physician,
      No mountebank bragger,
      Can cure the chill ague,

	Though 't be with the stagger.
Ditty:	Ale's a strong wrestler,
	Flings all it hath met,
	And makes the ground slippery
	Though 't be not wet.
Omnes:	But come, my boon, etc.
Ditty:	Ale is both Ceres
	And good Neptune too;
	Ale's froth was the sea
	From whence Venus grew.
Budget:	Ale is immortal
	And be there no stops,
	In bonny lads' quaffing,
	Can live without hops.
Omnes:	Then come, my boon fellows,
	Let's drink it around;
	It keeps us from the grave,
	Though it lays us o' th' ground.

THE LONDON CHANTICLEERS. A WITTY COMEDY, 14. 1659.

ANONYMOUS

The Sea Song.

Captain: To Tunis and to Argiers, boys.
          Great is our want, small be our joys;
          Let's then some voyage take in hand
          To get us means by sea or land.
             Come follow me, my boys, come follow me, *They*
             And if thou die, I'll die with thee.   *join in the*
                                                         close.

          Methinks, my boys, I see the store *He fixeth his eyes*
          Of precious gems and golden ore; *as upon objects*
          Arabian silks and sables pure   *in a landskip*
          Would make an haggard stoop to th' lure.

          No worthless mind e'er honour sought,
          Let's fight as if we fearèd nought;

If bullets fly about our ears
Let's laugh at death and banish fears.

Courage, my sparks, my knights o' th' sun,
Let Seville fame what we have done,
We'd better ten times fight a foe
Than once for all to Tyburn go.

Come let's away; mount, march away,
The calm portends a prosperous day.
When we return it shall be said
That by our voyage we are made.

But if we ne'er again return,
Inclose our ashes in an urn,
And with them spice a wassal cup,
And to good fellows drink it up.

No other obsequies we crave,
Nor quaint inscriptions on our grave;
A simple shroud's a soldier's share,
Which if he want, he needs not care.

LADY ALIMONY, iii. 3. 1659.

ANONYMOUS

So, so,
Lo lilies fade, before the roses show
Themselves in bow-dye, summer's livery.
    Feasting the curious eye
    With choice variety,
        While as before
        We did adore
            Narcissus in his prime.
        Now roses do delight
        The nicer appetite:
Such is the vast disparity of time.

So, so,
One woman fades before another know
What 'tis to be in love; but in a trice
All men do sacrifice
To th' latter and despise
Her whom before
They did adore
Like lilies in their prime.
Since now her sparkling eyes
Are darkened in disguise:
Such is the sad disparity of time.

MARCIANO, OR THE DISCOVERY, iii. 3. 1663.

3. bow-dye: *a scarlet dye.*

JOHN DRYDEN

1631-1700

Song is supposed sung by Aerial Spirits.

POOR mortals, that are clogged with earth below,
Sink under love and care,
While we, that dwell in air,
Such heavy passions never know.
Why then should mortals be
Unwilling to be free
From blood, the sullen cloud,
Which shining souls does shroud?
Then they'll show bright,
And like us light,
When leaving bodies with their care,
They slide to us and air.

THE INDIAN QUEEN, iii. 2. 1665.

AH fading joy! how quickly art thou past!
Yet we thy ruin haste.
And if the cares of human life were few,
We seek out new:
And follow fate, that does too fast pursue.

See, how on every bough the birds express,
In their sweet notes, their happiness.
They all enjoy, and nothing spare;
But on their mother nature lay their care:
Why then should man, the lord of all below,
Such troubles choose to know,
As none of all his subjects undergo?

Hark, hark, the waters, fall, fall, fall,
And with a murmuring sound
Dash, dash, upon the ground,
To gentle slumbers call.

THE INDIAN EMPEROR, iv. 3. 1667.

I FEED a flame within which so torments me
That it both pains my heart, and yet contents me:
'Tis such a pleasing smart, and I so love it,
That I had rather die, than once remove it.

Yet he for whom I grieve shall never know it,
My tongue does not betray, nor my eyes show it:
Not a sigh nor a tear my pain discloses,
But they fall silently like dew on roses.

Thus, to prevent my love from being cruel,
My heart's the sacrifice as 'tis the fuel:
And while I suffer thus to give him quiet,
My faith rewards my love, though he deny it.

On his eyes will I gaze, and there delight me;
While I conceal my love, no frown can fright me:
To be more happy I dare not aspire;
Nor can I fall more low, mounting no higher.

SECRET LOVE, OR THE MAIDEN QUEEN, iv. 2. 1668.

AH how sweet it is to love,
Ah how gay is young desire!
And what pleasing pains we prove

When we first approach love's fire!
    Pains of love be sweeter far
    Than all other pleasures are.

Sighs, which are from lovers blown,
Do but gently heave the heart:
Ev'n the tears they shed alone
Cure, like trickling balm, their smart.
    Lovers when they lose their breath,
    Bleed away in easy death.

Love and time with reverence use,
Treat them like a parting friend:
Nor the golden gifts refuse,
Which in youth sincere they send:
    For each year their price is more,
    And they less simple than before.

Love, like spring-tides full and high,
Swells in every youthful vein;
But each tide does less supply,
Till they quite shrink in again:
    If a flow in age appear,
    'Tis but rain, and runs not clear.

                    TYRANNIC LOVE, iv. 1. 1670.

You charmed me not with that fair face
    Though it was all divine:
To be another's is the grace
    That makes me wish you mine.

The gods and fortune take their part
    Who, like young monarchs, fight;
And boldly dare invade that heart
    Which is another's right.

First, and with hope, we undertake
    To pull up every bar;
But, once possessed, we faintly make
    A dull defensive war.

Now every friend is turned a foe
  In hope to get our store:
And passion makes us cowards grow,
  Which made us brave before.

AN EVENING'S LOVE, ii. 1671.

WHEREVER I am, and whatever I do,
  My Phyllis is still in my mind;
When angry, I mean not to Phyllis to go,
  My feet, of themselves, the way find:
Unknown to myself I am just at her door,
And, when I would rail, I can bring out no more
  Than, Phyllis too fair and unkind!

When Phyllis I see, my heart bounds in my breast,
  And the love I would stifle is shown;
But asleep, or awake, I am never at rest
  When from my eyes Phyllis is gone!
Sometimes a sad dream does delude my sad mind,
But, alas, when I wake, and no Phyllis I find
  How I sigh to myself all alone.

Should a king be my rival in her I adore,
  He would offer his treasure in vain:
O let me alone to be happy and poor.
  And give me my Phyllis again:
Let Phyllis be mine, and but ever be kind,
I could to a desert with her be confined,
  And envy no monarch his reign.

Alas, I discover too much of my love,
  And she too well knows her own power!
She makes me each day a new martyrdom prove,
  And makes me grow jealous each hour:
But let her each minute torment my poor mind,
I had rather love Phyllis, both false and unkind,
  Than ever be freed from her power.

THE CONQUEST OF GRENADA. PART ONE, iv. 2. 1672.

FAREWELL ungrateful traitor,
 Farewell my perjured swain,
Let never injured creature
 Believe a man again.
The pleasure of possessing
Surpasses all expressing,
But 'tis too short a blessing,
 And love too long a pain.

'Tis easy to deceive us
 In pity of your pain,
But when we love you leave us
 To rail at you in vain.
Before we have descried it,
There is no bliss beside it,
But she that once has tried it,
 Will never love again.

The passion you pretended
 Was only to obtain;
But when the charm is ended
 The charmer you disdain.
Your love by ours we measure,
Till we have lost our treasure,
But dying is a pleasure,
 When loving is a pain.

THE SPANISH FRIAR, v. 1681.

Mercury's song to Phædra.

FAIR Iris I love, and hourly I die,
But not for a lip, nor a languishing eye:
She's fickle and false, and there we agree;
But I am as false, and as fickle as she:
We neither believe what either can say;
And, neither believing, we neither betray.

'Tis civil to swear, and say things of course;
We mean not the taking for better for worse.
When present, we love; when absent, agree:

I think not of Iris, nor Iris of me:
The legend of love no couple can find,
So easy to part, or so equally joined.

AMPHYTRION, iv. 1. 1690.

*Enter Comus, with three Peasants, who sing the following
song in parts.*

Comus

YOUR hay it is mowed, and your corn is reaped:
Your barns will be full, and your hovels heaped:
  Come, my boys, come;
  Come, my boys, come;
And merrily roar out harvest home;
   Harvest home,
   Harvest home,
And merrily roar out harvest home.

1 Man

We have cheated the parson, we'll cheat him again,
For why should a blockhead have one in ten?
  One in ten,
  One in ten,
For why should a blockhead have one in ten.

2 Man

For prating so long like a book-learned sot,
Till pudding and dumpling burn to pot,
  Burn to pot,
  Burn to pot,
Till pudding and dumpling burn to pot.

3 Man

We'll toss off our ale till we cannot stand:
And hoigh for the honour of Old England:
  Old England,
  Old England,
And hoigh for the honour of Old England.

KING ARTHUR, OR THE BRITISH WORTHY, v. 1691.

No, no poor suffering heart, no change endeavour,
Choose to sustain the smart, rather than leave her;
My ravished eyes behold such charms about her,
I can die with her, but not live without her.
One tender sigh of hers to see me languish,
Will more than pay the price of my past anguish:
Beware, O cruel fair, how you smile on me,
'Twas a kind look of yours that has undone me.

Love has in store for me one happy minute,
And she will end my pain, who did begin it;
Then no day void of bliss or pleasure leaving,
Ages shall slide away without perceiving:
Cupid shall guard the door, the more to please us,
And keep out Time and Death, when they would seize us:
Time and Death shall depart, and say in flying,
Love has found out a way to live by dying.

CLEOMENES, ii. 2. 1692.

SIR GEORGE ETHEREGE

1635?-1691

They walk into an arbour. Letitia sings.

LADIES, though to your conquering eyes
Love owes his chiefest victories,
And borrows those bright arms from you
With which he does the world subdue,
    Yet you yourselves are not above
    The empire nor the griefs of love.

Then wrack not lovers with disdain,
Lest love on you revenge their pain;
You are not free because y're fair;
The boy did not his mother spare.
    Beauty's but an offensive dart;
    It is no armour for the heart.

LOVE IN A TUB, v. 6. 1664.

JOHN CROWNE

?-1703

A Song to be sung by the Levites at the Temple gates, on the opening of the scene.

DAY is dismounted on the watery plain,
  And Evening does begin to fold
  Up Light's rich cloth of gold,
And Nature's face the Night begins to stain.
  Holy angels round us keep,
  While our sense dissolves in sleep.
  While the half of us is dead
  Let the living half be led
  To your gardens, to your bowers,
  Where you pass your pleasing hours.
  Treat within your heavenly tents
    Your brethren spirits thus in state
        While they wait
  The leisure of their slumb'ring sense.

THE DESTRUCTION OF JERUSALEM. PART I, i. 7. 1677.

THOMAS PORTER

1636-1680

AWAY, away, flatter no more
MY easy faith, for now I see
  What thou in me seemed to adore
Thou makest thy pleasures' property;
  No more, no more will I believe
  The man that can so soon deceive.

  Nor was it flattery that did
Betray my heart, but that I loved,
  For which my reason hath been chid,
And I the sad effects have proved.
  Then go, and I no more will see
  The man that has abused me.

THE WITTY COMBAT, OR THE FEMALE VICTOR, iii. 3. 1663.

SEE where Calisto wheels about
  The Northern axle-tree of Heav'n,
And swift Bootes still doth rout
  Before his lash the glittering Seven.
    View then those eyes which are more fair
    Than any star that glitters there.

Fair Cassiopeia, wouldst thou gain
  The prize of glory in thy sphere?
Try then to borrow of these twain
  Two pair of eyes that shine more clear:
    For whilst they sparkle here below,
    Obscurer lights we cannot know.

In nights they far outshine the Moon,
  And render them like glorious days,
They may contend at height of noon
  To equalize the Sun's bright rays:
    Their coronet of hair, though brown,
    Does far outshine Ariadne's crown.

Then gently dart those beams; for know
  How quick and fiercely they surprise
The sentinels that expect below
  The dawning of your beauteous eyes.
    We are your plants, and if we thrive
    Tis by your influence that we live.

      (*The window opens quick*)

            THE VILLAIN, i. 1. 1663.

They all join hands and dance in a ring, answering all together at the Chorus.

Maria: AMARILLIS told her swain,
        Amarillis told her swain,   *Chorus etiam bis.*
        That in love he should be plain
        And not think to deceive her.
Chorus: Still he protested on his truth
        That he would never leave her.

If thou dost keep thy vow, quoth she,
And that thou ne'er dost leave me,   *Chorus bis.*
There's ne'er a swain in all the plain
That ever shall come near thee
Chorus: For garlands and embroidered scrips,
     For I do love thee dearly.

But Colin if thou change thy Love,
But Colin if thou change thy Love, *Chorus etiam bis.*
A tigress then I'll to thee prove
If e'er thou dost come near me.
Chorus: Amarillis fear not that,
     For I do love thee dearly.

THE VILLAIN, ii. 1.

Song within by the Boy.

BEYOND the malice of abusive fate
I now am grown, and in that state
My heart shall mourn the loss it has received,
When of its only joy it was bereaved;
The woods with echoes do abound,
And each of them returns the sound
Of my Amintor's name; alas, he's dead,
And with him all my joys are fled,
Willow, willow, willow, must I wear,
For sweet Amintor's dead, who was my dear.

THE VILLAIN, v. 1.

SIR CHARLES SEDLEY

1639-1701

AH Cloris! that I now could sit
As unconcerned, as when
Your infant beauty could beget
No pleasure, nor no pain.

When I the dawn used to admire,
  And praised the coming day;
I little thought the growing fire
  Must take my rest away.

Your charms in harmless childhood lay,
  Like metals in the mine,
Age from no face took more away,
  Than youth concealed in thine.

But as your charms insensibly
  To their perfections pressed,
Fond love as unperceived did fly,
  And in my bosom rest.

My passion with your beauty grew,
  And Cupid at my heart,
Still as his mother favoured you,
  Threw a new flaming dart.

Each gloried in their wanton part:
  To make a lover, he
Employed the utmost of his art,
  To make a beauty, she.

Though now I slowly bend to love,
  Uncertain of my fate,
If your fair self my chains approve,
  I shall my freedom hate.

Lovers, like dying men, may well
  At first disordered be,
Since none alive can truly tell
  What fortune they must see.

THE MULBERRY GARDEN, iii. 2. 1668.

THYRSIS, unjustly you complain,
  And tax my tender heart
With want of pity for your pain,
  Or sense of your desert.

By secret and mysterious springs,
    Alas! our passions move;
We women are fantastic things,
    That like before we love.

You may be handsome, and have wit,
    Be secret and well-bred,
The person love must to us fit,
    He only can succeed.

Some die, yet never are believed;
    Others we trust too soon,
Helping ourselves to be deceived,
    And proud to be undone.

BELLAMIRA, OR THE MISTRESS, iii. 1. 1687.

APHRA BEHN

1640-1689

A CURSE upon that faithless maid,
Who first her sex's liberty betrayed;
Born free as man to love and range,
Till nobler nature did to custom change.
Custom, that dull excuse for fools,
Who think all virtue to consist in rules.

From Love our fetters never sprung,
That smiling God, all wanton, gay, and young,
Shows by his wings he cannot be
Confinèd to a restless slavery;
But here and there at random roves,
Not fixed to glittering courts or shady groves.

Then she that constancy professed,
Was but a well dissembler at the best;
And that imaginary sway
She feigned to give, in seeming to obey,
Was but the height of prudent art,
To deal with greater liberty her heart.

THE EMPEROR OF THE MOON, i. 1. 1687.

THOMAS SHADWELL

1640-1692

LOVERS lament, lament this fatal day,
When Beauty's sweetest bud is snatched away:
Unhappy nymph, that could so wretched prove,
To suffer so for such a noble love;
A love that was her glory, not offence,
The gods will sure reward such innocence,
Within those ever springing groves, where she
Shall from disasters in her love be free;
Whither her loved Theander shall repair
In her eternal joy to claim his share.

THE ROYAL SHEPHERDESS, v. 1669.

ELKANAH SETTLE

1648-1724

Celia Sings.

LET us use time whilst we may;
Snatch those joys that haste away,
Earth her winter coat may cast,
And renew her beauties past;
But our winter come, in vain
We solicit Spring again.
And when our furrows snow shall cover,
Love may return, but never lover.

PASTOR FIDO OR THE FAITHFUL SHEPHERD, iii. 1677.

EDWARD RAVENSCROFT

Fl. 1671-1697

NYMPHS that now are in your prime,
Make, O make good use of time:
Each minute hastens your decay,

Beauty, like time, flies fast away.
  Nymphs that now are in your prime,
  Make, O make good use of time.

If you would know how youth did pass,
Look on the dial of your face,
Where, though no sudden change is found,
Yet still the sun is moving round.

But when it comes to be full noon,
The day grows short, and night comes soon;
The sun steals off by slow degrees,
And beauty fades, though no one sees.

Night's shades do pass, and day comes on,
But beauty has no second dawn;
The sun returns, but beauty never,
When beauty sets, it sets forever.
  Nymphs that now are in your prime,
  Make, O make good use of time.

THE ITALIAN HUSBAND. A TRAGEDY, ii. 1. 1698.

JAMES HOWARD

Fl. 1674

MY love and I a bargain made,
  It is well worth a-telling;
When one was weary we agreed
  To part both should be willing.

And thus our loves will longer last
  Than fools that still are pining;
We'll spend our time in joy and mirth,
  Whilst doaters do in whining.

ALL MISTAKEN, OR THE MAD COUPLE, ii. 1672.

THOMAS DUFFET?

Fl. 1678

I NEVER shall henceforth approve
The deity of Love
Since he could be
So far unjust as to wound me,
And leave my mistress free.
As if my flame could leave a print
Upon a heart of flint.
Can flesh and stone
Be e'er converted into one,
By my poor flame alone?
Were he a god, he'd neither be
Partial to her, nor me,
But by a dart
Directed into either's heart
Make both so feel the smart,
That being heated with his subtile fire,
Our loves might make us feel but one desire.

THE AMOROUS OLD WOMAN, iv. 4. 1674.

THOMAS OTWAY

1652-1685

PRINCES that rule and empires sway,
How transitory is their state!
Sorrows the glories do allay,
And richest crowns have greatest weight.

The mightiest monarch treason fears,
Ambitious thoughts within him rave;
His life all discontent and cares;
And he at best is but a slave.

Vainly we think with fond delight,
To ease the burden of our cares.

Each grief a second does invite,
And sorrows are each other's heirs.

For me my honour I'll maintain,
Be gallant, generous, and brave;
And when I quietude would gain,
At least I find it in the grave.

ALCIBIADES, v. 1. 1675.

THOMAS DURFEY

1653-1723

I'LL sail upon the Dog-star
  And then peruse the morning;
I'll chase the moon 'till it be noon,
  But I'll make her leave her horning.

I'll climb the frosty mountain
  And there I'll coin the weather;
I'll tear the rainbow from the sky,
  And tie both ends together.

The stars pluck from their orbs too,
  And crowd them in my budget;
And whether I'm a roaring boy,
  Let all the people judge it.

A FOOL'S PREFERMENT OR THE THREE DUKES OF DUNSTABLE, iv.
1688.

CELLADON, when Spring came on,
  Woo'd Silvia in a grove;
Both gay and young, and still he sung
  The sweet delights of love:
Wedded joys, in girls and boys,
  And pretty chat of this and that;
The honey kiss, and charming bliss
  That crowns the marriage bed.

He snatched her hand, she blushed and fanned,
   And seemed as if afraid;
"Forbear," she cries, "your fawning lies,
   I've vowed to die a maid."

Celladon at that began
   To talk of apes in Hell,
And what was worse, the odious curse
   Of growing old and stale:
Loss of bloom, when wrinkles come,
   And offers kind, when none will mind,
The rosy joy, and sparkling eye
   Grown faded and decayed.
At which, when known, she changed her tone
   And to the shepherd said:
"Dear swain, give o'er, I'll think once more
   Before I die a maid."

THE OLD MODE AND THE NEW, OR COUNTRY MISS WITH HER
FURBELOW, V. 2. 1709.

NATHANIEL LEE

1653?-1692

WEEP, weep, you Muses, drain the springs,
Such notes go warble to the strings,
Such dirges as the ravens sound
When ghosts run trembling through the ground:
The fairest of her sex is dead,
Her tender limbs are wrapped in lead;
Her eyes, stars envy, the earth's pride,
The broad black hand of Death does hide;
In Death's dark chamber, now she lies,
Pale as the snow, and cold as ice.

Chorus.

The grave, the lovely grave will bring us ease,
There we shall sweetly sleep in downy peace;
There no distractions, nor jealousies be,

But all from inordinate passions are free:
The cold tomb is free from hot love and desire;
It has ashes good store, but admits of no fire:
There men do never groan, nor women cry,
But all things, hushed, in solemn silence, lie.

THE TRAGEDY OF NERO, iii. 1. 1675.

CHARLES D'AVENANT

1656-1714

Orpheus Sings.

GIVE me my lute; in thee some ease I find,
  Eurydice is dead,
 And to that dismal country fled
Where all is sad and gloomy, as my mind.

The world has nothing worth a lover's care,
  None now by rivers weep:
 Verse, and the lute are both asleep;
All women now are false, and few are fair.

Thy sceptre, Love, shall o'er the aged be;
  Lay by thy useless darts,
 For all our youths will guard their hearts,
And scorn thy fading empire, taught by me.

Beauty the Thracian youth no more shall move,
  Now they shall sigh no more,
 But all my noble verse adore,
It has more graces than the Queen of Love.

CIRCE. A TRAGEDY, iv. 2. 1677.

GEORGE POWELL

1658?–1714

WHEN Sylvia is kind, and Love plays in her eyes,
I think 'tis no morning till Sylvia does rise;
Of Sylvia the hills and the valleys all ring,
Her beauty's the subject each shepherd does sing:
But, if she proves cruel, how little will move
Those charms which inspired us with raptures of love?
Thy rigour, dear Sylvia, will shorten thy reign,
And make our bright goddess a mortal again.

Love heightens our joys; he's the ease of our care;
Inspires the valiant and crowns all the Fair:
O seize his soft wings then before 'tis too late,
Or cruelty quickly will hasten thy fate.
'Tis kindness, dear Sylvia, 'tis kindness alone
Will add to thy lovers and strengthen thy throne:
In love as in empires, tyrannical sway
Will make loyal subjects forget to obey.

ALPHONSO KING OF NAPLES, i. 1. 1691.

ANONYMOUS

Urania discovered reading. A song within.

CORINNA, in the bloom of youth,
    Was coy to every lover;
Regardless of the tenderest truth,
    No soft complaints could move her:
Mankind was hers, and at her feet
    Lay prostrate and adoring,
The witty, valiant, rich and great
    Alike in vain imploring.

But now grown old she would repair
    The loss of time and pleasure;
With willing looks, and wanton air,
    Inviting every gazer.

But love's a summer flower, that dies
  With the first weather's changing.
The lover, like the swallow, flies
  From sun to sun still ranging.

Cloe, let this example move
  Your foolish heart to reason:
Youth is the proper time for love,
  And age is virtue's season.

ALPHONSO KING OF NAPLES, v. 2.

WILLIAM CONGREVE

1670-1729

LOVE's but the frailty of the mind,
  When 'tis not with ambition joined;
A sickly flame, which if not fed expires,
And feeding, wastes in self-consuming fires.

'Tis not to wound a wanton boy
  Or amorous youth, that gives the joy;
But 'tis the glory to have pierced a swain,
For whom inferior beauties sighed in vain.

Then I alone the conquest prize
  When I insult a rival's eyes:
If there's delight in love, 'tis when I see
That heart which others bleed for, bleed for me.

THE WAY OF THE WORLD, iii. 1. 1700.

RICHARD STEELE

1672-1729

WHY, lovely charmer, tell me why,
So very kind, and yet so shy?
Why does that cold forbidding air

Give damps of sorrow and despair?
Or why that smile my soul subdue,
And kindle up my flames anew?

In vain you strive with all your art,
By turns to freeze and fire my heart:
When I behold a face so fair,
So sweet a look, so soft an air,
My ravished soul is charmed all o'er,
I cannot love thee less nor more.

THE TENDER HUSBAND OR THE ACCOMPLISHED FOOLS, iv. 1. 1705.

GEORGE FARQUHAR

1678-1707

Enter Kite, with a Mob in each hand drunk. Kite sings.

OUR prentice Tom may now refuse
To wipe his scoundrel master's shoes;
For now he's free to sing and play,
Over the hills and far away.
   Over the hills, and over the main,
   To Flanders, Portugal, or Spain:
   The queen commands, and we'll obey,
   Over the hills and far away.

We all shall live more happy lives,
By getting rid of brats and wives,
That scold and brawl both night and day:
Over the hills and far away.
   Over the hills, and over the main,
   To Flanders, Portugal, or Spain:
   The queen commands, and we'll obey—
   Over the hills and far away.

THE RECRUITING OFFICER, ii. 2. 1706.

S.d. A Mob: *one of the mob or rabble.*

JOHN COREY

Fl. 1700

HAPPY was man ere cheated sense,
  By love's false fires misled,
From all the sweets of innocence
  To wilder passions fled.
Free from desire he knew no fear,
Enjoyment crowned the circling year.

Since art and wisdom cannot stay
  The too swift-footed hours,
Let us in pleasures melt the day
  While yet we call it ours.
He only truly knows to live
Who drinks, and scorns to love or grieve.

A CURE FOR JEALOUSY, ii. 1. 1701.

JOHN GAY

1685-1732

'TWAS when the seas were roaring
  With hollow blasts of wind;
A damsel lay deploring,
  All on a rock reclined.
Wide o'er the rolling billows
  She cast a wistful look;
Her head was crowned with willows
  That tremble o'er the brook.

Twelve months are gone and over,
  And nine long tedious days.
Why didst thou, venturous lover,
  Why didst thou trust the seas?
Cease, cease, thou cruel Ocean,
  And let my lover rest;
Ah! what's thy troubled motion
  To that within my breast?

The merchant, robbed of pleasure,
    Sees tempests in despair;
But what's the loss of treasure
    To losing of my dear?
Should you some coast be laid on
    Where gold and diamonds grow,
You'd find a richer maiden,
    But none that loves you so.

How can they say that Nature
    Has nothing made in vain;
Why then beneath the water
    Should hideous rocks remain?
No eyes the rocks discover,
    That lurk beneath the deep,
To wreck the wandering lover,
    And leave the maid to weep.

All melancholy lying,
    Thus wailed she for her dear;
Repaid each blast with sighing,
    Each billow with a tear;
When o'er the white wave stooping
    His floating corpse she spied;
Then like a lilly drooping,
    She bowed her head, and died.

THE WHAT D'YE CALL IT, ii. 8. 1715.

Mackheath: WERE I laid on Greenland's coast,
    And in my arms embraced my lass,
    Warm amidst eternal frost,
    Too soon the half-years' night would pass.

Polly: Were I sold on Indian soil,
    Soon as the burning day was closed,
    I would mock the sultry toil,
    When on my charmer's breast reposed.

Mackheath: And I would love you all the day,
Polly: Every night would kiss and play,

Mackheath: If with me you'd fondly stray
Polly: Over the hills and far away.

THE BEGGAR'S OPERA, i. 1728.

IF the heart of a man is depressed with cares,
The mist is dispelled when a woman appears;
Like the notes of a fiddle she sweetly, sweetly,
Raises the spirits, and charms our ears.
    Roses and lillies her cheeks disclose,
    But her ripe lips are more sweet than those.
        Press her,
        Caress her
        With blisses,
        Her kisses
Dissolve us in pleasure, and soft repose.

THE BEGGAR'S OPERA, ii.

How happy could I be with either,
  Were t'other dear charmer away!
But while you thus teaze me together,
  To neither a word will I say;
    But toll de rol, etc.

THE BEGGAR'S OPERA, ii.

    CEASE your funning;
    Force or cunning
Never shall my heart trepan;
    All these sallies
    Are but malice,
To seduce my constant man.

    'Tis most certain,
    By their flirting
Women oft have envy shown;
    Pleased to ruin
    Other's wooing;
Never happy in their own.

THE BEGGAR'S OPERA, ii.

O RUDDIER than the cherry,
O sweeter than the berry,
    O nymph more bright
    Than moonshine night,
Like kidling blithe and merry.
Ripe as the melting cluster,
No lily has such lustre,
    Yet hard to tame,
    As raging flame,
And fierce as storms that bluster.

ACIS AND GALATEA, ii. 1732.

JAMES THOMSON

1700-1748

WHEN Britain first, at Heaven's command,
    Arose from out the azure main,
This was the charter of the land,
    And guardian angels sung this strain:
    "Rule Britannia, rule the waves;
    Britons never will be slaves."

The nations, not so blest as thee,
    Must, in their turns, to tyrants fall;
While thou shalt flourish great and free,
    The dread and envy of them all.
    "Rule Britannia, etc."

Still more majestic shalt thou rise,
    More dreadful, from each foreign stroke;
As the loud blast that tears the skies,
    Serves but to root thy native oak.
    "Rule Britannia, etc."

Thee, haughty tyrants ne'er shall tame;
    All their attempts to bend thee down
Will but arouse thy generous flame;
    But work their woe, and thy renown.
    "Rule Britannia, etc."

To thee belongs the rural reign;
  Thy cities shall with commerce shine;
All thine shall be the subject main,
  And every shore it circles, thine.
    "Rule Britannia, etc."

The Muses, still with freedom found,
  Shall to thy happy coast repair;
Blest Isle! with matchless beauty crowned,
  And manly hearts to guard the fair.
    "Rule Britannia, rule the waves;
    Britons never will be slaves."

THE MASQUE OF ALFRED. 1740.

HENRY CAREY

?-1743

WHAT tho' they call me country lass,
I read it plainly in my glass,
That for a duchess I might pass:
    Oh, could I see the day!
Would Fortune but attend my call,
At park, at play, at Ring and ball,
I'd brave the proudest of them all,
    With a "Stand by—Clear the way."

Surrounded by a crowd of beaux,
With smart toupees, and powdered clothes,
At rivals I'll turn up my nose;
    Oh, could I see the day!
I'll dart such glances from these eyes,
Shall make some lord or duke my prize;
And then, Oh! how I'll tyrannize,
    With a "Stand by—Clear the way."

Oh! then for every new delight,
For equipage and diamonds bright,
Quadrille, and plays, and balls all night;
    Oh! could I see the day!

Of love and joy I'd take my fill,
The tedious hours of life to kill,
In everything I'd have my will,
    With a "Stand by—Clear the way."

COLLEY CIBBER'S THE PROVOKED HUSBAND, v. 3. 1753.

HENRY FIELDING

1707-1754

How unhappy's the fate
To live by one's pate,
And be forced to write hackney for bread!
An author's a joke,
To all manner of folk,
Wherever he pops up his head, his head,
Wherever he pops up his head.

Tho' he mount on that hack,
Old Pegasus' back,
And of Helicon drink till he burst,
Yet a curse of those streams,
Poetical dreams,
They never can quench one's thirst, one's thirst,
They never can quench one's thirst.

Ah! how could he fly,
On fancy so high,
When his limbs are in durance and hold?
Or how could he charm,
With genius so warm,
When his poor naked body's a cold a cold,
When his poor naked body's a cold.

THE AUTHOR'S FARCE, ii. 3. 1730.

THE dusky night rides down the sky,
    And ushers in the morn;
The hounds all join in glorious cry,
    The huntsman winds his horn:
        And a hunting we will go.

The wife around her husband throws
    Her arms, and begs his stay;
"My dear it rains, and hails, and snows,
    You will not hunt to-day."
      But a hunting we will go.

"A brushing fox in yonder wood
    Secure to find we seek;
For why, I carried, sound and good,
    A cartload there last week."
      And a hunting we will go.

Away he goes, he flies the rout,
    Their steeds all spur and switch;
Some are thrown in, and some thrown out,
    And some thrown in the ditch:
      But a hunting we will go.

At length his strength to faintness worn,
    Poor Reynard ceases flight;
Then hungry, homeward we return,
    To feast away the night:
      Then a drinking we will go.

           Don Quixote in England, ii. 5. 1734.

When mighty roast beef was the Englishman's food,
It ennobled our hearts, and enriched our blood;
Our soldiers were brave, and our courtiers were good.
    Oh the roast beef of Old England,
    And Old England's roast beef!

Then, Britons, from all nice dainties refrain,
Which effeminate Italy, France, and Spain;
And mighty roast beef shall command on the main.
    Oh the roast beef of Old England,
    Oh the roast beef of Old England.

           Don Quixote in England, v. 6.

ANONYMOUS

WHILE the sweet blushing spring glowing fresh in her prime,
  All nature with smiles doth adorn;
Snatch at each golden joy—check the ravage of time,
  And pluck every bud from the thorn.
In the May-morn of life, while gladsome and gay,
  Each moment, each pleasure improve,
For life we shall find is at best but a day,
  And the sunshine that gilds it is love.

The rose now so blooming, of nature the grace,
  In a moment is shrunk and decayed,
And the glow which now tinges a beautiful face,
  Must soon, alas! wither and fade.
In the May-morn of life then, while gladsome and gay,
  Each moment, each pleasure improve,
For life we shall find is at best but a day,
  And the sunshine that gilds it is love.

THE FATHERS; OR THE GOOD-NATURED MAN, i. 1. 1778.

DAVID GARRICK

1717-1779

COME, come, my good shepherds, our flocks we must shear;
In your holiday suits, with your lasses appear:
The happiest of folk are the guiltless and free,
And who are so guiltless, so happy as we.

We harbour no passions, by luxury taught,
We practice no arts, with hypocrisy fraught;
What we think in our hearts, you may read in our eyes;
For knowing no falsehood, we need no disguise.

By mode and caprice are the city dames led,
But we, as the children of nature are bred;
By her hand alone, we are painted and dressed,
For the roses will bloom, when there's peace in the breast.

That giant, Ambition, we never can dread;
Our roofs are too low, for so lofty a head;
Content and sweet cheerfulness open our door,
They smile with the simple, and feed with the poor.

When love has possessed us, that love we reveal;
Like the flocks that we feed, are the passions we feel;
So harmless and simple we sport, and we play,
And leave to fine folks to deceive and betray.

FLORIZEL AND PERDITA, ii. 1. 1758.

COME cheer up, my lads, 'tis to glory we steer,
To add something more to this wonderful year:
To honour we call you, not press you like slaves,
For who are so free as we sons of the waves?
    Heart of oak are our ships, heart of oak are our men,
  We always are ready; steady, boys, steady,
  We'll fight and we'll conquer again and again.

We ne'er see our foes but we wish them to stay;
They never see us but they wish us away;
If they run, why we follow, and run them ashore,
For if they won't fight us, we cannot do more.

They swear they'll invade us, these terrible foes,
They frighten our women, our children, and beaus;
But, should their flat bottoms in darkness get o'er,
Still Britons they'll find, to receive them on shore.

We'll still make them run, and we'll still make them sweat,
In spite of the devil, and Brussels gazette;
Then cheer up, my lads, with one heart let us sing,
Our soldiers, our sailors, our statesmen, and King.

HARLEQUIN'S INVASION. A CHRISTIAN GAMBOL. (See Notes.)

OLIVER GOLDSMITH

1728-1774

LET school-masters puzzle their brain,
    With grammar, and nonsense, and learning;
Good liquor, I stoutly maintain,
    Gives *genus* a better discerning.
Let them brag of their heathenish gods,
    Their Lethes, their Styxes, and Stygians;
Their qui's, and their quae's, and their quod's,
    They're all but a parcel of pigeons.
              Toroddle, toroddle, toroll.

When Methodist preachers come down,
    A preaching that drinking is sinful,
I'll wager the rascals a crown,
    They always preach best with a skinful.
But when you come down with your pence,
    For a slice of their scurvy religion,
I'll leave it to all men of sense,
    But you my good friend are the pigeon.
              Toroddle, toroddle, toroll.

Then come put the jorum about,
    And let us be merry and clever,
Our hearts and our liquors are stout,
    Here's the Three Jolly Pigeons for ever.
Let some cry up woodcock or hare,
    Your bustards, your ducks, and your widgeons;
But of all the birds in the air,
    Here's a health to the Three Jolly Pigeons.
              Toroddle, toroddle, toroll.

SHE STOOPS TO CONQUER, i. 11. 1772.

8. pigeons: *gulls, dupes.* 19. jorum: *a large drinking-bowl.* 24.
widgeons: *wild ducks.*

CHARLES DIBDIN

1745-1814

THEN farewell my trim-built wherry,
    Oars, and coat and badge, farewell;
Never more at Chelsea Ferry,
    Shall your Thomas take a spell.

But to hope and peace a stranger,
    In the battle's heat I go,
Where exposed to every danger,
    Some friendly ball shall lay me low.

Then mayhap when homeward steering
    With the news my messmates come;
Even you, the story hearing,
    With a sigh may cry—"Poor Tom"!

THE WATERMAN OR THE FIRST OF AUGUST, i. v. 1774.

BLOW high, blow low, let tempests tear
    The mainmast by the board;
My heart, with thoughts of thee, my dear,
    And love well stored,
Shall brave all danger, scorn all fear,
    The roaring winds, the raging sea,
        In hopes on shore
        To be once more
Safe moored with thee.

Aloft while mountains high we go,
    The whistling winds that scud along,
And the surge roaring from below,
        Shall my signal be,
        To think on thee,
And this shall be my song.
        Blow high, blow low, etc.

And on that night when all the crew
    The mem'ry of their former lives

O'er flowing cans of flip renew,
    And drink their sweethearts and their wives,
      I'll heave a sigh, and think of thee;
    And as the ship rolls through the sea,
    The burden of my song shall be—
      Blow high, blow low, etc.

THE SERAGLIO, i. 1776.

RICHARD BRINSLEY SHERIDAN

1751-1816

HERE's to the maiden of bashful fifteen;
    Here's to the widow of fifty;
Here's to the flaunting extravagant quean,
    And here's to the housewife that's thrifty.
Chorus: Let the toast pass,
        Drink to the lass,
I'll warrant she'll prove an excuse for a glass.

Here's to the charmer whose dimples we prize;
    Now to the maid who has none, sir;
Here's to the girl with a pair of blue eyes,
    And here's to the nymph with but one, sir.
Chorus: Let the toast pass,
        Drink to the lass,
I'll warrant she'll prove an excuse for a glass.

Here's to the maid with a bosom of snow;
    Now to her that's as brown as a berry;
Here's to the wife with a face full of woe,
    And now to the damsel that's merry.
Chorus: Let the toast pass,
        Drink to the lass,
I'll warrant she'll prove an excuse for a glass.

For let 'em be clumsy, or let 'em be slim,
    Young or ancient, I care not a feather;
So fill a pint bumper quite up to the brim,
So fill up your glasses, nay, fill to the brim,

And let us e'en toast them together.

Chorus: Let the toast pass,
                Drink to the lass,
I'll warrant she'll prove an excuse for a glass.

The School for Scandal, iii. 3. [1778?].

Had I a heart for falsehood framed,
  I ne'er could injure you;
For though your tongue no promise claimed,
  Your charms would make me true.

To you no soul shall bear deceit,
  No stranger offer wrong;
For friends in all the aged you'll meet,
  And brothers in the young.

But when they find that you have blest
  Another with your heart,
They'll bid aspiring passions rest,
  And act a brother's part.

Then, lady, dread not here deceit,
  Nor fear to suffer wrong;
For friends in all the aged you'll meet,
  And brothers in the young.

The Duenna, i. 6. 1783.

MATTHEW GREGORY LEWIS

1775-1818

Nought avails thy plaintive crying,
  Hush, dearest! Hush!
In the grave thy father's lying;
  Hush, dearest! Hush!
Tears and sighs in vain endeavour
Back to call the Loved-for-ever!
Never wilt thou see him, never!
  Hush, dearest! Hush!

See; no tears my grief are telling;
   Hush, dearest! Hush!
Hark; no sighs my breast are swelling;
   Hush, dearest! Hush!
No complaint nor murmur making,
Nought betrays my heart is aching;
Yet its breaking! breaking! breaking!
   Hush, dearest! Hush!

                RICH AND POOR, ii. 1. 1812.

ALFRED TENNYSON

1809-1892

Milkmaid (singing without)

SHAME upon you, Robin,
   Shame upon you now!
Kiss me would you? with my hands
   Milking the cow?
   Daisies grow again,
   Kingcups blow again,
And you came and kiss'd me milking the cow.

Robin came behind me,
   Kissed me well, I vow;
Cuff him could I? with my hands
   Milking the cow?
   Swallows fly again,
   Cuckoos cry again,
And you came and kiss'd me milking the cow.

Come, Robin, Robin,
   Come and kiss me now;
Help it can I? with my hands
   Milking the cow?
   Ringdoves coo again,
   All things woo again,
Come behind and kiss me milking the cow!

            QUEEN MARY, iii. 5. 1875.

HAPLESS doom of woman happy in betrothing!
Beauty passes like a breath and love is lost in loathing:
Low, my lute; speak low, my lute, but say the world is noth-
ing—
          Low, lute, low!
Love will hover round the flowers when they first awaken;
Love will fly the fallen leaf, and not be overtaken;
Low, my lute! Oh low, my lute! we fade and are forsaken—
          Low, dear lute, low!

                                     QUEEN MARY, v. 2.

Voices heard singing among the trees.

Duet.

1. Is it the wind of the dawn that I hear in the pine overhead?
2. No; but the voice of the deep as it hollows the cliffs of the
   land.
1. Is there a voice coming up with the voice of the deep from
   the strand,
   One coming up with a song in the flush of the glimmering
   red?
2. Love that is born of the deep coming up with the sun from
   the sea.
1. Love that can shape or can shatter a life till the life shall
   have fled?
2. Nay, let us welcome him, Love that can lift up a life from
   the dead.
1. Keep him away from the lone little isle. Let us be, let us
   be.
2. Nay, let him make it his own, let him reign in it—he, it
   is he,
   Love that is born of the deep coming up with the sun from
   the sea.

                                     BECKET, ii. 1. 1884.

ROBERT BROWNING

1812-1889

(The window opens softly. A low voice sings.)

THERE's a woman like a dew-drop, she's so purer than the
    purest;
And her noble heart's the noblest, yes, and her sure faith's the
    surest:
And her eyes are dark and humid, like the depth on depth of
    lustre
Hid i' the harebell, while her tresses, sunnier than the wild-
    grape cluster,
Gush in golden-tinted plenty down her neck's rose-misted mar-
    ble:
Then her voice's music . . . call it the well's bubbling, the
    bird's warble!

(A figure wrapped in a mantle appears at the window.)

And this woman says, "My days were sunless and my nights
    were moonless,
Parched the pleasant April herbage, and the lark's heart's out-
    break tuneless,
If you loved me not." And I who—(Ah, for words of flame)
    adore her,
Who am mad to lay my spirit prostrate palpably before her—

(He enters, approaches her seat, and bends over her)

I may enter by her portal soon, as now her lattice takes me,
And by noontide as by midnight make her mine, as hers she
    makes me!

(The Earl throws off his slouched hat and long cloak.)

A BLOT IN THE 'SCUTCHEON, i. 3. 1843.

WILLIAM SCHWENCK GILBERT

1836-1911

Patience.

I CANNOT tell what this love may be
That cometh to all, but not to me.
It cannot be kind as they'd imply,
Or why do these gentle ladies sigh?
It cannot be joy and rapture deep,
Or why do these gentle ladies weep?
It cannot be blissful as 'tis said,
Or why are their eyes so wondrous red?

    Though everywhere true love I see
    A-coming to all, but not to me,
    I cannot tell what this love may be!
        For I am blithe and I am gay,
        While they sit sighing all night, all day.
        Think of the gulf 'twixt them and me,
        "Fa la la la!"—and "Miserie!"

If love is a thorn, they show no wit
Who foolishly hug and foster it.
If love is a weed, how simple they
Who gather and gather it, day by day!
If love is a nettle that makes you smart,
Why do you wear it next your heart?
And if it be none of these, say I,
Why do you sit and sob and sigh?

    Though everywhere, etc.

                    PATIENCE, i. 1881.

Grosvenor.

PRITHEE, pretty maiden—prithee tell me true,
    (Hey but I'm doleful, willow willow waly!)
Have you e'er a lover a-dangling after you?

Hey willow waly O!
I would fain discover
If you have a lover?
Hey willow waly O!

Patience.

Gentle sir, my heart is frolicsome and free—
(Hey but he's doleful, willow willow waly!)
Nobody I care for comes a-courting me—
Hey willow waly O!
Nobody I care for
Comes a-courting—therefore,
Hey willow waly O!

Grosvenor.

Prithee, pretty maiden, will you marry me?
(Hey but I'm hopeful, willow willow waly!)
I may say at once, I'm a man of propertee—
Hey willow waly O!
Money, I despise it,
But many people prize it,
Hey willow waly O!

Patience.

Gentle sir, although to marry I design—
(Hey but he's hopeful, willow willow waly!)
As yet I do not know you, and so I must decline,
Hey willow waly O!
To other maidens go you—
As yet I do not know you,
Hey willow waly O!

PATIENCE, i.

Duet—Bunthorne and Grosvenor.

Bunthorne.

WHEN I go out of door,
Of damozels a score
(All sighing and burning
And clinging and yearning)

Will follow me as before.
I shall, with cultured taste,
Distinguish gems from paste,
    And "High diddle diddle"
    Will rank as an idyll,
If I pronounce it chaste!
    A most intense young man,
    A soulful-eyed young man,
An ultra-poetical, super-æsthetical,
    Out of the way young man!

Both.

A most intense young man, etc.

Grosvenor.

Conceive me, if you can,
An every-day young man:
    A commonplace type,
    With a stick and a pipe,
And a half-bred black-and-tan;
Who thinks suburban "hops"
More fun than "Monday Pops,"
    Who's fond of his dinner,
    And doesn't get thinner
On bottled beer and chops.
    A commonplace young man,
    A matter-of-fact young man,
A steady and stolid-y, jolly Bank-holiday
    Every-day young man!

Bunthorne.

A Japanese young man,
    A blue-and-white young man,
Francesca di Rimini, miminy, piminy,
    Je-ne-sais-quoi young man!

Grosvenor.

A Chancery Lane young man,
A Somerset House young man,

A very delectable, highly respectable,
Threepenny-'bus young man!

Bunthorne.

A pallid and thin young man,
A haggard and lank young man,
A greenery-yallery, Grosvenor Gallery,
Foot-in-the-grave young man!

Grosvenor.

A Sewell & Cross young man,
A Howell & James young man,
A pushing young particle—what's the next article—
Waterloo House young man!

ENSEMBLE

Bunthorne.

Conceive me, if you can,
A crotchety, cracked young man,
An ultra-poetical, super-æsthetical,
Out-of-the-way young man!

Grosvenor.

Conceive me, if you can,
A matter-of-fact young man,
An alphabetical, arithmetical,
Every-day young man!

PATIENCE, ii.

THOMAS HARDY

1840-

Tristram (singing)

LET's meet again to-night, my Fair,
Let's meet unseen of all;
The day-god labours to his lair,
And then the evenfall!

O living lute, O lily-rose,
  O form of fantasie,
When torches waste and warders doze
  Steal to the stars will we!

While nodding knights carouse at meat
  And shepherds shamble home,
We'll cleave in close embracements—sweet
  As honey in the comb!

Till crawls the dawn from Condol's crown,
  And over Neitan's Kieve,
As grimly ghosts we conjure down
  And hopes still weave and weave!

THE FAMOUS TRAGEDY OF THE QUEEN OF CORNWALL,
II. 1923.[1]

WILLIAM ERNEST HENLEY

1849-1903

WE hadn't been three days at sea before we saw a sail,
So we clapped on every stitch would stand, although it blew
    a gale,
And we walked along full fourteen knots, for the barkie she
    did know
As well as ever a soul on board, 'twas time for us to go.
        Time for us to go,
        Time for us to go,
    As well as ever a soul on board,
        'Twas time for us to go.

We carried away the royal yard, and the stunsail boom was
    gone;
Says the skipper, "They may go or stand, I'm damned if I
    don't crack on;
So the weather braces we'll round in, and the trysail set also,
And we'll keep the brig three p'ints away, for it's time for us
    to go."

Time for us to go,
Time for us to go,
And we'll keep the brig three p'ints away,
For it's time for us to go.

A quick run to the south we had, and when we made the Bight
We kept the offing all day long and crossed the Bar at night.
Six hundred niggers in the hold and seventy we did stow,
And when we'd clapped the hatches on, 'twas time for us
to go.
Time for us to go,
Time for us to go,
And when we'd clapped the hatches on,
'Twas time for us to go.

ADMIRAL GUINEA, ii. 6. 1884.[1]

AUGUSTA LADY GREGORY

YESTERDAY travelling Connacht,
Drogheda has me to-day;
My back to the empty pockets,
My face to the place will pay!

Just roving around,
To my grief and my sorrow,
Under a rock to-day,
Under a bush to-morrow.

Syrupy sweet to-day,
Sour as sloes to-morrow;
Sweet to the lads that pay,
Sour to the lads that borrow!

DERVORGILLA. 1912.

IT is pitiful and sharp to-day are the wounds of Ireland,
From Galway of white flaggy stones to Cork of the white
strand;
The branches that were full of leaves and honey on the leaves

Are torn and stripped and shortened by the stranger to our grief.

It is long, O Royal Ireland, you were mannerly and kind,
A nursing mother to your sons, fair, hospitable, wise;
Now you are wine spilled from a cup beneath the stranger's feet,
The English-speaking troops to-day have trodden down our wheat.

The wild white fawn has lost the shape was comely in the wood,
Since the foreign crow came nesting in the yew-tree overhead,
Since the red East wind brought to our hurt the troop of foreign rogues,
We are drifted like the wretched fur of a cat upon a bog!

DERVORGILLA.

ALL round my hat I wore a green ribbon,
All round my hat for a year and a day;
And if any one asks me the reason I wore it
I'll say that my true love went over the sea!

All in my hat I will stick a blue feather
The same as the birds do be up in the tree;
And if you would ask me the reason I do it
I'll tell you my true love is come back to me!

THE BOGIE MEN. 1913.

WILLIAM BUTLER YEATS

1865-

A Voice (close to the door)

THE wind blows out of the gates of the day,
The wind blows over the lonely of heart,
And the lonely of heart is withered away
While the faeries dance in a place apart,

Shaking their milk-white feet in a ring,
Tossing their milk-white arms in the air;
For they hear the wind laugh, and murmur and sing
Of a land where even the old are fair,
And even the wise are merry of tongue;
But I heard a reed of Coolaney say,
'When the wind has laughed and murmured and sung,
The lonely of heart is withered away!'

THE LAND OF HEART'S DESIRE. 1895.[1]

LAURENCE HOUSMAN

1865-

How now, everywhere up in air stars stare:
  On the roof shines the moon.
Little bird in your nest, are you there?
  Up, song, to her chamber go: say low, 'Down below,
  Thy love begs a boon.'
Little bird in your nest, are you there?

Sleep, sleep, for Love's sake let her wake,
  Say, 'Take no rest!'
Little bird in your nest, are you there?
  Tame heart, take heat, go beat in the small sweet breast.

Little dove, bird of Love, are you there?
Hour of night, at her bower go beat: say, 'Sweet, now rise!'
  Time flies! O Love, are you there?
Undo and renew to the night the light of your bright blue
  eyes!
For the man in the moon is here.
Do you hear? He is here!

PRUNELLA, ii. 1906.

JOHN GALSWORTHY

1867-

THE windy hours through darkness fly—
Canst hear them, little heart?
New loves are born, and old loves die,
And kissing lips must part.
The dusky bees of passing years—
Canst see them, soul of mine—
From flower and flower supping tears,
And pale sweet honey wine?

O flame that treads the marsh of time,
Flitting for ever low,
Where, through the black enchanted slime,
We, desperate, following go—
Untimely fire, we bid thee stay!
Into dark air above,
The golden gipsy thins away—
So has it been with love!

THE LITTLE DREAM, iii. 1911.

GORDON BOTTOMLEY

1874-

Blanid: THE bird in my heart's a-calling through a far-fled,
        tear-grey sea
    To the soft slow hills that cherish dim waters weary
        for me,
    Where the folk of rath and dun trail homeward si-
        lently
        In the mist of the early night-fall that drips from
        their hair like rain.

    The bird in my heart's a-flutter, for the bitter wind of
        the sea
    Shivers with thyme and woodbine as my body with
        memory:

I feel their perfumes ooze in my ears like melody—
　　The scent of the mead at the harping I shall not
　　　hear again.

The bird in my heart's a-sinking to a hushed vale hid
　　in the sea,
Where the moonlit dew o'er dead fighters is stirred by
　　the feet of the Shee,
Who are lovely and old as the earth but younger than
　　I can be
　　Who have known the forgetting of dying to a life
　　one lonely pain.

THE CRIER BY NIGHT. 1902.

CLEMENCE DANE

A Voice singing.

COME with me to London,
　　Folly, come away!
I'll make your fortune
　　On a fine day—
Daisy leave and buttercup!
Pick your gold and silver up,
　　In London, in London,
　　Oh, London town!
　　For sheep can feed
　　And robins breed
　　Without you, without you,
And the world get on without you—
　　Oh, London Town!

The Players singing.

Come with us to London,
　　Folly, come away!
We'll make your fortune
　　On a summer day.
Leave your sloes and mulberries!
There are riper fruits than these,

In London, in London,
Oh, London Town!
For winds will blow
And barley grow
Without you, without you,
And the world get on without you—
Oh, London Town!

Come away to London,
Folly, come away!
You'll make your fortune
Thrice in a day.
Paddocks leave and winter byres,
London has a thousand spires,
A-chiming, a-rhyming,
Oh, London Town!
The snow will fall
And cover all
Without you, without you,
And the world get on without you—
Oh, London Town!

WILL SHAKESPEARE, i. 1921.

Marlowe singing.

IF Luck and I should meet
I'll catch her tó me crying,
'To trip with you were sweet,
Have done with your denying!'
Hey, lass! Ho, lass!
Heel and toe, lass!
Who'll have a dance with me?

All together: Hey, Luck! Ho, Luck!
Ne'er say no, Luck!
I'll have a dance with thee!

When Death at last arrives,
I'll greet him with a chuckle,
I'll ask him how he thrives
And press his bony knuckle,

               With—Ho, boy! Hey, boy!
               Come this way, boy!
               Who'll have a drink with me?
Mary's Voice (on the stairs):
               Hey, Sir! Ho, Sir!
               No, no, no, Sir!
               Why should he drink with thee?
All together: Hey, Death! Ho, Death!
               Let me go, Death!
               I'll never drink with thee!

Mary singing: If Love should pass me by,
               I'll follow till I find him,
            And when I hear him sigh,
               I'll tear the veils that blind him.
               Up, man! Dance, man!
               Take your chance, man!
               Who'll get a kiss from me?
All together: Hey, Love! Ho, Love!
               None shall know, Love!
               Keep but a kiss for me!

                          WILL SHAKESPEARE, iii. 2.[1]

NOTES

Notes

COVENTRY PLAYS

Page 1. "As I out rode." In a *Dissertation on the Pageants or Dramatic Mysteries anciently performed at Coventry.* Pp. 115-118, 1825. Thomas Sharp printed for the first time this song and the two following ones. He took them from a MS. dated 1534, though the songs are dated 1591; yet the songs and the plays in which they are found undoubtedly belong to the fifteenth century. The songs are found at the end of the MS., "Lully, lulla" being No. 2 and coming between the shepherds' songs which are numbered 1 and 3. I have changed the order, because in the actual performance, the shepherds' songs followed one another and the lullaby was sung later.

In the MS. there is the following heading to the songs: "The first and the laste the shepheards singe (*i.e.,* Nos. 1 and 2 in this text), and the second or middlemost the women singe" (No. 3 in this text). Of course the women were personated by men and boys. All these songs are arranged for three parts, "the treble, the tenore the basse," to quote the MS. Novello and Co., London, have published Song 3 with the original music as transcribed by Sharp. Sir John Stainer has made it into a four part song and quite spoiled it. See Bramley and Stainer, *Christmas Carols New and Old.* No. LXI.

Immediately preceding "As I out rode" the angels have sung *Gloria in excelsis,* and the shepherds speak as follows:

Pastor II: "Glore, glorea in exselsis," that wase ther songe,
    How sey ye, fellois, seyde the not thus?
Pastor I: Thatt ys welseyd, now goo we hence
    To worschipe thatt chyld of hy manyffecence,
    And that we ma syng in his presence
    "Et in tarra pax omynibus."

There the schepphardis syngis "As I owte rodde."

Page 1. "Doune from heaven." The Virgin speaks before this song:

Mare: Now herdmen hynd for your comyng   (hynd: *courteous*)
    To my chylde shall I praye
    Asse he ys heyvin kyng to grant you his blessyng
    And to hys blys that ye may wynd at your last day.

There the schepphardis syngith ageyne and goth forthe of the place.

"Lully, lulla." For this song there is the following context:

Here the wemen cum in wythe there chyldur, syngyng them; and Mare and Josoff goth awey cleyne.

> Womon I: I lolle my chylde wondursly swete,
> And in my narmus I do hyt kepe,
> Be-cawse thatt yt schuld not crye.
> Womon II: Thatt babe thatt ys borne in Bedlem, so meke,
> He save my chylde and me from velany.
> Womon III: Be styll, be styll my lyttull chylde.
> That lorde of lordis save bothe the and me!
> For Erode hath sworne with wordis wyld
> That all yong chyldur sclayne they schalbe.

L. 18. Sharp prints: "morne and say." I have followed the reading suggested by Kittredge, and the spelling and punctuation of the songs as J. M. Manly prints them in his *Specimens of the Pre-Shakespearean Drama*, I, 152. Text in these notes from Sharp.

CHESTER PLAYS

PAGE 2. "The flood comes flitting." Noah's wife refuses to come into the ark unless she may take with her "my gossips everichon," with whom she sings this song.

Though the MS. from which this song is taken is dated 1592, the plays it contains probably date from the fifteenth century.

SKELTON

PAGE 3. "With ye, marry Sirs." Liberty sings this as he enters.

RASTELL

PAGE 3. "Time to pass." The music for this song, written for three voices, is printed in the text of the interlude. See J. C. Farmer's reprint of it in *The Tudor Facsimile Texts*. London. 1908.

BALE

PAGE 4. "Wassail, wassail." Sung off stage by Dissimulation just before he enters.

REDFORD

PAGE 4. "O lady dear." This interlude was not printed until 1848, when J. O. Halliwell-Phillipps edited for the *Shakespeare Society Publications*, No. 37, the sixteenth-century MS. of this Interlude.

Moros:	We will have drink if you be thirsty,
	For I love to drink without measure.
Ignorance:	You must begin for I can no skill,
	Yet I will jumble on as well as I can.
Cruelty:	We are indifferent, sing what ye will,
	We were brought up with a singing man.
Impiety:	We take our leave of you for this season,
	In time we will wait on you again.

Sing some merry song.

(This song is not given.)

TOM TYLER AND HIS WIFE

PAGE 10. "I am a poor tiler." The interlude from which this song is taken was published 1661, in black letter, by Francis Kirkman, who stated on the title-page that he was reprinting a piece that had been printed and acted "about one hundred years ago." This old edition which he used has never been found. Obviously this piece belongs to the period of the interludes; it may be dated *circa* 1560, which would correspond to Kirkman's "hundred years." *Cf.* E. K. Chambers, *The Elizabethan Stage*, IV, 50.

PAGES 11-12. "As many as match," "Let us sip." Trios sung by Strife, wife of "Tom Tyler, a labouring man"; Sturdie, "a gossip"; and Tipple, "an Ale-wife," to quote the *dramatis personæ*. The first song is thus introduced:

Tipple: Nay fall to singing and let us go dance.
Strife: By my troth chance, and let us begin,
Rise up gossips, and I will bring you in.

Here they sing.

After sixteen lines of conversation—and drinking—"Let us sip" follows the first song. There are seven songs in this interlude. It closes with two; in the final one a soloist sings "all alone with instruments, and all the rest within sing between every staff the first two lines."

MISOGONUS

PAGE 12. "Sing care away." This four-part song, sung by Misogonus, Orgalus, Cacurgus, and Oenophilus, is thus introduced:

Ca: Before I go hence, I must needs have a song.
Mi: A song with a horsenightcap sing they that list;
Till I see my trull. I'll neither sing nor say.
Oe: Lets haste then quickly, Cacurgus, or I'll be gone too,
And lets have such a one that will stir up delight.
Mi: Go to, I am content, then sing one and no more;
Begin you, Cacurgus, and take your tune right.

Ca: Fa, fa, fa, sol, sol, sol, Cods! that's too low;
    La, la, la, me, me, re, by th' mass, that's as high.
Mi: Take heed, sir, you go not too low for the crow.
Ca: And take heed, sir, you go not too high for the pie.
Or: None of us, to tell the truth, can sing well mean;
    Too high or too low we sing every one.
Ca: Well then, because you take me for your dean,
    I'll appoint the parts myself, by St. John!
    You shall sing the fr.e.de I mean, you know what:
    And thoust bear the bass because thou art trusty.
    The counterfet tenor is yours by your lot.
    Myself will sing the treble and that very trusty.

A song to the tune of "Heart's Ease."

Lawrence Johnson, Thomas Richards, and Laurence Bariona have all been suggested as the author of this play. See the article by G. L. Kittredge, *Journal of Germanic Philology*, III, 335; *cf.* E. K. Chambers, *E. S.*, IV, 31. For the tune of Heart's Ease, see Chappell, *O.E.P.M.*, I, 97. In the text here printed, one stanza has been omitted after l. 4 and one after l. 24.

LEWIS WAGER

PAGE 13. "Hey dery dery." The song is thus introduced:

Pride: I think it best that we three depart hence,
    And let mistress Mary come thither with Prudence.
Infidelity: Be it so, then you and I will come alone,
    I trust that by the way we will make one,
    Nay Mistress Mary we must have a song of four parts
    At your departing to rejoice our merry hearts.
Cupidity: The treble you shall, master Pleasure, sing,
    So freshly that for joy your heart shall spring.
    Utility can sing the bass full clean,
    And Noble Honor shall sing the mean.
Infidelity: Mistress Mary, will you help to sing a part?
Mary: Yea, sweet heart, with you with all my heart.
Infidelity: In faith we will have a song of your name.
    Come sirs, help I pray you to sing the same.

The song. "Hey dery dery."

JOHN PHILLIP

PAGE 14. "Be still my sweet sweeting." There are seven songs in this play. Four of them, Grissell sings; she also, as a long-suffering and obedient wife, joins the Marquis in a duo at his request. The stage direction before this song is: *Enter the nurse, bearing the child in her arms.* After a speech showing her affection for the "sweeting," the nurse sings.

PICKERING

PAGE 15. "Farewell, adieu." For Sellenger's Round see Chappell, *O.E.P.M.*, I, 256.

PAGE 16. "And was it not." In Marston's *Antonio and Mellida*, 1602, Felice sings "the old ballad" "And was not good King Solomon." The words unfortunately are not given; evidently this was a popular song.

Stanza 3, l. 6 (1567), reads "depayre"; stanza 4, l. 4, reads "depayred." I follow Brandl in emending to "desire" and "desired."

PAGE 17. "Stand back." I have changed one word in the last line.

THE TRIAL OF TREASURE

PAGE 19. "Hey ho, care away." Coming immediately after the prologue, this opens the interlude in which there are eight songs.

PAGE 19. "Am not I." A trio.

> *Lust:* Ah trusty treasure, ah pleasant pleasure,
> All wealth I possess now without measure,
> And seeing that the same shall firmly remain,
> To help me sing a song will you take the pain?
> *Treasure:* Even with all my heart, begin when ye will.
> *Inclination:* To it, and I will either help or stand still.
>
> *Sing this song.* "Am not I."

INGELEND

PAGE 20. "Spite of his spite." Sung by Youngman to Youngwoman whom he is determined to marry in defiance of his father. I have omitted three stanzas after l. 4, and also the stanza that concluded the song.

THE MARRIAGE OF WIT AND SCIENCE

PAGE 21. "Come, come, lie down." Sung by Idleness to Wit who falls asleep in her lap.

FULWELL

PAGE 21. "Good hostess." Sung by Cuthbert Cutpurse, Pierce Pickpurse and Nichol Newfangle, "as they go out from the place," to cite the stage directions.

WAPULL

Page 22. "We have great gain." A part song.

Courage: Nay soft, Profit, you must not go so,
You must help to sing a part or you go.
Profit: So it be short, I am well content.
Courage: And all the residue therto do consent.

The Song. "We have great gain."

Either Help or Futherance, who are both on the stage, must be the one of the "residue" to make the third in the song.

Page 23. "Though wastefulness." A four-part song.

Wantoness: But yet my friends before that you go,
Of a song help us to sing a part.
By my troth, husband, we must needs have a song,
Will you not help to further the same?
Wastefullness: Yes by my troth, so it be not too long,
Or else you might count me greatly to blame.
Courage: And I am content a part for to bear.
Help: Then be sure I will help in with a share.

THE CONTENTION BETWEEN LIBERALITY AND PRODIGALITY

Page 24. "As light as a fly." Sung by Money as he enters with Vanity.

Page 25. "The princely heart." In this song, Prodigality and Tenacity "plead in musical harmony," as Vanity expresses it, to Fortune for Money. Fortune listens to them, and in answer, commits her "dear son Money" to Prodigality.

This comedy was acted before Queen Elizabeth in 1601. "The characters are mainly abstract and the style archaic for the seventeenth century, and it is conceivable that the *Prodigality* of 1567-68 had been revived." Chambers, *E. S.*, IV, 26.

BRETON

Page 26. "In the merry month." This song began the "Third day's entertainment." It was sung at nine o'clock, as the Queen's window opened, when "three excellent musicians, . . . disguised in ancient country attire, did greet her with a pleasant song of Coridon and Phyllida, made in three parts of purpose." Elizabeth was delighted with both the words and music for "it pleased her Highness to command it again, and highly to grace it with her cheerful acceptance and commendation," to quote from the 1591 text of the entertainment.

The words of this song were printed in *England's Helicon*, 1600. There are two settings for it. One, by Michael East, is in his *Madrigals to 3, 4, and 5 parts.* 1604; the other, by Dr. John Wilson, is in J. Playford's *Select Musical Airs and Dialogues. Part III*, p. 27. 1653; this same setting, for three voices, is to be found also in J. Playford's *Catch that Catch Can or The Musical Companion*, p. 145. 1667.

RALEIGH?

PAGE 27. "Now what is love." In *England's Helicon*, 1600, appeared *The Shepherd's Description of Love*, a dialogue between Meliboeus and Faustus, beginning:

Mel: Shepherd, what's Love, I pray thee tell?
Faust: It is that fountain and that well
    Where pleasure and repentance dwell.

The poem has five stanzas and the first and last of these—with some changes in the text—make the song in Heywood's play.

As first printed in *England's Helicon*, Raleigh's initials were affixed to it, "but were obliterated by pasting over them a slip of paper with the word 'Ignoto.' The piece is marked W. R. in F. Davison's catalogue of the poems contained in *England's Helicon.*" John Hannah, *The Courtly Poets*, p. 77, note. 1870.

The poem was very beautifully set by Robert Jones in his *The Second Book of Songs and Airs*, 1601. All five stanzas are given.

ANONYMOUS

PAGE 27. *Two Italian Gentlemen.* This comedy has very interesting stage directions for the music to be played after each of the first four acts; the end of the fifth act is missing in the only known copy of the play. These directions read: "The first act being ended, the consort of music soundeth a pleasant Galliard." "The second act being ended, the consort soundeth again." "The third act being done, the consort sounds a solemn Dump." "The fourth act being ended, the consort soundeth a pleasant Allemaigne."

This comedy has been attributed to Munday, Gosson, and Chapman. *Cf.* E. K. Chambers, *E. S.*, IV, 13.

MUNDAY

PAGES 28-29. *John a Kent and John a Cumber.* This play was first published in 1851 by the Shakespeare Society, London; the only known MS. of it is somewhat damaged. Seven songs are given in full or indicated by stage directions, one of the songs being Welsh. "You that seek" and "You stole my love" are sung by spirits whom the magician John a Cumber summons. "Sleep sweetly" is sung by Shrimp, John a Kent's "boy."

PAGE 29. "Now wend we together." Taken from the masque given in honor of Sir John Jolles by his "worthy brethren, the truly honourable Society of Drapers," when he became Lord Mayor, 1615. Closing the brief entertainment, this lyric is introduced as follows:

> *Friar:* Thanks my dear Domine,
> And to you noble Homine,
> For to this indenter,
> Friar Tuck subscribes libenter.
> Now lest we offer wrong,
> Fall to your sing song.

PAGE 30. "Weep, weep, ye woodmen wail." This is evidently a chorus, for as Robin Hood dies, King John commands, "Fall to your wood-songs, therefore, yeomen bold," and the song follows. If compared with "Now wend we together," it would seem that both were by the same author. Though "The Death of Robert, Earl of Huntington," is attributed to Munday and Chettle, this song is probably Munday's; and Chettle apparently wrote that part of the play which follows the death of Robin Hood. *Cf. The Cambridge History of English Literature,* IV, 355.

LYLY

PAGE 30. In the first editions of Lyly's plays—*Sapho and Phao,* 1584; *Alexander and Campaspe,* 1584; *Endymion,* 1591; *Midas,* 1592; *Galathea,* 1592; *Mother Bombie,* 1594; *Love's Metamorphosis,* 1601—no songs appeared. In the *Woman in the Moon,* 1597, were two songs printed as prose. In all these plays, however, stage directions, such as "song" or "Trico singeth," call for lyrics, yet none are given. In 1632, under the title *Six Court Comedies,* Blount published in a single volume the first six of these plays; and in them, twenty-one songs appear for the first time, while the context shows that three, and possibly four songs, are still missing from them. These recovered songs, with one slight exception, are in their proper places and fit their context exactly; yet it has been maintained that they were not written by Lyly.

In an article in the *Modern Language Review,* Vol. I, No. 1, October, 1905, pp. 43-52, W. W. Greg rejects Lyly's authorship, basing his arguments on the style and the language of these songs; on their belated publication; and on the absence of contemporary allusions to Lyly as a lyric poet. Professor Albert Feuillerat, in his *John Lyly,* p. 403, note, summarizes and accepts these arguments. I cannot feel that Greg has proved his point. His conclusions drawn from the style and the language are unconvincing; the notes in this volume to the lyrics of Heywood and Fletcher will show that it was not unknown for the songs of a play to be found and restored

to the text long after the play had been printed without them;
while the absence of contemporary allusions to Lyly's lyrics is not
in the least surprising. It is difficult to find allusions to the songs of
any of the Elizabethan dramatists. For the best argument in favor of
Lyly's authorship, see W. J. Lawrence, "The Problem of Lyly's
Songs," *London Times Literary Supplement*, December 29, 1923, p.
894. I accept his conclusions.

PAGE 30. "O for a bowl." This trio, ending the scene, is introduced
by the following lines:

Psyllus: For joy of Grannichus let's sing.
Manes: My voice is as clear in the evening as in the morning.
Granichus: An other comedy of emptiness.

> Song. "O for a bowl."

At the end of the second quarto, 1640, of Middleton's *A Mad
World my Masters* this song was inserted, with two changes from
the text here printed: l. 2, "Aristippus" for "Palermo"; l. 16,
"come" for "leap."

PAGE 31. "Cupid and my Campaspe." This song ends the act. In
The Wandering Lover, iv, 3. 1658, Thomas Meriton has appropri-
ated this song, changing it to "Cupid and my Greceana played"!

PAGE 31. "What bird so sings." The context of this lyric is interesting. Sylvius has brought his three sons to Diogenes to be taught by
him.

Sylvius: Now shall you hear the third, who sings like a nightingale.
Diogenes: I care not: for I have heard a nightingale sing herself.
Sylvius: Sing, sirra.

> Trico singeth. "What bird so sings."

Sylvius: Lo Diogenes, I am sure thou canst not do so much.
Diogenes: But there is never a thrush but can.

This song, with many variations in the text, appears in Ford and
Dekker's *Sun's Darling*, ii, 1656. *Cf.* the article by Lawrence cited
above.

PAGE 32. "Merry knaves." The context for this song:

Criticus: Be not choleric; you are wise: but let us take up this matter with a song.
Calypho: I am content, my voice is as good as my reason.
Molus: Then shall we have sweet music. But come, I will not break
off.

> Song. "Merry knaves."

This ends the scene.

PAGE 32. "O cruel Love." This is called for at the close of the scene by the stage direction *The Song;* but from the dialogue it is evident that Sapho who sings it must fall asleep before the scene ends. Eighteen lines before the scene closes there is the following:

> *Sapho:* But give me my lute, and I will see if in song I can beguile my own eyes.
> *Milet:* Here Madam.

Probably the song should be sung at this point.

PAGE 33. "Stand, who goes there." This song, ending the scene, has the following context:

> *Dares:* But come on Master Constable, shall we have a song before we go?
> *Constable:* With all my heart.
>
> *Song.* "Stand, who goes there."

PAGE 34. "Pinch him." It is interesting to compare this with the "sham fairy song" in the *Merry Wives of Windsor*, v, 5. W. J. Lawrence, *Thomas Ravenscroft's Theatrical Associations* in *Modern Language Review*, XIX, 4, p. 421, suggests that at a revival of *Endymion* in 1600, "Pinch him, pinch him" was replaced by a song beginning "Dare you haunt our hallowed green," set by Thomas Ravenscroft and printed in his *A Brief Discourse*, Part III, No. 16, 1614.

PAGE 34. "Rocks, shelves, and sands." The singers of this trio have just escaped from a shipwreck. Their song ends the act. At the very close of the play, Venus appears with them and the following dialogue takes place:

> *Venus:* Can you sing?
> *Rafe:* Basely.
> *Venus:* And you?
> *Dick:* Meanly.
> *Venus:* And what can you do?
> *Robin:* If they double it, I will treble it.
> *Venus:* Then shall ye go with us, and sing Hymen before the marriage. Are you content?
> *Rafe:* Content, never better content, for there we shall be sure to fill our bellies with capons rumps, or some such dainty dishes.
> *Venus:* Then follow us.
>   *Exeunt.*

This ends the play. There is no stage direction for a song, but it seems improbable that the trio which had sung "Rocks, shelves, and sands" should be given merely these well-worn puns. I believe the play ended, as did so many, in a song.

PAGE 35. "O yes, O yes!" This opens the scene.

PAGES 35, 36. "My Daphne's hair," "Pan's Syrinx." In the first of these songs, Apollo accompanies himself on the lute, saying, "Then thus I begin my song and my play." Pan begins thus:

Pan: Now let me tune my pipes. I cannot pipe and sing, that's the odds in the instrument, not the art: but I will pipe and then sing; and then judge both of the art and instrument.

He pipes, and then sings.

The nymphs award the prize to Apollo; but Midas, to his misfortune, declares in favor of Pan.

PAGE 36. "Sing to Apollo." When the ass's ears, with which Apollo punished Midas, "fall off," as the stage direction has it, Midas in his gratitude says:

"So blessed be Apollo, quiet be Lesbos, happy be Midas: and to begin this solemnity, let us sing to Apollo, for, so much as music, nothing can content Apollo."

They sing all. "Sing to Apollo." *Exeunt.*

This is one more instance of a play ending with a chorus.

PAGE 37. "O Cupid!" This ends the scene.

PAGE 37. "Full hard did I sweat." Rixula has been jesting with the "four pages," wishing they "may hang in a halter." He continues:

But harken to my song.

Cantant. "Full hard."

WATSON

PAGE 38. "With fragrant flowers." Sung at the "First Day's Entertainment" by six virgins, representing the Graces and the Hours. "With flowery garlands on their heads, and baskets full of sweet herbs and flowers upon their arms," they walked before the Queen "towards the house, strewing the way with flowers, and singing a sweet song of six parts to this ditty which followeth:"

"With fragrant flowers."

In *England's Helicon*, 1600, this song is printed as Watson's. It is also ascribed to Watson in Francis Pilkington's *The First Book of Songs or Airs of 4 parts*, 1605. As Pilkington's book appeared in the reign of James I, Watson's refrain "O beauteous Queen" is changed in Pilkington's setting to "O gracious king." Byrd, in his *Psalms, Songs, and Sonnets*, 1611, has set a madrigal presumably by Watson, which has the same refrain, "O beauteous Queen." *Cf.* E. H. Fellowes, *English Madrigal Verse 1588-1632*, pp. 63, 257, 574, 626.

LODGE

PAGE 38. "Beauty, alas!" is sung to the King of Cilicia by Aluida:

> *Aluida:* Hear me but sing of love, then by my sighs,
>   My tears, my glancing looks, my changed cheer,
>   Thou shalt perceive how I do hold thee dear.
> *King:* Sing Madam, if you please, but love in jest.
> *Aluida:* Nay. I will love, and sigh at every rest.

On its title-page this play is ascribed to Thomas Lodge and Robert Greene; but as this song is thoroughly in the style of Lodge, it is here attributed to him. Bell, *Songs from the Dramatists*, ascribes the song to Greene, because the lyrics of Lodge "were generally of a higher and more imaginative cast."

PEELE

PAGE 39. *The Arraignment of Paris.* The title-page of the play informs the reader that it was "presented before the Queen's Majesty by the Children of her Chapel." With choristers for his actors, it was natural that Peele should introduce in this play a large number of songs and choruses, two of which, unfortunately, are merely mentioned, not printed.

PAGE 39. "O Ida, O Ida." Immediately preceding this song is the very interesting stage direction: "*An artificial charm of birds being heard within, Pan speaks*":

> *Pan:* The silly birds make mirth; then should we do them wrong,
>   Pomona, if we nill bestow an echo to their song.

The songs in this play are printed in italics. Despite the fact that "O Ida, O Ida" is not so printed, it is obvious both from its stage direction and its meter that it was intended to be sung.

PAGE 40. "Fair and fair." "Cupid's curse," l. 13, is explained by the following passage that introduces the song:

> *Œnone:* There is a pretty sonnet, then, we call it Cupid's curse:
>   They that do change old love for new, pray gods they change for worse.
>   The note is fine and quick withal, the ditty will agree,
>   Paris, with that same vow of thine upon our poplar tree.
> *Paris:* No better thing; begin it then, Œnone thou shalt see
>   Our music figure of the love that grows 'twixt thee and me.

PAGE 43. "His golden locks." Sir Henry Lee, considered by De Champany, the ambassador of France to Elizabeth's court, to be "the most accomplished cavaliero I had ever seen," had organized each year a tournament in honour of the Queen's birthday. In 1590, feeling too old to take part in such a dangerous contest as tilting, he resigned his leadership in the tournament and the Earl of Cumberland succeeded him. A full account of this ceremony is printed in Sir William Segar's *Honor Military and Civil*, Book III, chapter 54, 1602. Here we are told that at the end of the tournament "Her Majesty beholding these armed knights coming toward her, did suddenly hear a music so sweet and secret, as everyone thereat greatly marvelled. And harkening to that excellent melody, the earth as it were opening, there appeared a pavillon . . . like unto the sacred temple of the Virgins Vestal. . . . The music aforesaid was accompanied with these verses, pronounced and sung by M. Hales her Majesty's servant, a gentleman in that art excellent, and for his voice both commendable and admirable:

"My golden locks time hath to silver turned,
(O time too swift, and swiftness never ceasing)
My youth 'gainst age, and age at youth hath spurned,
But spurned in vain; youth waneth by increasing.
Beauty, strength, and youth, flowers fading been,
Duty, faith and love, are roots and ever green.

"My helmet now shall make an hive for bees,
And lovers songs shall turn to holy psalms:
A man-at-arms must now sit on his knees, [*sic*]
And feed on pray'rs that are old age's alms.
And so from court to cottage I depart,
My Saint is sure of mine unspotted heart.

"And when I sadly sit in homely cell,
I'll teach my swains this carol for a song—
Blest be the hearts that think my Sovereign well,
Curst be the souls that think to do her wrong.
Goddess, vouchsafe this aged man his right,
To be your beadsman now that was your night."

Peele's *Polyhymnia Describing the honourable Triumph at Tilt*, 1590, is merely a description in blank verse of the thirteen pairs of knights who jousted at Sir Richard Lee's last tournament, and of his resigning his place to the Earl of Cumberland. Nothing is said of the masque or of the music that was a part of it. On the last page is printed "A Sonnet"—"His golden locks time hath to silver turned," with no indication that it was sung at this tournament. John Dowland, *First Book of Airs*, 1597, has given it a beautiful setting. See E. H. Fellowes, *The English School of Lutanist Song Writers*, Part II, No. 18. Fellowes believes it doubtful whether at Lee's tournament Dowland's setting of the song was used, for if the "M. Hales" who sang it "is to be identified with Robert Hales it is likely that he set it to music himself." The third lyric in Dowland's *A Musical Banquet*, 1610, was set by Robert Hales. *Cf.* Fellowes, *English Madrigal Verse*, p. 614.

PAGE 43. *The Hunting of Cupid.* This play was licensed in 1591; but no printed copy of it has been found. Fragments of it are included in the MS. commonplace book of William Drummond of Hawthornden (now in the library of the Society of Scottish Antiquaries) where they are entered under the heading "The Hunting of Cupid by George Peele of Oxford, A Pastoral." I take the text from A. H. Bullen, *The Works of George Peele*, II, 366-369. London, 1888.

PAGE 43. "What thing is love." The first seven lines of this song, with slight variations in lines 1, 2, and 7, are to be found in the first act of the anonymous play *The Wisdom of Dr. Dodypoll*, 1600. The same seven lines, with variations in lines 1 and 7, are to be found in John Bartlet's *A Book of Airs*, 1606.

PAGE 44. "Melampus, when will love." Drummond gives but the subtitle and four lines of the song. The complete song is taken from *England's Helicon*, 1600, which also printed "O gentle love" and "Melpomene" from the *Arraignment of Paris*.

PAGE 44. "Whenas the rye." The context shows this to be a part song:

> *Fantastic:* Sirrah Frolic, I am sure thou art not without some round or other; no doubt but Clunch can bear a part.
> *Frolic:* Else think you me ill brought up, so set to it when you will. (*They sing.*)

PAGE 44. "All ye that lovely lovers be." This stanza and the following one are separated by some three hundred lines of dialogue.

PAGE 45. "Hot sun, cool fire." This song of Bethsabe's opens the play.

LOCRINE

PAGE 45. For a discussion of the authorship of this play, often ascribed to Greene, *cf.* C. F. Tucker Brooke, *The Shakespeare Apochrypha*; E. K. Chambers, *E. S.*, IV, 26.

MAIDS METAMORPHOSIS

PAGE 46. "Ye sacred fires." Orestes and Phylander tell Eurymine they have made an oath to their master, the Duke, to kill her because she has won the love of Ascanio, the Duke's son. She pleads in vain for her life:

> *Eurymine:* Then since there is no remedy, I pray
> Yet good my masters, do but stay so long

> Till I have ta'en my farewell with a song,
> Of him whom I shall never see again.
>
> *Phylander:* We will afford that respite to your pain.
> *Eurymine:* But lest the fear of death appall my mind,
> Sweet gentlemen let me this favour find:
> That you will veil mine eye-sight with this scarf:
> That when the fatal stroke is aimed at me,
> I may not start, but suffer patiently.
> *Orestes:* Agreed, give me, I'll shadow ye from fear,
> If this may do it.
> *Eurymine:*   O I would it might,
> But shadows want the power to do that right.
>
> *She sings.* "Ye sacred fires."
>
> *Orestes offers to strike her with his rapier, and is stayed by Philander.*

The song saves her.

PAGE 47. "Terlitelo," "Can you blow the little horn," "Fortune my foe." It is evident that the first and fourth lines of "Terlitelo" are composed of two lines run together; and we have here two four-line stanzas. This is the same meter as Frisco's "Can you blow your little horn" and I believe that both Mopso and Frisco are singing the same song. It has not been identified; but from its style, one would date it *circa* 1550.

"Fortune my foe" was probably as widely known and sung as any song of its period. William Byrd arranged it for the virginals. See W. Chappell, *O.E.P.M.*, II, 76, for the melody and for many references to it by Elizabethan dramatists.

PAGE 47. "By the moon." Sung to the "boys," Mopso, Frisco, and Joculo. Thomas Ravenscroft, in his *A Brief Discourse*, 1614, No. 8 of *Part III for Dancing*, has arranged this song for four voices. In l. 3, Ravenscroft prints "frisk" for "dance."

PAGE 48. "Round about, round about." Sung to the same boys.

> 2 *Fay:* O you must needs dance and sing:
> Which if you refuse to do,
> We will pinch you black and blue,
> And about we go.
>
> "Round about, round about."

In the play, the first stanza is repeated. This song, set by John Bennet for four voices, is in Ravenscroft's *Brief Discourse*, Part III, No. 9.

PAGE 48. "Amidst the mountain." Apollo, alone on the stage, sings this:

I'll sit me down, and wake my griefs again,
To sing awhile, in honour of thy name.

    The Song. "Amidst the mountain."

PAGE 48. "As little lambs." This duo is sung by Gemulo, a shepherd, and Silvio, a forester, to "call in carol from her quiet cote" Eurymine, whom they both love. Evidently for at least a part of this song there was a flute accompaniment, since Gemulo, as he begins, says:

    Now Pan pipe in thy sweetest reed,
    And as I love, so let thy servant speed.

PAGE 49. "All hail fair Phœbus." Sung by the Muses, and by Gemulo, Silvio, and Ascanio, to invoke Apollo:

1 Muse: Sing therefore, and each party from his heart,
    In this our music, bear a cheerful part.

    Song. "All hail fair Phœbus."

    Phœbus appears.

PAGE 49. "Since painful sorrow's date hath end." This chorus brings the play to a close. From the speech of Phœbus which introduces it, there was evidently a harp accompaniment to it. This is one of the earliest instances of the use of that instrument on the stage. *Cf.* W. J. Lawrence, *Welsh Song in the Elizabethan Drama, London Times Literary Supplement,* December 7, 1922. The speech of Phœbus is as follows:

Then Ladies gratulate this happy chance,
With some delightful tune and pleasant dance.
Mean space, upon his harp will Phœbus play,
So both of them may boast another day
And make report, that when their wedding chanced,
Phœbus gave music, and the Muses danced.

Acted by the Children of Pauls, this play had, in addition to the songs here reprinted, three choruses of shepherds and woodmen (Act i), the words of which are not given; and a four-line solo by Eurymine (Act iv) beginning "Since hope of health my froward stars deny."

The authorship of this play is still an open question, though it is now generally agreed that Lyly did not write it. Gosse suggests that it may be a youthful work of John Day, and Bullen, in the introduction to his reprint of the play, agrees with him. A. H. Bullen, *A Collection of Old English Plays,* I, 99, 1882. *Cf.* Chambers, *E. S.,* IV, 28.

WILY BEGUILED

PAGE 49. "Satyrs sing." The singers of this chorus are sent by Sylvanus

"Out of their bowers to tune their silver strings,
And with sweet sounding music sing,
Some pleasing madrigals and roundelays,
To comfort Sophos in his deep distress."

PAGE 50. "Old Tithon." This song is used to separate two scenes. Immediately before it are the following lines:

Sophos: Then let us solace, and in love's delight,
And sweet embracings spend the live long night.
And whilest love mounts her on her wanton wings,
Let descant run on music's silver strings.

Exeunt.

THE THRACIAN WONDER

PAGE 50. Kirkham, who obtained the MS. of this play and published it in 1661, stated on its title-page that it was written by Webster and Rowley. No one believes this. In the *Modern Language Review*, Vol. 88, pp. 34-38, Brereton suggests that Robert Greene is the author of the play because "it is little more than a dramatic adaptation of Greene's pastoral romance," *Menaphon.* J. Q. Adams, Jr., in *Modern Philology*, III, 317-325, believes that the play is not by Greene but by some one who boldly plagiarized from his *Menaphon.* Fleay identifies the play with a lost comedy by Thomas Heywood, *War without Blows and Love without Suit,* acted 1599. *Cf.* Chambers, *E. S.*, IV, 49.

PAGE 50. "Love is a law." Sung by Titterus, "a merry shepherd," to quote the *dramatis personæ*, who has in all eleven songs. This is not called in the text a song, nor is there any indication of music. To introduce this, Titterus says, "I'll tell thee my opinion now of Love," and this poem is called an "invective." However, when Titterus concludes, Pallamon says: "See Orpheus, you have drawn listeners," which points to music; and in Act ii, Titterus speaks of himself as having been a "singing satire against all women."

PAGE 51. "Art thou gone in haste." Sung by Pallamon, "stark mad" for love—an agreeable change from the love-crazed heroine.

PAGE 51. "Love's a lovely lad." Sung by Titterus to Ariadna, ending the act. He talks with her between several of the stanzas.

DANIEL

PAGE 53. "Are they shadows." Tethys and her nymphs, reposing after their second dance, are "entertained with this song."

PAGE 53. "Had sorrow." This song is introduced as follows:

Thirsis: Come boy, whilst I contemplate these remains
Of my lost love, under this myrtle tree,
Record the dolefull'st song, the sighingst notes,
That music hath to entertain bad thoughts.
Let it be all at flats, my boy, all grave,
The tone that best befits the grief I have.

Previous to this passage, there is no mention of the boy either in the text or in the stage directions.

PAGE 54. "Love is a sickness" is sung at the close of Act i, after all the actors have left the stage. There is no allusion to this chorus in the text, and neither the dialogue nor the action leads directly to it. It is a song sung between the acts. We know that the musicians at times played between acts, but singing between the acts is not often as clearly indicated as it is here. In this play there is a song after every act, and it ends with a chorus.

PAGE 54. "Eyes hide my love" immediately follows this passage:

Thirsis: And yet Palamon stay; perhaps you may
By charms you have, cause sleep to close mine eyes;
For you were wont, I do remember well,
To sing me sonnets which in passion I
Composèd in my happier days, when as
Her beams inflamed my spirits, which now are set.
And if you can remember it, I pray
Sing me the song which thus begins: "Eyes hide my love"
Which I did write upon the earnest charge
She gave unto me to conceal our love.

Song.

Palamon: So now he sleeps, or else does seem to sleep.

PAGE 54. "Were ever chaste and honest hearts"—another song between the acts.

SHAKESPEARE

PAGE 55. "When daisies pied." "When icicles." These two songs, ending the play, are thus introduced by Armado:

But most esteemed greatness, will you hear the dialogue that the two learned men have compiled, in praise of the owl and the cuckoo? it should have followed in the end of our show.
King: Call them forth quickly; we will do so.
Armado: Holla! approach.

Enter all.

> This side is Hiems, Winter. This Ver, the Spring: the one
> maintained by the owl, th'other by the cuckoo. Ver, begin.
>
> *The Song.*

PAGE 56. "You spotted snakes." "Titania Queen of Fairies," who
has entered "with her train," calls for a "roundel and a fairy song":

> Sing me now asleep:
> Then to your offices, and let me rest.
>
> *Fairies sing.*

In the first folio there is, at the end of this song, the stage direction
She sleeps.

PAGE 57. "The ousel cock." Sung by the "translated" Bottom, who
prefaces his song with these lines:

> I see their knavery. This is to make an ass of me, if they could; but
> I will not stir from this place, do what they can. I will walk up and
> down here, and will sing that they shall hear I am not afraid.

Between the first and second stanzas, Titania calls out: "What
angel wakes me from my flowery bed?"

PAGE 57. "Tell me where." In both the first quarto and the first
folio, line 4 of our text is printed on the margin of line 3. Probably
it is a part of the song and not a stage direction. Noble, *Shakespeare's Use of Song*, p. 49, accepts the suggestion of W. J. Lawrence
that "Reply, reply" was possibly a refrain sung by "All." I agree
with him. Putting it in the margin in the MS. might have been
merely a reminder that the solo was interrupted at this point.

In line 5, the first quarto reads "eye"; the reading of the first
folio, "eyes," has been followed to make the triple rhyme, corresponding with the first three lines of the song.

In both the quarto and the folio, "I'll begin it," line 9, is
printed in a different case from the rest of the song. Apparently it
was spoken, not sung.

It is held by many critics that this song gives Bassanio the right
clue; he chooses the casket that does not appeal to the eyes.

PAGE 57. "Sigh no more." This song, overheard by Benedict, is sung
by Balthazar at the request of the Prince: "Come Balthazar, we'll
hear that song again." Balthazar demurs because he has "so bad a
voice" and "There's not a note of mine that's worth the noting." At
the conclusion of the song the Prince remarks "By my troth, a good
song."

Nineteen lines before the song the first quarto has the stage direction *Enter Balthasar with music.* The first folio omits this, but
six lines further back prints the direction *Enter Prince, Leonato,*

Claudio and Jack Wilson. Plainly in the acting version of the play printed in the first folio, Wilson took the rôle of Balthazar. There was a John Wilson, son of Nicholas Wilson, Minstrel, born 1585; and also the better known Dr. John Wilson (1594-1673), composer and Professor of Music at Oxford. As Daniel observes in his reprint of the first quarto of this play, "It is evident from the birth dates of these two individuals that neither of them could be the original personator of Balthasar; but either might, for anything we know to the contrary, have taken the part at some revival of the play. Hence the insertion of the name in the theatrical copy of the first Folio." *Cf.* Chambers, *E. S.*, II, 349.

PAGE 58. "Pardon goddess of the night." Sung at the supposed tomb of Hero at the command of Claudio, "Now music sound and sing your solemn hymn."

PAGE 58. "How should I." The three sources for the songs in Hamlet are the first quarto of the play, 1603, the second quarto, 1604, and the first folio, 1623. "How should I," "And will he not," "Tomorrow is Saint Valentine's day" are taken from the 1603 quarto; "They bore him" does not appear in the 1603 quarto; and our text is taken from the 1604 quarto. "In youth when I did love" is taken also from the 1604 quarto, for the 1603 quarto omits the first two stanzas, and gives the last stanza twice.

PAGE 58. "How should I." In line 2, the 1603 quarto reads "another man," which we have changed to "another one," following the reading of the 1604 quarto and the first folio. In both the 1604 quarto and the first folio, stanzas two and three of our text are transposed; and these two editions contain the following variants: 1604, 1623, l. 5, "as the mountain snow"; 1604, l. 6, "larded all"; 1604, l. 7, "to the ground"; 1604, 1623, l. 8, "true love's."

PAGE 58. "And will he." 1604, ll. 1, 2, "will a"; 1604, 1623, l. 3, "No, no, he is dead"; 1604, 1623, "Go to thy death bed"; 1604, 1623, l. 5, "He never"; 1604, l. 6, "beard was"; 1604, l. 7, "Flaxen was"; 1604, 1623, "He is gone, he is gone"; 1623, l. 10, "Gramercy on."

PAGE 59. "Tomorrow is Saint Valentine's day." 1604, 1623, l. 3, "And I a maid"; 1604, 1623, l. 5, "Then up he rose"; 1604, 1623, l. 10, "Alack, and fie"; 1604, 1623, "if they"; 1604 inserts "(He answers)" before l. 15; 1604, 1623, l. 16, "And thou."

For an early setting to these words, see V. Jackson's *English Melodies from the 13th to the 18th Century. One Hundred Songs*, p. 36, 1910.

Page 59. "They bore him," 1623, has four lines, the second reading "Hey non nony, nony, hey nony."

Page 60. "And let me the cannikin clink." Sung by Iago to incite Cassio to drunkenness. There are the following variants in the first folio, 1623: l. 2, "cannikin clink"; l. 3, "Oh, man's life."

Page 60. "The poor soul." Before singing this song, Desdemona speaks the following lines:

My mother had a maid called Barbara,
She was in love: and he she loved proved mad,
And did forsake her. She had a song of Willow,
An old thing 'twas, but it expressed her fortune,
And she died singing it. That song to-night
Will not go from my mind. I have much to do
But to go hang my head all at one side
And sing it like poor Barbara: prithee, dispatch.

In the quarto, 1622, this passage ends with "mind," l. 6, and the song is omitted; consequently in Act v of the quarto Emilia makes no allusion to the song as she dies. In the 1623 folio, which first printed the song, Emilia dies singing the refrain "Willow, Willow, Willow." For the music of this song see the Appendix by E. H. Fellowes to Noble's *Shakespeare's Use of Song*. Shakespeare has here adapted a popular song of his day, the lament of a forsaken man, not woman. For his original, see *A Lover's Complaint* in Percy's *Reliques*. In l. 1, most editors follow the reading of the 1630 quarto "sat sighing."

Page 60. "Come unto these yellow sands." Probably Ariel did not sing the two-line burden, for his name is repeated immediately after it.

Between this song and "Full fathom five" there is the following speech by Ferdinand, and nothing more:

Where should this music be? I' th' air, or th' earth?
It sounds no more: and sure it waits upon
Some God o' th' island, sitting on a bank,
Weeping again the King my Father's wrack.
This music crept by me upon the waters,
Allaying both their fury, and my passion
With its sweet air: thence I have followed it
(Or it hath drawn me rather) but 'tis gone.
No, it begins again.

Page 61. "Full fathom five." As in the previous song, probably the "burden" was sung not by Ariel but by other musicians. Ferdinand's comment on this song shows that the singers must have been in the balcony or the musicians' room:

The ditty does remember my drowned father,
This is no mortal business, nor no sound
That the earth owes: I hear it now above me.

A melody for this song as well as for "Where the bee sucks" was written by Robert Johnson (*circa* 1550-1625) and arranged for three voices by Dr. John Wilson in his *Cheerful Airs or Ballads, first composed for one single voice, and since set for three voices.* 1660. See Sir Frederick Bridge, *Shakespearean Music in the Plays and Early Operas*, chapter 4. 1923. For Wilson's melody, see Bridge, *Songs from Shakespeare*, n.d, p. 23. It is also found in J. Playford's *Catch that Catch Can*, p. 126, 1667.

PAGE 61. "No more dams I'll make." Singing this song and shouting "Freedom, high-day," Caliban leads Stephano off the stage, ending the act.

PAGE 61. "Where the bee sucks." Sung by Ariel while Prospero is attiring himself as the Duke of Milan. Bridge, *Shakespearean Music*, p. 28, gives a facsimile of Johnson's setting for this song; he believes that Arne knew it and used it for his own setting of this lyric.

PAGE 61. "Who is Sylvia." Musicians, brought by Thurio, perform this serenade. When the song is ended, they continue playing while the host and Julia speak some sixteen lines.

PAGE 62. "Fie on sinful fantasy." Though the quarto edition of this play, 1602, gives no songs, it prints in Act v two stage directions that call for singing: "*Enter Sir Hugh like a satyr, and boys dressed like fairies, Mistress Quickly like the queen of Fairies. They sing a song about him, and afterwards speak.*" "*Here they pinch him and sing about him.*" The first folio omits both these stage directions and prints only the song we give. It is called for by Mistress Quickly:

About him, Fairies, sing a scornful rime,
And as you trip, still pinch him to your time.

Cf. Lyly's song, "Pinch him, pinch him, black and blue."

PAGE 62. "Take, Oh take those lips away." This song opens the act. This stanza, with a second one beginning "Hide, Oh hide those hills of snow," was sung in Fletcher's *Bloody Brother*, v, 2, first printed in 1639. It is generally assumed that Fletcher took the first stanza from Shakespeare and wrote the second one himself. It is certainly strange that Fletcher, who had a facile pen and a lyric gift inferior only to Shakespeare's, should have found it necessary to borrow from any one when he needed a song. For John Wilson's setting of this song, see Playford's *Select Musical Airs and Dialogues, Book I*, p. 24. 1653. *Cf.* Vincent Jackson, *E. M.*, p. 94.

PAGE 62. "Under the greenwood tree." After Amiens sings the first stanza of this song, he converses with Jaques, who asks for more of it. Amiens replies, "I'll end the song," and he evidently joins the other singers in the second stanza. At its close, Jaques says:

I'll give you a verse to this note,
That I made yesterday in despite of my invention.

to which Amiens replies, "And I'll sing it."

From the phrase with which Jaques introduces his parody—"Thus it goes"—it is not clear whether he recites or sings it.

PAGE 63. "Blow, blow." Sung by Amiens when the Duke says: "Give us some music, and good cousin, sing."

For Arne's setting, see Jackson, *op. cit.*, p. 172.

PAGE 64. "It was a lover." Sung by two pages "both in a tune like two gypsies on a horse" when Touchstone bids them "Come sit, sit, and sing a song."

In the original, stanza four of our text is stanza two. This song is the only one of Shakespeare's that was printed with a musical setting in his lifetime. "It was a lover" is No. 6 of Morley's *The First Book of Airs with little short songs to sing and play to the lute with the bass-viol. 1600.* For Morley's melody see Bridge, *Songs from Shakespeare,* p. 7.

PAGE 64. "O mistress mine." Sung by Feste in the drinking scene with Aguecheek and Sir Toby Belch, who calls for "A love song, a love song."

In 1599 Thomas Morley published his *The First Book of Consort Lessons, made by divers exquisite Authors for six Instruments to play together.* It contains an air entitled "O Mistress mine" but there are no words with it. The *Fitzwilliam Virginal Book (circa 1550-1620)* has a set of variations to this air by William Byrd, showing it was a popular one. The question arises, Is Morley's air the one to which this song was sung on Shakespeare's stage? Dr. E. H. Fellowes is inclined to doubt it. "It can be no more than pure conjecture as to whether Morley was setting Shakespeare's words—there is no evidence whatsoever beyond whether the words will fit or no, and as far as one can see they do not fit exactly." Noble's *Shakespeare's Use of Song,* p. 82. On the other hand, Sir Frederick Bridge believes that Morley's air goes with Shakespeare's words. See *Shakespearean Music,* pp. 10-16, 77-78. In Morley's *First Book of Airs,* 1600, No. 8 is "Mistress mine"; but the words of this are not Shakespeare's.

PAGE 65. "Come away." The Duke calls for this song:

Give me some music; Now good morrow friends.
Now good Cesario, but that piece of song,
That old and antique song we heard last night;
Me thought it did relieve my passion much,
More than light airs, and recollected terms
Of these most brisk and giddy-paced times.
Come, but one verse.

While Feste, who sings it, is being sent for, the Duke bids the musicians "play the tune the while." On Feste's arrival the Duke comments further on this song:

O fellow come, the song we had last night:
Mark it Cesario, it is old and plain;
The spinsters and the knitters in the sun,
And the free maids that weave their thread with bones,
Do use to chant it: it is silly sooth,
And dallies with the innocence of love,
Like the old age.

PAGE 65. "I am gone." There is no indication in the text that this is sung, but the meter suggests singing. With it Feste takes leave of Malvolio.

PAGE 65. "When that I was." Sung by Feste as an epilogue after all the actors have left the stage. It is interesting to compare the stanza of the fool in *King Lear*, iii, 2.

He that has and a little tiny wit,
With heigh-ho, the wind and the rain,
Must make content with his fortunes fit,
Though the rain it raineth every day.

PAGE 66. "When daffodils." Autolycus opens the scene and makes his first entrance with this song. Of the six songs in this play, he sings five and joins Dorcas and Mopsa in the sixth. No other character in Shakespeare's plays sings so many times.

PAGE 67. "Jog on." Autolycus makes his exit with this quatrain. It is set for three voices by John Hilton in J. Playford's *Catch that Catch Can*, p. 85. 1667.

PAGE 67. "Get you hence." One of the songs Autolycus is peddling:

Autolycus: This is a merry ballad, but a very pretty one.
Mopsa: Let's have some merry ones.
Autolycus: Why this is a passing merry one, and goes to the tune of two maids wooing a man: there's scarce a maid westward but she sings it: 'Tis in request, I can tell you.
Mopsa: We can both sing it: if thou'lt bear a part, thou shalt hear; 'tis in three parts.
Dorcas: We had the tune on't, a month ago.

Autolycus: I can bear my part, you must know 'tis my occupation: Have at it with you.

> *Song.* "Get you hence."

PAGE 68. "Will you buy any tape." With this song Autolycus makes an exit.

PAGE 68. "Come thou monarch." Sung on Pompey's galley at the feast he made for Cæsar and Antony:

Enobarbus: All take hands:
Make battery to our ears with the loud music,
The while I'll place you, then the boy shall sing.
The holding every man shall beat as loud
As his strong sides can volley.

PAGE 68. "Hark, hark, the lark." A serenade arranged for Imogen by the foolish Cloten.

Cloten: I would this music would come: I am advised to give her music a mornings, they say it will penetrate. (*Enter musicians*) Come on, tune: If you can penetrate her with your fingering, so: we'll try with tongue too: if none will do, let her remain: but I'll never give o'er. First, a very excellent, good conceited thing; after, a wonderful sweet air, with admirable rich words to it, and then let her consider.

> *Song.*

PAGE 69. "Fear no more." Though this dirge over Imogen bears in the first folio the title *Song*, the context shows that it was spoken, probably because Shakespeare's company, when the text of the folio was performed, did not have for the rôles of Guiderius and Arviragus actors who could sing. It is interesting to notice from the context how a song could be changed to recitation:

Arviragus: And let us, Polidore, though now our voices
Have got the mannish crack, sing him to th' ground
As once to our mother: use like note, and words,
Save that Euriphile must be Fidele.
Guiderius: Cadwall,
I cannot sing: I'll weep, and word it with thee;
For notes of sorrow, out of tune, are worse
Than priests and fanes that lie.
Arviragus: We'll speak it then. . . .

   .   .   .   .   .

We'll say our song the whilst: Brother begin.

CAMPION

PAGE 69. "Of Neptune's empire." In Davison's *Poetical Rhapsody,* 1602, this poem is signed Thomas Campion and after it is this notice: "This hymn was sung by Amphitrite, Thamesis, and other sea-

nymphs in Gray's Inn Masque, at the Court, 1594." This masque
was not printed until 1688; and in this printed copy the song lacks
Campion's name and is marred by obvious misprints. *Cf.* W. W.
Greg's reprint of *Gesta Grayorum.*

PAGE 70. "Now hath Flora." According to the stage directions this
song was a trio. Descending from a hill, come

> *First Zephyrus and Flora, the two Silvans with baskets after them:
> Four Silvans in green taffata, and wreaths, two bearing mean lutes, the
> third a bass lute, and the fourth a deep Bandora. As soon as they came
> to the descent toward the dancing place, the consort of ten ceased, and
> the four Silvans played the same air, to which Zephyrus and the two
> other Silvans did sing these words in a bass, tenor, and treble voice, and
> going up and down as they sang, they strowed flowers all about the
> place.*

Campion composed the music for his own words. It was printed
with the masque.

PAGE 71. "Tell me gentle hour." This is the concluding song of
the masque. The text says of it: "This chorus was performed with
several echoes of music, and voices." The music for this is not
printed with the text.

PAGE 71. "Night as well as brightest day." This was sung by a
"Traveller, Gardener, and Cynic." The context is:

> *Gardener:* Let us all therefore join together sociably in a song, to
> the honour of good fellowship.
> *Cynic:* A very musical motion, and I agree to it.
> *Traveller:* Sing that sing can, for my part I will only while you sing
> keep time with my gestures. *A la more* [*mode*] *du
> France* [*sic*].

PAGE 72. "Woo her and win her." The music for this song is
printed at the end of Campion's "Mask . . . At the Marriage of
the Earl of Somerset and the Lady Frances Howard," 1614, added
to it "to fill up these empty pages."

PAGE 73. "While dancing rests," "Come ashore." At the end of the
masque, the music for these two songs is printed, with the note:
"These songs following were composed by Mr. Coprario, and sung
by Mr. John Allen, and Mr. Lanier." *Cf.* Smith, *Mus. Ant.*, p. 61.

PAGE 74. "Robin is a lovely lad." This is No. VI in a little book
entitled *The Airs that were sung and Played at Brougham Castle,*
1618, by George Mason and John Earsdend. Percival Vivian, *The
Works of Thomas Campion*, pp. li-lii, attributes this song to Campion because of its style. *Cf.* Smith, *op. cit.*, p. 156.

NASHE

PAGE 74. "Fair Summer droops." At the close of this song, Will Summers comments on it as follows:

"The rest of the green men have reasonable voices, good to sing catches, or the great Jowben by the fire's side, in a winter's evening."

PAGE 75. "Spring, the sweet Spring." Summers remarks on this:

"By my troth, they have voices as clear as crystal; this is a pratty thing, if it be for nothing but to go a-begging with."

For an interesting bird song contemporary with this play, see "Cuckow" from a MS. in the British Museum (*circa* 1610), published by Laudy and Co., London.

PAGE 76. "Adieu, farewell." The following is the context:

Summer:　　To weary out the time until they come,
　　　　　　　Sing me some doleful ditty to the lute,
　　　　　　　That may complain my near approaching death.

The Song. "Adieu, farewell."

Summer:　　Beshrew me, but thy song hath moved me.
Will Summers: Lord have mercy on us, how lamentable it is!

PAGE 77. "Autumn hath all." At the end of this song, which closes the play, Will Summers asks:

"How is't? how is't? You that be of the graver sort, do you think these youths worthy of a *Plaudite* for praying for the Queen, and singing of the Litany?"

McKerrow offers evidence to show that this play was performed October, 1592, before the Archbishop of Canterbury in his palace at Croydon.

MIDDLETON

PAGE 78. "Love for such a cherry lip." Sung by the courtezan Imperia to Fontinelle, a French prisoner.

Imp: Will my sweet prisoner entertain a poor Italian song?
Font: O most willingly, my dear Madonna.
Imp: I care not if I persuade my bad voice to wrestle with this music, and catch a strain: so, so, so; keep time, keep time, keep time.

Sings. "Love for such."

There is a setting for this song by Edward Pearce in Thomas Ravenscroft's *A Brief Discourse, etc.* 1614.

PAGE 78. "Happy times." A chorus sung by reapers, first heard off stage.

Simplicity: Hark, the reapers begin to sing; they're come nearer, methinks, too.

Song. "Happy times."

Simplicity: These reapers have the merriest lives; they have music to
all they do.

The title-page of the masque assigns it to Middleton and Rowley
and it is quite possible that Rowley wrote this song.

PAGE 79. "Weep eyes." Sung by Moll, supposed to be dying.

PAGE 79. "In a maiden time." Sung by Isabella who says:

I care not if I try my voice this morning;
But I have got a cold sir, by your means.

PAGE 79. "Black spirits and white." In *Macbeth*, iv, 1. 1623, there
is the following stage direction: "*Music and a Song. Black Spirits,
etc.*"; and in iii, 5, is the stage direction: "*Sing within. Come away,
come away, etc.*" The words of these two songs are not given.

In *The Witch*, iii, 3, is a song (not included in this volume)
which begins:

Come away, come away,
Hecate, Hecate, come away.

Bullen believes that neither this song nor "Black spirits and white,"
of our text, were the ones sung in *Macbeth*; but that Middleton took
phrases from Shakespeare's songs—now lost—and expanded them
into the songs in *The Witch. Cf.* A. H. Bullen, *The Works of
Thomas Middleton, I, Introduction,* lii-lviii.

The Witch was not printed in the seventeenth century. The MS.,
undated, says it was "long since acted by His Majesty's Servants at
the Black Friars."

PAGE 80. "How round about." The title-page of this play ascribes
it to Jonson, Fletcher, and Middleton. Probably either Jonson or
Fletcher would have written better lyrics than these.

DEKKER

PAGE 81. "O, the month of May." The 1600 edition of *The Shoemaker's Holiday* was not divided into acts and scenes. This song and
the following one were printed together, preceding the play.

PAGE 82. "Cold's the wind." After the phrase *The second Three
Mans Song*, the 1600 quarto has the line *This is to be sung at the
latter end.* In stanza 3, "Close with the tenor, boy" is printed in
italics as though it were another stage direction, similar to ll. 14 and
15; yet it is probably a part of the song, "boy" giving the rhyme
for "joy.'

PAGE 82. "Fortune smiles." Immediately preceding this song is the stage direction *Enter a Gardener, a Smith, a Monk, a Shepherd all crowned, a Nymph with a globe, another with Fortune's wheel, then Fortune . . . The foremost come out singing.* At the very end of the play this song is repeated with "Fortune" changed to "Virtue," and the last four lines, sung by "All," omitted.

PAGE 83. "Virtue's branches wither." Immediately before this song, Vice and her attendants enter with "a fair tree of gold with apples on it"; Virtue and her nymphs follow, bringing "a tree with green and withered leaves mingled together, and little fruit on it." Fortune commands that both trees be planted:

> Apply your tasks; whilst you are labouring,
> To make your pains seem short, our priest shall sing.

> *The Song.* ("Virtue's branches.") *Whilst he sings, the rest set the trees into the earth.*

PAGE 83. "Virtue stand aside." This is sung to the sleeping Andelocia. According to the stage direction, after the first stanza she "wakens and stands up." Immediately before the song is the stage direction: *Enter Fortune, Vice, Virtue, the Priest, Satyrs with music, playing as they come in before Fortune. They play awhile.* Fortune, Virtue, and Vice speak a line apiece, and then comes the stage direction *Music awhile and then cease.* After this prelude, the song is sung, introduced by the following:

> *Vice:* Sweet tunes, wake him again.
> *Fortune:* Vice sets too heavy on his drowsy soul,
> Music's sweet concord cannot pierce his ear.
> Sing, and among your songs mix bitter scorn.
> *Virtue:* Those that tear Virtue, must by Vice be torn.

PAGE 84. "Art thou poor." Henslowe's diary records that on December 19, 1599, Henry Chettle, W. Haughton, and Thomas Dekker received fifty-one shillings of "good and lawful money" "in earnest of Patient Grissill." As the songs in this play have all the traits of Dekker's style and thought, I assume he wrote them.

That this is a part song is indicated by the lines of Janiculo that introduce it:

> Let not thy tongue go so; sit down to work,
> And that our labour may not seem too long,
> We'll cunningly beguile it with a song.

> "Art thou poor."

Before line 8, "Work apace," the quarto has the word "foot," meaning that this and the two following lines are the burden or chorus of the song.

PAGE 84. "Golden slumbers." This had a lute accompaniment. The lines that precede it are:

> *Janiculo:* Lay them both softly down, Grissill sit down,
>   Laureo, fetch you my lute. Rock thou the cradle.
>   Cover the poor fool's arm, I'll charm their eyes
>   To take a sleep by sweet tuned lullabies.

PAGE 85. "Beauty arise." Janiculo's third song. The Marquis bids him sing it as a "bridal song" at the Marquis's supposed marriage— the final test of Grissill.

> *Marquis:* Janiculo, here is a bridal song,
>   Play you the lark to greet my blessed sun.
>   Grissill, are you returned? Play you the morning
>   To lead forth Gratiana my bright bride.
>   Go in and wait on her. Janiculo,
>   Sing Hymaneus hymns, Music, I say.

After the song, the Marquis asks Janiculo, "Art thou as glad in soul as in thy song?"

PAGE 85. "Oars, Oars." Probably this lyric is by Dekker rather than by Webster, whose songs are invariably tragic. It is printed at the end of the play, after the final *Exeunt*. Five lines before it, Parenthesis says, "Gentlemen, hasten to his rescue some, while others call for oars."

PAGE 85. "Brave iron." There are but two copies extant of *London's Tempe*. Our text is taken from Shepherd's edition of Dekker, 1873. This song is from the "Fourth Presentation," and is sung in the "Lemnian forge." The stage directions:

> *In it are Vulcan, the smith of Lemnos, with his servants . . . working at the anvil. . . . A fire is seen in the forge, bellows blowing, some filing, some at other works; thunder and lightning on occasion. As the smiths are at work, they sing in praise of iron, the anvil and hammer.*

PAGE 87. "Fancies are but streams." This opens the play; it is preceded by the following lines:

> *Enter the Priest of the Sun. Raybright discovered sleeping.*

> *Priest:* Let your tunes, you sweet-voiced spheres,
>   Overtake him:
>   Charm his fancies, ope his ears,
>   Now awake him. Begin.
> *Song.* "Fancies are but streams."

Ford collaborated with Dekker in this play; surely the songs are by Dekker.

PAGE 87. "Haymakers, rakers." The stage directions for this song are:

Hautboys. The Sun takes his seat above. Enter Summer, Raybright, Humor, Plenty, Folly, Country-fellows and Wenches.

PAGE 88. "Cast away care." Solo by Folly, who says his music is "natural, and came by inheritance, my father a French nightingale, and my mother an English wagtail."

THOMAS HEYWOOD

PAGE 90. "Pack, clouds, away." *The Rape of Lucrece* offers a good example of the way songs disappeared from plays. In 1608 was published the first edition, containing a preface by Heywood himself. In it the poet explains that he is printing his drama because some of his plays "have (unknown to me and without any of my direction) accidentally come into the printer's hands, and therefore so corrupt and mangled (copied only by the ear) that I have been as unable to know them as ashamed to challenge them. This therefore I was the willinger to furnish out in his native habit." After such an explicit statement, one would naturally expect that all the songs of this play would be printed, especially as the title-page contains the phrase "With the several songs in their apt places." Moreover, at the end of the last act two more songs are given "because we would not that any man's expectation should be deceived in the ample printing of this book, Lo (Gentle Reader) we have inserted these few songs which were added by the stranger that lately acted Valerius his part in form following." Evidently this edition was to be a complete one.

It contained twelve songs, as did the second edition, 1609. But in 1630 there appeared what is called on the title-page the fourth edition, though no third edition appearing between 1609 and 1630 is known. This so-called fourth edition contained four songs that were not included in the previous editions. To introduce three of these lyrics, lines were added to the text. Some of these passages are so inappropriate that they may prove the new songs following them were not Heywood's but were lyrics interpolated at some revival of the play by another "stranger that lately acted Valerius his part." But this supposition does not account for one of these four songs; since in the first edition, 1608, there appeared the following:

Brutus: What so early, Valerius, and your voice not up yet? Thou wast wont to be my lark and raise me with thy early notes.

Valerius: I was never so hard set yet, my Lord, but I had ever a fit of mirth for a friend.

Brutus: Prithee, lets hear it then whilst we may, for I divine thy music and my madness are both short lived; we shall have something else to do ere long, we hope Valerius.

Horatius: Jove send it.

It is perfectly plain that Valerius should sing at this point, yet in the first edition no song is given or even indicated by a stage direction, and Brutus continues the conversation.

In the 1630 edition, immediately after "Jove send it," Valerius sings "Pack, clouds, away, and welcome, day." Heywood was the author of this song for it appears in a little volume he published, *Pleasant Dialogues and Dramas*. 1637. It is equally plain that it fits the context perfectly. Thus Heywood, for all his professions in the title-page and preface of his first edition of *Lucrece*, had neglected to print in it one of his finest lyrics.

The following passage, taken also from the first edition, evidently calls for a part song:

Horatius: The news, the news, if it have any shape
    Of sadness, if some prodigy have chanced,
    That may beget revenge, I'll cease to chafe,
    Vex, martyr, grieve, torture, torment myself,
    And tune my humour to strange strains of mirth;
    My soul divines some happiness, speak, speak:
    I know thou hast some news that will create me
    Merry and musical for I would laugh,
    Be new transhaped. I prithee sing, Valerius,
    That I may air with thee.

No song is given; but in the 1638 edition these lines are followed by a very wretched lyric beginning: "I'd think myself as proud in shackles." One may well doubt that Heywood wrote it.

Thus the first edition of this play, 1608, contained twelve songs; the edition of 1630 reprinted these and added four more; and to these sixteen, the edition of 1638 added five more, each of them bearing the title "the first new song," "the second new song," and so on. This was evidently to justify the statement on the title-page: "The copy revised, and sundry songs before omitted, now inserted in their right places." So a play that had twelve songs in its first printing appears thirty years later with twenty-one, and though some of these are plainly later additions, at least one undoubtedly should have been printed in the first edition. This is a striking example of the way songs were omitted and interpolated. For a song, not by Heywood, introduced in this play, see "Now what is love," p. 27 and notes.

In Heywood's *Pleasant Dialogues and Dramas*, pp. 262-263, 1637, "Pack, clouds, away" is printed as *A Nuptial Song devoted to the Celebration of a marriage between Master James and Mistress An. W. A Song at their uprising.* This *Nuptial Song* has two variants from the text of the play, 1630: l. 3, "larks"; l. 10, "them both I'll."

PAGE 91. "Come list and hark." Not printed in the 1608 or 1609 quarto. To introduce this song, the 1630 quarto inserted the following:

Valerius: Nay if he be dying as I could wish he were, I'll ring out his funeral peal, and this it is. "Come list and hark."

PAGE 91. "We that have known." Solo by Amphrisa.

THOMAS HEYWOOD?

PAGE 92. "Ye little birds." The song is thus introduced:

Enter Frank singing.

Frank: "Ye gods of love that sit above, and pity lovers' pain,
Look from your thrones upon the moans that I do now sustain."
Was ever man thus tormented with love?

Song. "Ye little birds."

The Fair Maid of the Exchange was published anonymously. For the question of Heywood's authorship, see Chambers, *E. S.,* IV, 13.

PAGE 93. "Phœbus unto thee." Sung by a page of Apollo in a contest with a clown who has a worthless song, though the "champion" of Pan. Heywood's claim to *Love's Mistress* is a doubtful one. *Cf.* Chambers, *E. S.,* III, 346.

JONSON

PAGE 93. "Slow, slow, fresh fount." Sung by Echo as a "mourning strain" over the "watery hearse" of Narcissus. The context shows that this song had a full accompaniment:

Mercury: Begin, and (more to grace thy cunning voice)
The humourous air shall mix her solemn tunes,
With thy sad words: strike music from the spheres,
And with your golden raptures swell our ears.

Song. "Slow, slow, fresh fount."

There is a contemporary setting for this song in Henry Youll's *Canzonets to three Voices* (No. VIII), 1598.

PAGE 94. "O that joy." Sung by Hedon.

Hedon: I made this ditty and the note to it upon a kiss that my honour gave me; how do you like it, sir?
Amorphus: A pretty air; in general, I like it well. But in particular, your long die-note did arride me most, but it was somewhat too long. I can show one, almost of the same nature, but much before it, and not so long; in a composition of mine own: I think I have both the note, and the ditty about me.

PAGE 94. "Thou more than most sweet glove." Sung by Amorphus to show Hedon "a composition of mine own." He reads it aloud before singing it.

PAGE 94. "Queen and Huntress." In the first quarto, 1592, this is entitled *Hymnus*. It is sung to Cinthia by Hesperus, whose only part in the play is this song.

PAGE 95. "If I freely may discover." A duo, Crispinus singing the first stanza, Hermogenes the second.

PAGE 95. "Love is blind." Sung by Crispinus to viol accompaniment. From the dialogue it appears that, as he sings, Crispinus himself plays "the pretty instrument."

PAGE 96. "Wake our mirth," "Then in a free." In the play, these two songs are separated by but four lines of prose. The first is a solo; from the dialogue preceding it, evidently Albius, dressed as Vulcan, sings it. The second song is sung by Hermogenes and Crispinus, judging by the context.

PAGE 96. "Fools they are" is part of the entertainment "invented" by Mosca to please his master, Volpone.

PAGE 97. "Come, my Celia" is sung as Volpone tempts her. There is a contemporary setting, possibly the one used in the play, in Alfonso Ferrabosco's *Airs* (No. 6), 1609.

PAGE 97. "So Beauty." The text of the masque states that this was sung by a "loud tenor."

PAGE 98. "If all these Cupids." The purpose of this and the two following songs was to permit the Queen and her fifteen ladies to rest after their dancing, which had been "exquisitely performed." The music for the five songs from the masque here reprinted, may be found in Ferrabosco's *Airs* (Nos. xviii-xxii). 1609.

PAGE 99. "Buzz, quoth the Blue-Fly." The music for this song, composed by Edmund Nelham, is to be found in Playford's *Catch as Catch Can*, p. 75. 1667.

PAGE 99. "Still to be neat." The very first words of the play concern this song:

Clerimont: Ha' you got the song yet perfect I ga' you, boy?
Boy: Yes, sir.
Clerimont: Let me hear it.
Boy: You shall, sir; but i' faith let no body else. . . .
Clerimont: . . . Sing, sir.

Boy sings.

The words are not printed until two pages further, when Clerimont says to a friend who joins him: "I have made a song, I prithee hear it, o' the subject," and the song is given. The full context shows that the boy sings the same song both times.

In this lyric, Jonson has imitated "Semper munditias," an anonymous poem found in an edition of *Petronius*, 1585. *Cf. Notes and Queries*, September 29, 1900. A setting for "Still to be neat" is found in John Playford's *Select Airs and Dialogues*, 1669.

PAGE 100. "See the chariot." Apparently this is the song which Manly sings to attract Mrs. Fitz-dottrell to his friend, Wittipol. Wittipol has given Manly "a paper wherein is the copy of a song."

> Read those.
> They'll go unto the air you love so well.
> Try 'em unto the note, may be the music
> Will call her sooner: light, she's here! Sing quickly.
> *Mrs. Fitz:* How! Music? then he may be there: and is sure.

> *Manly sings.*

The words of the song are not printed; but at the end of the scene Wittipol says:

> Lady
> Shall I, with what I have made today here, call
> All sense to wonder, and all faith to sign
> The mysteries revealed in your form?
> And will Love pardon me the blasphemy
> I uttered when I said a glass could speak
> This beauty, or that fools had power to judge it?

He then recites the last two stanzas of this song. The opening stanza was first printed in the *Underwood*, 1640.

For an interesting contemporary setting of this song, ascribed to Robert Johnson, see Vincent Jackson, *E. M.*, pp. 40-41. In Suckling's tragedy, *The Sad One*, iv, 3. 1659, the third stanza is imitated in his *Song to a Lute*, beginning

> Hast thou seen the down ith' air
> When wanton blasts have tossed it.

This song is parodied in William Cavendish's *The Variety*, iv, 1. 1649.

PAGE 101. "The faery beam." Sung by Patricio, one of the gypsies. In his *Night-piece to Julia* Herrick has imitated this song; he also took hints from "Still to be neat" for his *Delight in Disorder*.

PAGE 101. "Though I am young." Sung by Karolin to "divert" the grief-crazed Æglamour. The stage direction is *Sings while Æglamour reads the song.* Probably it was read aloud, then sung. Jonson did this more than once, as these notes show, evidently not wishing the words of his songs to be missed by the audience. *Cf.* W. J. Law-rence, "First Read then Sing," in *The Stage,* January 29, 1920.

The music for this song, by Nicholas Laniere, is in Playford, *Select Musical Airs and Dialogues,* Part II, p. 21. 1653. It is also found, arranged for four voices, in Playford, *Catch as Catch Can,* p. 216. 1667.

PAGE 102. "An eye of looking back." This song had the following stage direction:

> *Here they danced with the Ladies, and the whole revels followed; which ended, Mercury called to him* [Hercules] *in the following speech: which was afterwards repeated in song by two trebles, two ten-ors, a bass, and the whole chorus.*

The "Hill" of l. 11 was "the Mountain Atlas," which was the "scene" of the masque.

RETURN FROM PARNASSUS

PAGE 104. "How can he sing." "Fiddlers" play the accompaniment for Philomusus, whose voice, he says, has been "quite untuned" by "the cold of woe":

> Time was in time of my young Fortune's Spring,
> I was a gamesome boy and learned to sing.

For the authorship of this play, see Chambers, *E. S.,* IV, 38.

EVERY WOMAN IN HER HUMOUR

PAGE 104. "Sister, awake." This song, and the two following ones, are sung by Philautus, who is constantly warbling. He is proud of his skill, of the beauty of his "relish," and his first entrance is marked by a lyric, or at least by the opening line of one. Sometimes he ap-parently sings but the first phrase of a song—"Sleep, wayward thoughts," from John Dowland's *First Book of Songs or Airs,* 1597; the ever popular "Fortune my foe"; or "Here's none but only I," "Is it not most aimiable and fair," "All hail to my beloved," "Sad despair doth drive me hence, For all must be to no effect," four songs I have not identified. It is probable from the "&c" of the text that he sings all of the first two songs here printed. "Sister, awake" is from Thomas Bateson's *First Set of English Madrigals,* 1604. "My love can sing no other song" is plainly "My mistress sings no other song" from Robert Jones's *First Book of Songs and Airs,* 1600. Philautus sings it before Cæsar to gain his liberty.

There were other songs in this play, indicated by the stage di-rections, though even their first words are not given. What is most interesting in this comedy is the proof it offers that the lyrics from the contemporary song books were heard on the stage. This was a simple expedient and it was but natural that the theatre should add to its attractions by offering the favorite songs of the day.

In *Modern Philology*, X, 413, J. Q. Adams, Jr., argues that Lewis Machin was the author of this play. *Cf.* Chambers, *E. S.*, IV, 11.

MARSTON

PAGE 106. "O Love" is sung to Beatrice by Frevill:

> By your sorrows leave,
> I bring some music, to make sweet your grief.
>
> *He sings, she swoons.*

PAGES 106, 107. "The nut-brown ale," "Holiday, O blessed morn." It is generally believed that Marston was not the author of *Histriomastix*; and that it was an old play which he revised. I assume the songs are his. *Cf.* Chambers, *E. S.*, IV, 17.

THE MONTEBANKS MASQUE

PAGE 107. "The hour of sweety night." This song ends the masque, which was not printed until the last century. It is sometimes attributed to Marston. *Cf.* Brotanek, *Die Englischen Maskenspiele, Wiener Beiträge*. 1902. Bullen suggests this song may be by Campion.

ROWLEY?

PAGE 108. "Oh, sorrow." It is not indicated who sings this; possibly Onælia and her maid, for a few lines after the end of this duo Onælia says, "I'll sing any song." At its close, Cornego enters and asks, "No lesson, Madam, but Lachrymæ's?"

L. 3 of the quarto's text reads "furier face." On the pages of this play the title is changed to *The Noble Spanish Soldier*. Concerning its authorship, Bullen writes: "*The Noble Spanish Soldier* bears Samuel Rowley's initials on the title page of the old edition; but there are good reasons for ascribing it—in whole or part—to Dekker. It was entered on the Stationer's Register as a work of Dekker in May, 1631, and again in December, 1663." *Lyrics from the Elizabethan Dramatists*, p. 294. *Cf.* Chambers, *E. S.*, III, 300.

PAGE 108. "Trip it." Solo by Sancho.

PAGE 109. "Come follow." The stage direction calls for the entrance of nine characters "and others" "with the following song":

> "Come follow."

The title-page of this play ascribes it to Middleton and Rowley, but Bullen believes that the gypsy scenes are Rowley's. For the air of this song, see Chappell, *O.E.P.M.*, I, 1867.

WEBSTER

Page 110. "Call for the robin." Probably this lyric was sung. A few lines before it, the stage directions call for a song which, however, is omitted in the text. There is no such stage direction for this passage but immediately preceding it Cornelia says:

I'll give you a saying which my grandmother
Was wont, when she heard the bell toll, to sing o'er unto her lute.

Page 111. "Hark now everything is still." Shortly before this lyric is the mad song "O let us howl some heavy note," with the stage direction, *Here (by a mad-man) this song is sung to a dismal kind of music.* It is not clear that "Hark now everything" is sung, for though printed in italics, as were songs in general, there is no indication of music. The lines immediately preceding it are:

Bosola:　　　　　'Twas to bring you
　　By degrees to mortification. Listen.

The word "listen" may indicate that the song is sung off stage; or that Bosola recites it.

In iii, 4, of this play is a "ditty sung (to very solemn music) by divers churchmen." On the margin of the song is printed "The author disclaims this ditty to be his."

BELCHIER

Page 111. "Walking in a shadowed grove." Printed at the end of the play with no indication of how or where it was sung. The stage directions call for six songs—a "tawny Moor," Abnidaræs Quixot,—sings three times in half a page—but this is the only song whose words are given.

Following Bullen, "shadowe," l. 1, has been changed to "shadowed."

MASSINGER

Page 113. "Why art thou slow." Sung by the Empress, Athenais, falsely accused by a jealous husband. At the end of her song she says:

Thus like a dying swan, to a sad tune
I sing my own dirge.

Page 113. "Though we contemplate" is sung by two boys.

Landislaus: Pallas, bound up in little volume,
Apollo with his lute attending on her,
Serve for the induction.

PAGE 114. "The blushing rose." Hearing this sung by some one unseen, Matthias exclaims:

A song too: certainly be it he or she
That owns this voice; it hath not been acquainted
With much affliction: Whoso'er you are
That do inhabit here, if you have bodies
And are not mere aerial forms, appear!

MASSINGER?

PAGE 111. "Turn, turn thy beauteous face." Sung by Piorato to Malroda, "a wanton mistress of Vitelli."

Though *Love's Cure* appeared in the Beaumont and Fletcher folio, 1647, scholars are pretty generally agreed that Fletcher had no hand in the play. It has been attributed to Massinger. *Cf.* A. H. Bullen, "John Fletcher" in *The Dictionary of National Biography*.

MASSINGER AND FIELD

PAGE 115. "Fie, cease to wonder." Four songs, of which this is the first, precede the play. There is no indication where they belong.

TOMKIS

PAGE 115. "Sing sweetly." Sung by a chorus off stage. The play was presented before King James by the "Gentlemen of Trinity College," Cambridge.

BEAUMONT

PAGE 115. "Come, sleep." Sung by Oriana, "the Duke's Mistress," to Gondarino, the "Woman Hater." The context follows:

Oria: Or let my voice, set to some pleasing cord, sound out
The sullen strains of my neglected love.
Gond: Sing till thou crack thy treble string in pieces,
And when thou hast done, put up thy pipes and walk,
Do any thing, sit still, and tempt me not.
Oria: I had rather sing at doors for bread than sing to this fellow
but for hate:

Song. "Come sleep."

Gond: Have you done your wassyl? 'Tis a handsome drowsy ditty
I'll assure ye, now I had as leave hear a cat cry, when her
tail is cut off, as hear these lamentations, these lousy lovelays, these bewailments.

PAGE 116. "Shake off your heavy trance." Sung by twelve priests, "every priest playing upon a lute." The text of this song and of the two following ones is taken from the quarto entered on S. R., 1613, but printed undated; Beaumont supplied a preface for it.

PAGE 116. "Ye should stay longer." The quarto has the following heading for this song:

The knights take their ladies to dance with them Galliards, Durets, Cirantoes etc. and lead them to their places. Then loud music sounds, supposed to call them to their Olympian games. (Cf. 1. 5.)

The folios, issued after Beaumont's death, makes several changes in this song: "And" for "but," l. 5; " 'em" for "them," ll. 7, 10; "clip" for "cut," l. 9.

PAGE 116. "Peace and silence." The priests sing this chorus which ends the masque.

PAGE 116. " 'Tis mirth." One of Merry-thought's songs. As Bullen observes, "aches," l. 11, is dissyllabic.

PAGE 117. "Tell me, dearest." This duo has the following context:

Luce:　　　　I cannot sleep.
　　　　Indeed I cannot friend.
Jasper: Why then we'll sing
　　　　And try how that will work upon our senses.
Luce: I'll sing, or say, or anything but sleep.
Jasper: Come little mermaid, rob me of my heart
　　　　With that enchanting voice.
Luce: You mock me, Jasper.

Song. "Tell me."

In Fletcher's *The Captain*, ii, 2, 1647, is the following version of this song (*Cf.* Smith, *Musica Antiqua*, p. 55):

A Duo. Enter at Window Frank and Clora.

1.　Tell me, dearest, what is love?
2.　'Tis a lightning from above,
　　'Tis an arrow, 'tis a fire,
　　'Tis a boy they call desire.
Both:　　'Tis a grave,
　　　　Gapes to have
　　Those poor fools that long to prove.

1.　Tell me more, are women true?
2.　Yes, some are, and some as you.
　　Some are willing, some are strange,
　　Since you men first taught to change.
Both:　　And till troth
　　　　Be in both,
　　All shall love, to love anew.

1.   Tell me more yet, can they grieve?
2.   Yes, and sicken sore, but live:
       And be wise, and delay,
       When you men are as wise as they.
Both: Then I see,
                Faith will be,
       Never till they both believe.

PAGE 117. "Come you whose loves." A dirge, sung by Luce over the coffin supposed to hold the dead Jasper. "Mourning," l. 8, is probably a mistake for "moaning"; yet the 1635 quarto and 1679 folio both read "mourning."

PAGE 118. "Better music." This chorus practically ends the play, for after it there is but the brief epilogue of the citizen's wife. The song is thus introduced:

Old Merry-thought: Methinks all we, thus kindly and unexpectedly
                        reconciled, should not part without a song.
Merchant: A good motion.
Old Merry-thought: Strike up then.

                Song. "Better music."

The punctuation of the last three lines of the song follows that of the 1679 folio. The quarto of 1613, with a period after "crying" and "mirth" is plainly wrong.

   C. M. Gayley, *Beaumont the Dramatist, Book II*, has summed up the results of recent studies on the collaboration of Beaumont and Fletcher. In deciding what plays shall be attributed to their joint authorship, and what plays shall be assigned to them individually, I have followed Gayley's conclusions. *Cf.* Chambers, *E. S.*, III, 215-218.

BEAUMONT AND FLETCHER

PAGE 118. "Lovers, rejoice!" Solo by a boy.

Priest of Cupid: Now boy sing to stick our hearts
                        Fuller of great Cupid's darts.

                Song. "Lovers, rejoice!"

PAGE 118. "Cynthia, to thy power" is a "great chorus" from a masque presented in the play.

PAGE 119. "Lay a garland," "I could never." These two songs and the lines introducing them (printed below) are omitted from the first edition of the play, the quarto of 1619. They were printed, together with these lines, for the first time in the 1622 quarto.

Aspasia: "Lay a garland on my hearse of the dismal yew."
Evadne: That's one of your sad songs, Madam.
Aspasia: Believe me, 'tis a very pretty one.
Evadne: How it is, Madam?

Song. "Lay a garland."

Evadne: Fie on't, Madam, the words are so strange they are able to make one dream of hobgoblins. "I could never have the power." Sing that, Dula.

Song. "I could never."

L. 4. The quartos 1622, 1630, 1638, 1650, as well as the 1679 folio, read "lay lightly" not "lie lightly," as often printed. The editions of 1622, 1630, read "gently earth"; the editions of 1638, 1650, 1679, "gentle earth."

JOHN FORD

Page 119. "Fly hence, shadows" is sung to "soft music" by a "Boy that sings." The music continues after the song through eight lines of the dialogue to the stage direction *Cease music.*

Page 120. "Can you paint a thought" has this stage direction: *During which time* [*i.e.*, the singing of this song], *Enters Prophilus, Bassanes, Penthea, Grausis, passing over the stage; Bassanes and Grausis enter again softly, stealing to several stands, and listen.*

Page 120. "Comforts lasting" is sung by Orgilus:

That these in presence may conclude an omen,
Thus for a bridal song I close my wishes.

"Comforts lasting."

Page 121. "Oh no more, no more." Philema and Christalla tell how Penthea died "within" to the music of this song:

Phil: She called for music,

And begged some gentle voice to tune a farewell
To life and griefs: Christalla touched the lute,
I wept the funeral song. *Chris:* Which scarce was ended
But her last breath sealed up these hollow sounds.

Page 121. "Glories, pleasures, pomps" is sung at Calantha's command:

Cal: One kiss on these cold lips, my last; crack, crack.
Argos now's Sparta's king: command the voices
Which wait at th' altar, now to sing the song
I fitted for my end. *Nearchus:* Sirs, the song.

As it is being sung, she dies.

FIELD

PAGE 122. "They that for worldly wealth." Sung as the guests gather for the marriage of Bellafront and Count Eredick.

PAGE 122. "Rise, lady mistress." Before this is "sung by the Boy," it is read aloud. The context is the following:

> *Bould:* Hark, what's here? music. (*music*)
> *Enter Subtle with a paper, and his Boy with a cloak.*

When Subtle has read the song aloud, he gives it to the boy, who sings it. As in other instances in the drama of this period, the boy only sings and does not speak a word.

BROWNE

PAGE 123. "Steer hither." Sung by a siren sitting on "a cliff of the sea," "a sea being done in perspective at one side." The two-line refrain was "repeated as from a grove near, by a full chorus."

PAGE 124. "What sing the sweet birds." Sung from "among the trees" to the accompaniment of eight musicians standing "upon hillocks." They were clad in "crimson taffeta robes with chaplets of laurel on their heads."

HOLIDAY

PAGE 124. "Tobacco's a musician." Solo by Phlegmaticao, who enters with "his hat beset round about with tobacco pipes: with a can of drink hanging at his girdle." The stage directions are: *He takes tobacco, drinks, and then spawles. He drinks again and sings.*

As the poem is too long, we have omitted in the text the last stanza:

> Tobacco is a whiffler,
> And cries Huff Snuff with fury;
>   His pipe's his club and link,
>   He's the visor that does drink,
> Thus arm'd I fear not a jury.

E. F. Rimbault, *A Little Book of Songs and Ballads*, p. 175, reprints this song from a "MS set of Part-books, in the handwriting of Thomas Weelkes, 1609."

PAGE 125. "The black jack." Sung by Poeta, Geographus, and Geometres:

> *Geom:* Prethee, Poeta, do thou sing a catch alone and we'll sing the close with thee.
> *Poeta:* A match, hay boys!

"The close" was the last four lines of each stanza; in the 1618 edition they are repeated, each time with the stage direction: "*Poeta Geog. Geom. simul.*"

The title-page informs the reader that this play was acted by the students of Christ Church, Oxford, before the University at Shrovetide.

SWETNAM, THE WOMAN HATER

Page 126. "Whilst we sing." Sung in a short "Dumb Show," thus described in the stage directions: *Enter two mourners, Atlanta with the axe, Leonida all in white, her hair loose, hung with ribbons, supported on either side by two ladies, Aurelia following as chief mourner. Pass softly over the stage. A song in parts.*

SAMPSON

Page 127. "When from the wars." This song satirizes the Puritans as well as the army, for it is sung by Joshua, a Puritan "painter-stainer by art," who had been impressed and here returns from fighting.

GOFFE

Page 128. "Drop golden showers." The stage direction: *This song is to be sung in the music room to soft music; now when she looks, she's dreaming sent to Elysium.* In the margin is the single word "Dreams," deleted in the second edition, 1656. Evidently the original song for this passage was

"Now when she looks, she's dreaming
    Sent to Elysium."

At some revival of the play, the present song, "Drop golden showers," was substituted for it; but inadvertently the stage direction calling for the original song, "Dreams," was not changed.

Page 128. "Lullaby, lullaby baby." Sung at Electra's command:

Yes, nurse, sit down and sing, look to the babe,
I'll only with my uncle change a word.

T. G.

Page 129. "Grieve not, fond man." This song, which begins the play, has the following stage direction: *Music having played a little, Philaretus is discovered discontented in his couch while one sings the ensuing song.*

The speech of Philaretus at the end of the song shows that he was quite familiar with *Twelfth Night:*

Play on, let music feed the ear, which is
Denied his mistress' voice. That strain again: (*They play it again*)
O 'tis composed of harmony, it has
The magic of a siren's note. So, so.   (*The music ceases*)
Now let them sing what in my sleep I dreamt
Of Cupid's cruelty.

The song that follows is a poor one.

PAGE 129. "Come, shepherds, come" begins the second act.

Two songs of this play, "Now fie on love" and "I am in love" are printed with Shirley's lyrics. They appeared, with some textual changes, in a volume of *Poems* which he published in 1646.

The initials T. G. on the title-page of this play have generally been considered as standing for Thomas Goffe; but in the *London Times Literary Supplement*, July 24, 1924, p. 463, W. J. Lawrence shows that the author of this play, produced *circa* 1632, could not have been Goffe, who died 1629. T. G. was alive at the time of this production.

QUARLES

PAGE 131. "How blest are they." Queen Augusta bids her maid sing this: My heart's much oppressed with melancholy! Come Phonilla; sing the song the King likes so well.

This song is found also in Brome's *Queen and Concubine*, 1659.

CAVENDISH

PAGES 131-132. "Thine eyes to me," "I'd have her merry." These two songs are performed by a boy, one of the musicians brought in by Newman for a serenade. Before "I conjure thee," a song that preceded these two, Newman says, "Now boy, the song I made to the window, while I muffle myself with the fiddlers." Before "Thine eyes to me," he says of the fiddlers, "Till they have my liveries, I'll maintain 'em in songs; wind up your voice again." Before "I'd have her merry," "Another song, and direct your voice to the lady."

In the 1649 edition, the first line of the final stanza of "Thine eyes to me" reads "For four lines"—a mistake which I have corrected.

MAY

PAGE 133. "Not he that knows." Sung at a banquet given Antony by Cleopatra. The music continues playing at the close of the song, for after a few lines, Cleopatra commands: "Let this soft music cease and louder sound."

PAGE 133. "Dear, do not your fair beauty wrong." This is read, not sung, by Euphues, who remarks: "The song's a good one." In the previous act of this play a song is introduced as follows:

Theodore: But hark, hark friend, what ravishing sound is that?
Eugeny: Ha! wondrous sweet! 'Tis from the adjoining thicket.

Song. "This is not the Elysian grove."

Evidently there was no singer among the actors and the song from "the adjoining thicket" is merely one more song performed "within." (But *cf.* Smith, *Musica Antiqua*, p. 53.)

SHIRLEY

PAGE 133. "Woodmen, shepherds." A chorus first heard off stage, thus introduced:

Cornelio: Hark, I hear the shepherds' music and voices too; lets sit down, I pray.

L. 13, 1631, reads "joy drown our bowers"; this is intelligible, yet I prefer Bullen's emendation, "crown our bowers."

PAGE 134. "Melancholy, hence!" has this context:

Eugenia: I prithee try
Thy voice, to put my heart in better tune;
There is a power of harmony some say
To charm the unruly motions of the brain:
Love is itself a melancholy madness;
Why should not music cure the wound of love?

Maid sings within.

"Melancholy, hence!"

PAGE 134. "If Love his arrows." Introduced as follows:

Enter Servant

Servant: Sir, 'tis done.
Gerard: I prithee let it be undone, as I am.
Servant: The song . . .
Gerard: I gave to be taught music. I'll hear't anon. I prithee go.
Servant: Whither?
Gerard: To prison . . .
                              Let me see't,
It is the same: first read it; reach the chair:
'Tis yet no song: infuse a soul into it.

(Servant sings)

"If Love his arrows."

(Gerard sleeps)

This song is printed in the 1646 edition of Shirley's poems, with some slight changes in the text, the most important being ll. 5-6:

And it appears too true in me,
Cupid wants no artillery.

PAGE 135. "Love, a thousand sweets" is another song "within." The context:

Fowler: Ha! are we entertained with music?

> *Song.*
>
> "Back, back again, fond man forbear,
> Buy not a minute's play too dear:
> Come with holy flame and be
> Welcome to Virtue and to me."

Fowler: Come with holy flame, and be
Welcome to virtue and to me . . .
Again?

> *Song.* "Love, a thousand sweets."

These are the only songs in the play. In Shirley's *Poems,* 1646, "Love, a thousand sweets" is the second stanza, and "Melancholy, hence!" the first stanza of the poem *Upon his Mistress Sad.*

PAGE 135. "Come away, away." This, the ninth and the last song, is headed: *The Masquers are called from their revels by other voices.*

PAGE 136. "I neither will lend" is sung by the Bard as he makes his last exit—"And so I take my leave." Of the thirteen songs in the play, he sings eight.

In the 1640 edition, l. 3 reads: "This pleasure." I have changed it to " 'Tis pleasure."

PAGE 136. "Cease warring thoughts" is sung to the sleeping Paris. The title-page of *The Triumph of Beauty* states that it was "Personated by some young Gentlemen for whom it was intended at a private recreation."

PAGE 137. "Beauty, and the various graces" is sung as the four "bandits" enter in "quaint disguises."

PAGE 137. "You virgins, that did late despair" is a chorus for a triumphal entry of "Men, with boughs of laurel, singing before the Duke." It appeared first in Shirley's *Poems,* 1646.

PAGE 137. "O fly my soul" is a song that prepares the entrance of the Abbess, her nuns, and Juliana.

PAGE 138. "Come my Daphne." Hernando and Placentia, the lady in waiting to the Duchess, hear a lute "within" where the Cardinal and the Duchess are together.

Her: They have music.
Pla: A lute only.

Her: Gentle Lady, a voice too?

Song within. "Come, my Daphne."

Her: If at this distance I distinguish, 'tis not
Church music, and the air's wanton, and no anthem
Sung to't, but some strange ode of love and kisses.

This song is printed in Shirley's *Poems*, 1646, where l. 13 reads "In thy perfumed bosom then I'll stray." For its setting, see John Playford, *Airs and Dialogues, Book II*, p. 4, 1653, "For treble, bass and instrument" by William Lawes. (Also in John Playford's *Catch that Catch Can or The Musical Companion, Part II*, p. 90, 1667: *Musical Companion, Part II*, p. 63, 1672.)

PAGES 139-140. "Now fie on love," "I am in love." These two lyrics are printed in Shirley's *Poems*, 1646, and apparently are his. This is merely another instance of the interpolation of songs in plays. In the *Poems* ll. 7-10 of "Now fie on love" are omitted. "I am in love" is a speech—with many changes in the text—from *The Triumph of Beauty* printed in the *Poems*. In T. G.'s play it is thus introduced:

Arismena: This place will yield an echo to thy voice,
Come therefore Graculus, let's pass the time
More pleasantly. You have a merry song I know.
Graculus: Truth mistress, you know they are rude yet such as Nature, not Art, hath taught me I'll pour into your ears.

PAGE 140. "The glories of our blood" is sung by Calchas "before the body of Ajax" as it is borne on the stage. A note at the end of the song reads: "This was afterwards sung in parts, the music excellently composed by Mr. Ed. Coleman." This music is in John Playford's *Catch that Catch Can or The Musical Companion*, p. 146, 1667. The first four lines of each stanza are arranged for two voices, the last four lines of each being a "chorus" for three voices. This setting also appears on p. 156 of Playford's *Musical Companion*, 1673. A MS. note by Oldys on p. 485 of Langbairn's *Account of English Dramatic Poets* (British Museum) reads: "In the *Contention* is the fine song which old Bowman used to sing to King Charles, and which he has often sung to me, 'The glories etc.' "

The title-page of this masque states that it was "nobly represented by young Gentlemen of quality, at a private entertainment of some persons of Honour." As but five lines are spoken after it, this song practically ends the masque.

FLETCHER

PAGE 142. "Come, shepherds." Sung by Cloe, alone on the stage.

PAGE 142. "Do not fear." Sung to Amoret by the River God.

PAGE 143. "Drink to-day." A chorus by the master cook and other servants.

PAGE 143. "Take, Oh take." Edith, planning to murder Rollo, Duke of Normandy—"His heaven forgot, and all his lusts upon him"— bids her boy "entertain him" with this song. It is generally assumed that Fletcher added the second stanza to the first stanza written by Shakespeare. See Shakespeare's "Take, Oh take" and note, p. 280.

There are two obvious misprints in the 1639 edition of *The Bloody Brother*: stanza 1, l. 5, "being again" for "bring again"; and stanza 2, l. 2, "frozen blossome" for "frozen bosom."

"The origin of both verses may be traced to the fragment *Ad Lydiam*, ascribed to Cornelius Gallus. The . . . corresponding passages . . . discover a resemblance too close to have been accidental," R. Bell, *Songs from the Dramatists*, p. 148, note.

PAGE 144. "Away, delights." A solo, sung to Lelia, "a cunning, wanton widow," who is pretending to be grief-stricken. The 1647 quarto, last line of song, prints "in the day,"; also a comma, not a semicolon, after "thee."

PAGES 144-145. "Now the lusty spring," "Hear, ye ladies." These two songs, sung continuously, are from the scene in which Lucina is tempted. She comments on them:

> I like the air well,
> But for the words they are lascivious,
> And over light for ladies.

"Hear, ye ladies" l. 19, 1647, "short tower"; 1679, "short hour."

PAGE 145. "Care-charming Sleep" is sung to the Emperor, dying of poison. The stage direction: *Enter Emperor, sick in a chair, with Eudoxia the Empress, and Physicians, and attendants. Music and song.*

In l. 5, Bullen, to make the rhyme, reads "light" for the "sweet" of the text.

PAGE 146. "God Lyæus." A song at the banquet which concludes the play.

PAGE 146. "Orpheus I am" is sung to Memnon, "the mad lover," by Stremon, "a soldier that can sing," who has dressed himself "like Orpheus."

PAGE 147. "Charon, O Charon." This follows immediately the preceding song. Stremon sings these with the purpose of humouring and subduing the "mad lover."

PAGE 148. "Arm, arm." Sung at Memnon's command, probably by Stremon:

> *Memnon:* Sing me the battles of Pelusium
> In which this worthy died.

As this song is not at all in the style of Fletcher's other lyrics there is a possibility he did not write it. *Cf.* note to Davenant's "Run to Love's lottery," a song in the same style. Though Fletcher had collaborators—Massinger, Rowley, Field, and others—in several of the plays here attributed to him, I have placed under Fletcher's name the lyrics in them. *Cf. Cambridge History of English Literature*, VI, 5, appendix; also pp. 140-141, same volume; M. Chelli, *Le Drame de Massinger*, pp. 80-81, 348-350. 1647, l. 13, reads "in boys, in boys"—clearly wrong. I change it to the reading of the second folio.

PAGE 149. "Rise from the shade below." This is part of the magician's conjuring. It is not certain who sings it; or whether the "Answer" was sung or recited. "Answer," l. 2, "e're day," 1647; "the day," 1679; "one Hell," 1647; "our Hell," 1679.

PAGE 150. "O fair sweet face." This is sung by Lopez to his sleeping wife:

> I'll sing thy sweets a requiem,
> But will not waken thee.

The 1647 folio, l. 9, reads "rest about these sweets"; the reading of our text is from the 1679 folio.

PAGE 150. "Look out bright eyes." A song for Cleopatra, who is in her room:

> *Apollodorus:*   I have prepared
> Choice music near her cabinet, and composed
> Some few lines (set unto a solemn tune)
> In the praise of imprisonment. Begin Boy.
>
>   *Song.* "Look out bright eyes."

PAGE 150. "Make room." One of the songs commanded by Ptolemy to entertain Cæsar.

PAGE 151. "Come away." At the close of this song, occurring in the first few minutes of the play, Dinant breaks in on the wedding procession and upbraids the false Lamira.

PAGE 151. "This way." Sung "within" while the stage is empty.

PAGE 152. "Cast our caps" is a chorus by gypsies, "crowning their good king." 1647 folio, l. 15, "all offices"; 1679 folio, "all officers." This song is set for two voices by Dr. John Wilson in J. Play-ford's *Musical Companion, Part II*, p. 70. 1672.

PAGE 152. "Adieu, fond love." This song occurs in a passage in which a friar tells Clarange that Lidian, his rival for the love of Olinda, has turned hermit:

> Ere he entered
> His solitary cell, he penned a ditty,
> His long, and last farewell to love and women,
> . So feelingly, that I confess however
> It stands not with my order to be taken
> With such poetical raptures, I was moved,
> And strangely with it.

Clarange: Have you the copy?
Friar: Yes, sir;
> My novice too can sing it, if you please
> To give him hearing.
Clarange: And it will come timely,
> For I am full of melancholy thoughts,
> Against which I have heard with reason, music
> To be the speediest cure; 'pray you apply it.

> *Song by the Novice.* "Adieu, fond love."

Friar: How do you approve it?
Clarange: To its due desert,
> It is a heavenly hymn, no ditty, father,
> It passes through my ears unto my soul
> And works divinely on it.

It is needless to say that the "novice" appears only in this passage to sing the song.

PAGE 153. "This late and cold." A lute is heard outside the door; then this song is sung by the dead host, who presently enters and asks that he be reburied in hallowed ground.

L. 5, 1647, "beds of wanton down the best." The reading in our text is from the 1675 quarto. L. 17, 1647, has "Welcome"; second folio, "Welcome, welcome."

PAGE 153. "Oh turn thy bow." The stage direction for this is: *Enter . . . six woman maskers . . . the first woman singing and playing.*

PAGE 153. "Hence all you vain delights." Sung by the "passionate cousin, rudely and carelessly apparelled, unbraced and untrussed." He is the only person on the stage when he sings this; he later sings two other short songs.

It is obvious that Milton's *Il Penseroso* owes much to this song; possibly it was inspired by Fletcher's lyric.

PAGE 154. "Come follow me." Sung by Gerasto. The play from

which this is taken was written by Rowley and Fletcher. Bullen "suspects" this song "may be by William Rowley."

In l. 2 of the second stanza, Bullen changes "gazes," folios 1647, 1679, to "grazes."

PAGE 154. "Dearest, do not you." Sung by Landro to attract Amaranta, the wife of a covetous lawyer:

> Landro: Now, if I could but see her: she's not this way:
> I'll in, and strike my lute; that sound may call her.
> *(Exit)*
> *Lute and Song.* "Dearest, do not you."
>
> Amaranta: He keeps very close: Lord, how I long to see him!
> A lute struck handsomely, a voice too; I'll hear that:
> These verses are no law, they sound too sweetly.

For an early setting of this song, see Henry Lawes, *Airs and Dialogues*, p. 20, 1653. In the index this song is attributed to "Mr. Henry Harrington, son to Sir Henry Harrington." Lawes says that he gives the names of the persons "from whose hands I received them" [the songs].

PAGE 155. "Let the bells ring." Sung to the curate by singers brought in by four parishioners to "appease his spirits" by giving him "the best song."

This song, set for three parts by Dr. Rogers, is in John Playford's *Musical Companion*, p. 170, 1673.

PAGE 155. "Weep no more." When the song ends, Agenor speaks:

> These heavy airs feed sorrow in her, Lady,
> And nourish it too strongly; like a mother
> That spoils her child with giving on't the will.
>
> *A lighter song.*
> "Court ladies laugh and wonder."

At the end of this "lighter song" (which is not included in this volume), Beliza commands "Some lighter note"; probably the viols continued playing a while during the dialogue.

In the *Maid's Tragedy* Fletcher again contrasts two songs, one "sad" and one "light," a device Shakespeare never employs. It is interesting to notice that "Dearest, do not you," "Let the bells ring," and "Weep no more" were first printed in their plays in the 1679 folio; they do not appear in the 1647 folio.

FLETCHER?

PAGE 156. "Orpheus with his lute." The third act of the play begins:

Notes 311

The Queen and her women, as at work.

Q. Kath: Take thy lute, wench: my soul grows sad with troubles.
Sing and disperse 'em, if you canst: leave working.

Song. "Orpheus with his lute."

A setting for three voices, by Matthew Locke, is in J. Playford's
Catch that Catch Can or The Musical Companion, p. 174, 1667.

Critics are generally agreed that Fletcher had a share in this play.
From its style, this lyric may be his rather than Shakespeare's.

PAGE 156. "Roses, their sharp spines." This song, opening the play,
is sung in the wedding procession by *"a boy, in a white robe before,
strewing flowers,"* to quote from the stage directions.

The following textual changes are universally accepted:

L. 9, "harebells" for "her bels," 1634; l. 14, "chough hoar," for
"Clough hee," 1634.

The stage direction *"music,"* indicates not only that this song had
an accompaniment but that the music played for the entrance of the
bridal train.

PAGE 157. "Urns and odours" has the following heading: *Enter
the Queens, with the hearses of their knights, in a funeral solemnity.*

CAREW

PAGE 157. "From whence was first." This chorus ends the play. It
is thus introduced:

Hermit: Let all men sing, and in full chorus join, and detest this
crime. An ancient Druid left this sacred hymn, and against jealousy
commanded all to sing full chorus round the Temple.

The Song in Parts. "From whence."

In a note, printed immediately after the last line of the chorus,
Killigrew writes as follows: "This Chorus was written by Mr.
Thomas Carew, Cup-bearer to Charles the First; and sung in a
Masque at White-hall, Anno 1633. And I presume to make use of it
here, because in the first design, 'twas writ at my request upon a dis-
pute held betwixt Mistress Cicilia Crofts and myself, where he was
present; she being then Maid of Honour: this I have set down, lest
any man should believe me so foolish as to steal such a poem from
so famous an author; or so vain as to pretend to the making of it
myself; and those that are not satisfied with this apology, and this
song in this place, I am always ready to give them a worse of mine
own.

Written by Thomas Killigrew Resident for Charles
the Second in Venice, August 1651."

As Killigrew has stated, correctly, his own songs are very much worse than this one, and accordingly I have not included any of them in this collection.

This song appeared in Carew's *Poems*, 1640, with some few variations in the text, as in the last line, "And raging."

HENRY SHIRLEY

PAGE 159. "What are earthly honours." Before this song are the following stage directions:

"*As he is writing an angel comes and stands before him: soft music; he astonished and dazzled.*" "*He falls flat on the earth, and whilst a song is heard, the angel writes, and vanishes as it ends.*"

BROME

PAGE 159. "You say my love." Sung by Mistress Trainwell "above."

PAGE 160. "A bonny, bonny bird." Sung by Constance, mad for love. From Skelton's time, Philip seems to have been the popular name for a pet sparrow. *Cf.* Cartwright, *Lesbia on her Sparrow*, in his *Poems*, 1651:

He would from my trencher feed,
Then would hop, and then would run,
And cry "Philip" when h' had done.

PAGE 161. "Peace, wayward barne." Sung, off the stage, by the distracted Constance.

PAGE 161. "Come, come away." A chorus by "Four especial beggars" who leave the stage singing it. This song ends the act but for three lines of prose.

PAGE 162. "A round, a round." Set for three voices by William Lawes in J. Playford's *Catch that Catch Can or The Musical Companion*, p. 79. 1667.

COX

PAGE 162. "Come you young men." *Actæon and Diana* is but ten pages in length. The first stanza of this song has the heading "*1. Country Wench.*" Probably each of the three women sang a stanza in turn (though only the first stanza has a stage direction) and all joined in the two-line refrain.

For Cox, see G. H. Nettleton, *English Drama of the Restoration and Eighteenth Century*, pp. 15-19.

PETER HAUSTED

PAGE 163. "Drowsy Phœbus" has this stage direction:

Venus (being Phosphorus as well as Vesper) appearing at a window above as risen, calling to Sol who lay in Thetis' lap at the east side of the stage, canopied with an azure curtain: at the first word that Venus sung, the curtain was drawn, and they discovered.

PAGE 164. "Have pity grief" is sung by a boy to lute accompaniment at his master's command:

Lucius: Where is my boy Luscinio? Call him in,
That he may touch a string which may dissolve me
Into a flood of tears—come on my boy,
O teach that hollow pensive instrument
To give a true relation of my woes
Whilst I lie here, and with my sighs keep time.

PAGES 164-165. "Cupid if a God"; "But why"; "Have you a desire." These three songs were sung at the close of Acts 1, 3, and 4, respectively. It was not unusual for the musicians to play between the acts; here apparently songs divided them.

The title-page of *The Rival Friends* states that the play was acted in Cambridge in 1631 before Charles I and Henrietta Maria; but it was "cried down by boys, faction, envy and confident ignorance, approved by the judicious and now exposed to public censure."

DAVENPORT

PAGE 166. "Matilda, now go take thy bed." Shortly before this song, the body of Matilda, to "the sad music of flutes" is brought on the stage, and a song in parts, with a chorus, is sung. Thus the singers are on the stage for this song which ends the play.

GOMERSALL

PAGE 166. "How I laugh" is thus introduced:

Sforza: Why stayst thou, my Aurelio? good boy
I'll see no bed tonight; then go, yet stay,
If they have not escaped thy memory
Sing me those verses which you made of sleep.

Song. "How I laugh."

Sforza: Pretty philosophy! go boy, go sleep.
Enjoy the good thou sing'st—this boy can sleep,
Sleep quietly, and sing himself to sleep,
Making that gentle rest unto his song.
But I'll go read.

During his long soliloquy which follows, Sforza is confronted by the ghost of his nephew whom he had murdered.

STRODE

PAGE 167. "Once Venus' cheeks" has this context:

> *Fancie:*   Kill me, but kill me
> With some sad strain under this spreading oak.
> *Amorphus:* I hope 'twill ease, not kill you.
> Sing of Venus.
>
>   *Musician sings.* "Once Venus' cheeks."

PAGE 167. "Come heavy souls" is thus introduced:

> *Desperato:*   And before our death
> A hymn is necessary. Then sing, good fellow.
>
>   *An attendant sings in a bass.* "Come heavy souls."

The Floating Island was performed at Oxford, 1636, before Charles I by the students of Christ Church. The "airs and songs" were "set by Mr. Henry Lawes." See H. Lawes's *Airs and Dialogues*, p. 28. 1653, where the song is entitled, "Desperato's Banquet" and set "For a bass alone."

HEMING

PAGE 168. "Come, blest virgins." Sung by "two nuns in white" as Aphelia is led to execution.

MAYNE

PAGE 168. "Time is a feathered thing." The song is thus introduced:

> *Orythia:* You two sing us asleep; and when y'have done,
> Go walk the round, and see the watch relieved.
>
>   *Exeunt.* [*i.e.,* All except the two singers]

This song occurs at the end of a short scene and the following one opens with this stage direction: *Having changed clothes to their doublets, enter Callias, Neander, Artops.* This scene with the song was designed to give these characters time to change their costumes; they left the stage immediately before the singing.

HABINGTON

PAGE 170. "Fine young folly."

> *Sanmartino:* Boy, sing those verses were presented me
> This morning.

<pre>
Dwarf: I will creep behind a bush,
            And then for voice, vie with the nightingale.
            If seen, I am so bashful.
Sanmartino: Take your way.
</pre>

Song without. "Fine young folly."

This song, set for three voices by William Howes, is to be found in John Playford's *Catch that Catch Can*, p. 182, 1667. There is an earlier setting for three voices by William Tompkins in J. Playford's *Select Musical Airs and Dialogues, Book III*, p. 23. 1653.

THOMAS NABBES

PAGE 171. "Flow, flow delight" has this stage direction:

During the following song, the third scene is discovered, being a pleasant arbour, with perspectives behind it, of a magnifique building: in the midst thereof Sensuality sits.

PAGE 171. "Beauty, no more" has the following stage direction:

To them Sophonisba, ladies all in white, and veiled: who to the music of the song, place themselves in a figure for a dance. The Song.

PAGE 172. "What a dainty life" is sung "within" by Cicely, the milkmaid. It is preceded by "singing within, a far off." The frightened Bellamie hears the song:

New fears assault me. 'Tis a woman's voice.
She sings; and in her music's cheerfulness
Seems to express the freedom of a heart
Not chained to any passions. Be propitious
Thou regent o'er my fate, and guide her hither
Unto my comfort.
       The Song within.

RANDOLPH

PAGE 172. "Slaves are they." Sung by "two schollars."

PAGE 173. "We care not for money." This chorus is sung "within," and ends the play but for a short speech of eleven lines.

KILLIGREW

PAGE 173. "Chloris, we see the offended gods." This song is preceded by the following lines:

Ordella: I have much to say to you Brother, pray stay my return: good Selindra, entertain him in my chambre with Cleonel's last melancholy song I like so well. (*Phillocles and Selindra sit within the scene.*)

DAVENANT

PAGE 174. "This lady." The only song in the play, introduced as follows:

> *Alteza:* Hast thou Lucio call'd, and bid Pythe mix
> With him in a sad song?
> *Niente:* I have, Madam.

The boys take no part in the dialogue.

PAGE 174. "Weep no more" has this context:

> *Corsa:* Sing gentle youth; who knows if I shall live
> T'employ thy voice again.

Song. "Weep no more."

Enter Foreste

> *Foreste:* This is your dirge.
> *Corsa:* Hah! who is there?
> *Foreste:* Tis I. Dismiss that trifle hence, and shut
> The door.
> *Corsa:* Farewell youth! Get thee to bed. (*Exit boy*)

She is brutally murdered by Foreste, her brother. As she dies, there are the following stage directions: "*Recorders, sadly.*" "*She dies. Still music above.*"

PAGE 175. "My lodging." Sung by the "distracted" Celania, one more insane yet melodic heroine. At the end of the song is the stage direction: *That done, she lies down and falls asleep.* By singing this song, Mary Davis captivated Charles II. James Howard in his *All Mistaken, or The Mad Couple*, Act 5, 1672, parodied it:

> "My lodging is on the cold boards
> And wonderful hard is my fare."

Chappell, *O.E.P.M.*, II, 137, gives the air of this song. For attributing this play, published anonymously, to Davenant, see Logan and Maidment, *The Dramatic Works of William D'Avenant*, V, 215-217.

PAGE 175. "The bread is all baked." Sung by Don John and others at "a table spread with linen" on which were trencher, spoons, and a sack-posset.

> *Don John:* I'll give you a song if you will call for music.
> *Sancho:* Firk your fiddles.

Song. "The bread is all baked."

PAGE 177. "Run to Love's lottery," " 'Tis in good truth." These two songs are not to be found in either the first (1643) or the second (1649) edition of *The Unfortunate Lovers*, but were first printed in the 1673 folio. As the songs are not in the first two editions, neither are the two characters connected with them—"Orna, Cousin to Amaranta" "who sings them, and Phœbe, a maid who brings in Orna." The following interesting context to the songs is naturally missing in the quartos of 1645 and 1649:

Enter Amaranta, Phœbe.

Phœbe: Madam, your little cousin, Orna, is
Without, and comes to visit you.
Amar: Attend her in. (*Exit Phœbe*)
This dreadful storm of war has frighted her.
Can childhodd, in a cloister bred, fear danger;
Not being grown to the unhappy sence
Of love neglected and disdained.   (*Enter Orna*)
Orna: How do you, Madam?
Amar: Alas, sweet cousin, you look pale.
Orna: We have been praying all night in the nunnery
For fear of the soldiers.
Amar: The soldiers will not hurt ye.
Orna: I hear they are cruel black men, Cousin.
Amar: Fear nothing, you are safe.
Orna: I can stay anywhere but in the dark.
Amar: You come in season hither; prethee sing
That song which Gartha taught thee e're she died.
Orna: I'm out of breath.
Amar: Pause and recover it.

The Song. "Run to Love's lottery."

Enter Page

Page: Madam, your father expects you in the garden.
Amar: I fear his pity of me will undo him.
Orna: I pray, desire him speak to the King
That soldiers may leave drumming. I'm sure
We can't sing matins for 'em in the nunnery.
Amar: Come Cousin, I will teach you grief betimes,
Lest when your growth admits of love, it then
Should meet you unprepared.
                                iii. 1.
(*Exeunt*)

Enter Amaranta, Phœbe, Orna.

Amar: Send back my little Cousin to her cloister;
She has a soul too musical for mine.
Phœbe: Shall she go tonight, Madam?
Amar: Aye, presently. My discords are
Unfit companions for her harmony.
Orna: Call for the coach. I am grown weary of you.
'Tis merrier being in the nunnery
Than here. Phœbe pray call for the coach!

Phœbe: First sing the song to her you promised me.
It may put her out of this dull humour.
Orna: Cousin, leave your melancholy and hear me.

The Song. " 'Tis in good truth."

Amar: Music to her who does all comforts lack
Is like to whistling winds before a wrack.
Orna: Cousin farewell. I'll go sing with the nuns.

(Exeunt several ways) iv. 1.

It is an interesting speculation whether Davenant, or some other
writer, added this dialogue and the two songs after the 1649 edition
appeared; or whether they were in the first MS. of the play and
were omitted for practical reasons. Both the 1643 and 1649 editions
print in v, 1, the following stage directions: "*Strange music is heard
above. The Song to a Horrid Tune*"; and they both print three stanzas of a very poor song. The 1673 folio has the same stage directions (omitting "*to a horrid tune*"), but in printing the song, it adds
to each of the three stanzas a four-line chorus. Evidently when the
1643 and 1649 text was used, the musical possibilities of the company were slight. The meter and style of " 'Tis in good truth" are
certainly of the Restoration period; and "Run to Love's lottery"
seems an equally late production. Davenant died five years before
these songs were first printed.

It is interesting to notice that the song "Arm, arm" in Fletcher's
The Mad Lover, V, 1. 1647, is not at all in the style of his other
lyrics; and that it closely resembles, both in spirit and technique,
these two songs from Davenant's play. It is quite possible that the
same person wrote all three.

PAGE 178. "Wake all the dead." The context:

Viola: Sister, I have got verses. Signor Lucio
Made them; he and Balthazar are within.
Beatrice: Is Lucio become a man of metre?
That's the next degree upward to the giddy
Station of a foolish lover. They are
Composed into a song too. Sing it, Viola.

Song. "Wake all the dead."

LUMINALIA

PAGE 179. "In wet and cloudy mists." This song opens the masque,
which R. Brotanek attributes to Davenant. See *Beiblatt zur Anglia*,
XI, 177-181, and *Die Englischen Maskenspiele. Wiener Beiträge*,
XV, 1902.

CORONA MINERVÆ

PAGE 180. "Those flowers." This song has the following stage direction:

Here are sung the several songs by several voices, with symphonies betwixt, and a Chorus: during which, Time peruseth the several presents, as he discovers them orderly: All which are expressed in the Song.

The songs of Summer and Autumn are not interesting and have been omitted. In the 1655 text, the Chorus is repeated after each of the two stanzas of Spring and the one stanza of Winter.

CHAMBERLAIN

PAGE 181. "Be not so cruel." The following lines occur immediately before and after the song:

Sabina: 'Tis very true, come reach me my lute—prethee sing, Betty.

Song.

Sabina: 'Twas well sung.
Betty: No indeed, forsooth my voice is quite gone; Chambermaids have occasion you know, forsooth, now and then to sit up in the nights when they have business to do, and that spoils a maid's voice quickly, forsooth.

Betty has but two other short appearances in this play, and is evidently a character brought in simply to sing.

PAGE 181. "Farewell this company." A solo by Sportlove.
I have made some changes in the text of these two songs. In the first song, 1640 edition reads, l. 4, "sorrow's flow"; l. 6, "appears"; ll. 11-12, no quotation marks; l. 12, "and dies." In the second song, l. 7, "let us."

COKAYNE

PAGE 182. "The spheres are dull." Sung at a banquet by musicians to whom Polidacre says:

Play a more merry tune. I do abhor whatever relishes of melancholy. Sing *The Spheres are dull.* Apply it to yourself that best deserve it.

MILTON

PAGE 182. "Sweet echo." Sung by the Lady, to call her brothers to her.

PAGE 183. "Sabrina fair." Sung by the "Attendant Spirit," a part taken by Henry Lawes, who composed the music for these songs.

PAGE 183. "O'er the smooth enamelled green," "Nymphs and shepherds." *The Arcades,* from which these songs are taken, was performed probably in 1633, while *Comus* was acted in 1634; yet *The Arcades* was not published until eight years after *Comus.*

KING AND QUEENS ENTERTAINMENT

PAGE 184. "Did not you once." The first part of this "Entertainment," in which this song occurs, was reprinted in 1673 as "Wiltshire Tom" in *The Wits, or Sport upon Sport. Being a curious collection of several Drolls and Farces . . . written I know not when, by several persons, I know not who; but now newly collected by your old friend to please you, Francis Kirkman.*

A note at the end of the 1636 edition praises the "music which prepared and commended the numbers to the ears of the auditors and was excellently composed by Master Charles Coleman." The *Dictionary of National Biography,* in its sketch of Coleman, makes no allusion to this piece. Coleman's setting for "two voices and instrument" is in John Playford's *Select Musical Airs and Dialogues, Book II,* p. 10. 1653.

SUCKLING

PAGE 185. "Why so pale." It is worth giving all the context of this famous song:

Semanthe: Come, my Lord, the song then.
Orithie: The song.
Orsames: A vengance take this love, it spoils a voice.
              I have got such a cold with rising
              and walking in my shirt a nights, that
              a bittern whooping in a reed is better music.
Orithie: This modesty becomes you as ill, my Lord,
              as wooing would us woman; pray, put's not to it.
Orsames: Nay ladies, you shall find me
              as free as the musicians of the woods
              themselves; what I have, you shall not need to call for,
              nor shall it cost you anything.

Song. "Why so pale."

Orithie: I should have guessed it had been the issue of
              your brain, if I had not been told so.
Orsames: A little foolish counsel, Madam, I gave a friend
              of mine four or five years ago, when he was
              falling into a consumption.

In Thomas Forde's *Love's Labyrinth,* iv, 3, 1660, there is an imitation of this song beginning "Why so nice and coy, fair Lady," while in George Coleman's *New Brooms,* 1776, there is a poor adaptation of it.

PAGE 186. "No, no, fair heretic." This is the context:

Enter Aglaura and a Singing Boy.

Boy: Madam, 'twill make you melancholy,
I'll sing the Prince's song, that's sad enough.
Aglaura: What you will, sir.

Song. "No, no, fair heretic."

Aglaura: Leave me! for to a soul, so out of tune
as mine is now, nothing is harmony.

There is a setting for this song by Henry Lawes in J. Playford's *Select Musical Airs and Dialogues, Book I*, p. 12. 1653.

PAGE 186. "Come let the state stay" is sung as a "round." *The Discontented Colonel* has no date on its title-page; it was licensed 1642. This play was reissued in 1646 as *Brennoralt*.

RUTTER

PAGE 187. "Shall I because my love." Thyrsis calls for this song:

Come boy, and under this same hanging bow,
The note which thou attemperest to my words,
Sing, and be happier than thy master, boy.

"Shall I because."

PAGE 187. "Tell me what you think." This duo opens the third act.

PAGE 189. "Hymen, god of marriage-bed." A solo.

Mirtillus: And in the honour of your nuptials
I have a song, which if your Grace will hear,
'Twill entertain the time.
Sylvia: Let it be sung.

"Hymen."

PAGE 189. " 'Twas not his person." Cimeia bids his page sing this:

Take your lute, boy, and sing the song I gave you,
It suits my present state.

" 'Twas not."

CARTWRIGHT

PAGE 190. "A pox on our gaoler." This song, opening the play, is sung by "four Ephesian captives." The stage directions are: "*A city in the front, and a prison on the side;*" and captives "*singing in the prison, Molops harkening without.*" As Molops, the gaoler, hears the words he says: "That's I," "I again; good, good."

In John Hilton's *Catch that Catch Can or a Choice Collection of*

Catches, Rounds and Canons for 3 or 4 voices, p. 29, 1652, this song is set for three voices by Hilton himself; it is set for four voices by W. Lawes in J. Playford's *Catch that Catch Can,* p. 74, 1667.

PAGE 190. "Come, my sweet" is sung by a boy whom Praxaspes calls in and bids sing "Your last new song, that which I gave you, sirrah." The purpose of this lyric is to tempt the king. There is a setting for it in Henry Lawes's *Airs and Dialogues,* p. 32, 1653.

PAGE 191. "Now that the sun is fled." Another song by the "captives," who call in fiddlers to play for their carousing. The context:

> *Philotas:*   Let's have a song between, and then have at you.
> *Leocrates:* Fiddlers, employ your throats and sing awhile;
>   you shall drink with 'em after.
> *Stratocles:* Sing that which I made in the prison; 'tis
>   seasonable enough.

> *Song.* "Now that the sun."

The title-page of *The Royal Slave* states that it was "presented to the King and Queen by the students of Christ Church in Oxford, August 30, 1636. Presented since to both their Majesties at Hampton Court by the King's servants." The Queen was so delighted with the college performance that through Archbishop Laud's persuasion, the Vice Chancellor of the University loaned the play, the costumes and the scenery to the King's Servants for another presentation at Hampton Court. The professionals did not equal the amateurs, for Laud wrote in his diary: "All said that the Queen's players came short of the University actors." The players tried it a second time, with a considerable expenditure for "the charge of the alterations, reparations, and additions which were made unto the scene, apparel, and properties"; possibly they were nettled by such criticism as Laud recorded.

PAGE 192. "To carve our loves." This is a song to the lute as shown by the lines addressed to Eumelia immediately before she sings it:

> I prethee
> Take up the lute there, and lets hear the ode
> That thou didst promise us; I hope 'tis sad.

PAGE 192. "Wake my Adonis." Another song to the lute, thus introduced:

> *Lucasia:*   We'll divert
>   This anxious fear. Reach me the lute, Eumelia.
>   Have you not heard how Venus did complain
>   For her belov'd Adonis? The young poet

That was desired to give a language to
Th' afflicted Goddess, thought her words were these.

A setting for this song by Coleman is in J. Playford's *Select Musical Airs and Dialogues, Book I*, p. 26, 1653.

PAGE 193. "Seal up her eyes." Sung by a boy "in the habit of a virgin," at the command of Misander, Tyrant of Thrace, to put to sleep Leucasia, whom he has wounded. These lines introduce the song:

Prithee sing
And try if in this habit thou canst woo
Her weary thoughts into a gentle slumber.

After the song is this stage direction: *As she falls asleep, Misander seats himself just over against her, and looks immoveably upon her, not regarding anything done in the next scene.*

Evidently Cartwright's songs were highly regarded by his contemporaries. In lines prefixed to Cartwright's *Comedies, Tragi-Comedies, with other Poems*, 1651, Jasper Mayne writes:

Witness thy other poems too, and songs,
Such as turned deserts heretofore to throngs;
And tun'd to the music of a Thracian string,
Made wild men tame, and peace from discord spring.

Another admirer, addressing the dead poet, says "The young adored thy song"; while still another writes that Cartwright "sweetly guides the nimble lyric feet." The title-page to the 1651 edition states that "The airs and songs" were "set by Mr. Henry Lawes, Servant to his late Majesty, in His Public and Private Music."

RICHARDS

PAGE 194. "Helpless wretch." Immediately following this song is a quaint stage direction:

After this song (which was left out of the play in regard there was none could sing in parts) Enter the ghosts.

I have omitted a half line, "Friends all are dead," which in the 1640 edition preceded l. 3 of our text. It is plainly an error.

FISHER

PAGE 194. "At the Spring." The best of the twelve songs in this play, which, as the title-page states, was: "Publically represented by the Gentlemen Students of Magdalene College in Oxford." In Thomas Meriton's *Love and War. A Tragedy*, i, 7. 1658, there is a very poor imitation of this song. The first verse of it is typical:

Shout aloud,	While with mirth
Let a cloud	We on earth,
Distill rain	Mercy, Peace,
To the plain,	Each embrace.

Let him want mercy, peace, and voice,
That cannot play when we rejoice.

In *Fuimus Troes*, v, 3, is a doggerel song which is worth quoting because of the stage direction:

Eulinus in a night cap, unbraced. Viol. Poinard. Plays and sings to the viol.

So the silver-feathered swan,
Both by death and colour wan,
Loves to sing before she die,
Leaving life so willingly.
But how can I sing a note
When dead hoarseness stops my throat?
Or how can I play a stroke
When my heart-strings all are broke?

Eulinus follows this song with a two-page soliloquy—then stabs himself and dies.

GLAPTHORNE

PAGE 196. "Great Pan, to thee." The stage direction to this song is: *Enter Kalender, Argalus, Philarchus, Castalia, singing;* yet this chorus is evidently sung by the shepherds who are on the stage, not by these gentlefolk. At the conclusion of the song, Kalender says: "Shepherds, we owe our gratitude to your thanks." Evidently the stage direction should read: *Castalia. Singing.*

SHARPE

PAGE 196. "Tell me, Jove." A serenade, thus introduced:

Honorio: These are the princess' lodgings,
That her window! Come boy, breathe
Out my sorrows in a mournful air.

"Tell me."

PAGE 197. "Charm, O charm." Sung by a lady to comfort the sorrowing princess:

I'll try my voice to charm
Your eyes and heart with pleasing slumbers.

The song lulls her to sleep.

TATHAM

PAGE 197. "I will follow." Sung by Cloe. The title-page of the play informs the reader that it is a "Pastoral presented by the Scholars of Bingham in the County of Nottingham in the year 1632."

BURNELL

PAGE 197. "Love's far more powerful" has this context:

Fatyma: I heard no mean physician often say, Sir,
That music and mirth were good for sickly men.
Reymer: Bid the boy sing the song we made of Love.

"Love's far more powerful."

A note at the end of the play informs the reader that it was first acted on St. Patrick's day, 1639, in Dublin, where it was published.

DENHAM

PAGE 198. "Somnus, the humble God." Sung to Prince Mirza, dying of poison:

Prince: Sleep to these empty lids
Is grown a stranger . . .
O happiness of poverty! that rests
Securely on a bed of living turf . . .
Call in some music, I have heard soft airs
Can charm our senses, and expell our cares.

Enter Music. "Somnus, the humble God."

Servant: So now he sleeps, lets leave him
To his repose.

COWLEY

PAGE 198. "The merry waves." Sung by "Alupis, a merry shepherd."

PAGE 199. "It is a punishment." Sung by Bellula, though she fears to forfeit her "little skill in singing" by doing it.

BOYLE

PAGE 199. "Since you will needs" has this context:

Enter Music and Dancers.

Plot: Will you have a merry song, or a sad one?
Mrs. Philadelphia: We'll have the last song that Mr. Plot made on his own heart. . . . Come, come, the Song, the Song.

Song. "Since you will needs."

PAGE 200. "Why was I doomed." A serenade, thus introduced:

> *Lycidor:* This is the window, Page; under that light
> Go sing the song that I composed tonight.
> Solemnize every accent with a groan,
> And make the tune sad as th' occasion.
>
> "Why was I."

The page has no part in the dialogue and is brought in merely to sing this song. *Altemira* was revised and put on the stage by the author's grandson, Charles Boyle, in 1702.

FLECKNOE

PAGE 201. "Love and Death." This song, "in the narrative style" as its subtitle reads, is printed at the end of the play with no indication of its position in the text. The subject of this song is taken from the *Elegies* of Johannes Secundus, Book II, No. 6. *Cf.*

> Cupid once more has changed his shafts with death,
> And kills instead of giving life.
> > Dekker, *The Virgin Martyr.* iv. 2. 1632.

THOMPSON

PAGE 201. "What need we." In the chorus of this song, two of the women of the play take part. "Aye, aye; come, come, we'll help to make a chorus."

PAGE 202. "Come let us be frolic." This is played and sung in the tavern by the "old musicians" whom Plot-thrift learns are not "employed." Sending for them he says: "Then come, musicians, let's hear the tavern catch I gave you when I was here last." *Musicians:* "Yes sir," and this song follows.

PAGE 203. "O sweet Diana." Sung by Maria, who is brought into the play to sing this song to the lute. Apart from her request to her maid for her lute—"Now give it me; is it in tune?"—she speaks but ten other lines.

THE LONDON CHANTICLEERS

PAGE 203. "Submit, bunch of grapes." With a short speech of nine lines following this song, the play ends. This chorus is started by Ditty:

> *Ditty:* In the meantime, let's have one on the genius of good ale.
> *Omnes:* Begin't, begin't.

Ditty, a "Ballad-man," has two good snatches of song in the second
scene, "Once did I love a maiden fair" and "My love and I to
Medley."

LADY ALIMONY

PAGE 204. " To Tunis and Argiers." This song is sung by the "*Captain, trapanners, tarpaulins, with other renegados orderly marching.*"
It is thus introduced:

1. *Trapan:* Let us have a sea-sonnet before we launch forth in our
Adventure Frigate. They say the sirens love singing.
Captain: Agreed, wags; but which shall we have?
1. *Trapan:* That old catch of Tunis and Argiers; good Captain, it
suits best with our voyage.
Captain: To't then my Hectors; and keep your close as you do
your march. The sirens will not relish you if you sing
out a tune.

One stanza has been omitted after l. 6; one after l. 14; three after
l. 26; and two after l. 30. In the text, the chorus is repeated after
every stanza.

MARCIANO

PAGE 205. "So, so." Sung "behind the arras." This play was performed at Edinburgh by a "Company of Gentlemen" at "the Abbey
of Holyrood House" before "His Majesty's High Commissioner
and others of the nobility," to quote from the title-page.

DRYDEN

PAGE 206. "Poor mortals." Sung by spirits whom Ismeron thus
invokes:

You spirits that inhabit in the air,
With all your powerful charms of music try
To bring her soul back to its harmony.

Sir Robert Howard collaborated with Dryden in this play; I assume
this lyric to be by Dryden.

PAGE 206. "Ah fading joy" has the following stage direction:

*A pleasant grotto discovered; in it a fountain spouting; round about
it Vasquez, Pizarro, and other Spaniards, lying carelessly unarmed, and
by them many Indian women, one of which sings the following song.*

PAGE 207. "I feed a flame" is sung by Asteria, "the Queen's confidante":

Asteria: Shall I sing the song you made of Philocles,
    And called it *Secret Love?*
Queen: Do, for that's all kindness; and while thou sing'st it,
    I can think nothing but what pleases me.

Song. "I feed a flame."

PAGE 207. "Ah how sweet" is sung by the evil spirit, Damilcar, to the sleeping St. Catharine in order to tempt her. Evidently Damilcar's part was taken by a singer, not an actor, for the name is not given in the list of "Persons represented."

PAGE 208. "You charmed me once" is sung by Wildblood to Donna Jacintha.

Wildblood: Or let us encourage one another to a breach by the dangers of possession. I have a song to that purpose.
Jacintha: Pray let me hear it: I hope it will go to the tune of one of our Passa-calles.

Song. "You charmed me not."

PAGE 209. *"Wherever I am." The context (Cf.* Smith, *Mus. Ant.* p. 170):

(*Music without*)

Lyndaraxa: Music! and I believe addressed to me.

Song. "Wherever I am."

PAGE 210. "Farewell ungrateful traitor." Sung to the Queen by her "woman."

Queen: To soothe my sadness
   Sing me the song which poor Olympia made
   When false Bireno left her.

Song. "Farewell ungrateful traitor."

PAGE 210. "Fair Iris I love." The music for this song is at the end of the play, after a separate title-page: "The Songs to Amphitryon with the music composed by Mr. Henry Purcell."

PAGE 211. "Your hay it is mowed." The last three lines of each stanza after the first are repeated as a chorus. The lively and popular music for this song was composed by Henry Purcell. Gay used it for "Despair leads to battle" in *Polly,* 1729. For Purcell's music, see Vincent Jackson, *E. M.,* p. 146.

PAGE 212. "No, no" was performed by a singer, not an actor, as were most of Dryden's lyrics. The stage direction is: *The scene opens and discovers Cassandra's appartment. Musicians and dancers.*

ETHEREGE

PAGE 212. "Ladies, though to your conquering eyes." Sung by Letitia, "a girl waiting upon Aurelia," to Graciana:

> *Grac:* Come then into the arbour girl, and there
> With thy sweet voice refresh my wearied soul.

> *Song.* "Ladies, though to."

The best remembered song of Etherege's, "Ye happy swains whose hearts are free," was not written for a play. In Playford, *Theatre of Music, The Fifth Book,* p. 18, 1684, it may be found set as a solo by Damasene and beginning "You happy youths whose hearts are free."

CROWNE

PAGE 213. "Day is dismounted." This chorus opens the play.

THOMAS PORTER

PAGE 213. "Away, away." Thomas Porter was the son of Endymion Porter, Herrick's patron and friend. This song was sung "above" by the adventuress, Madam Modes, to ensnare Young Carleton, who "loves a good voice as I love my life." He exclaims after the first verse, "Excellent, excellent"; after the second, "Incomparable! the voice of Nightingales are hoarse to hers; shall I see her, sister?" In l. 10, quarto, 1663, prints "said effects."

PAGE 214. "See where Calisto." This is part of a serenade of vocal and instrumental music by a boy and "fiddlers"—musicians "bespoken" by three officers. It is thus introduced:

> *Lamarch:* Plague o' your tuning, ye Dogs,
> Cannot your instruments stand in tune
> One quarter of an hour?
> *Delpeche:* Prethee, Lamarch, be silent.

> "See where Calisto."

PAGE 214. "Amarillis told her swain." These lines lead to this song:

> *Francibel:* Fie, fie, Gentlemen, come give me your hands again;
> Sister, prethee one song *à la Ronde.*

> "Amarillis."

PAGE 215. "Beyond the malice." Mariana has just sung a rather indifferent song in an attempt to "still the spirits" of Charlotte, crazed by grief. The lines immediately preceding and following this song are:

Charlotte: Away, thou art out of tune and sense,
        If I must needs hear music,
        Let it be my poor boy's voice;
        He once could please me with his melancholy songs,
        Pray let him sing.
D'Orvile: Any thing to please thee, poor Charlotte.

Song within by the Boy.

Francibel: She's fallen into a slumber.
D'Orvile: No noise; make the room dark you do convey her to.

(Exeunt)

In this play there is much music, both vocal and instrumental. Pepys saw it and wrote in his diary, October 20, 1662, "There is good singing in it."

SEDLEY

PAGE 215. "Ah Cloris." These verses by Wildish are sung by Victoria, whom he bids "put a tune to 'um, 'tis an easy stanza."

PAGE 216. "Thyrsis, unjustly." The stage directions and context are:

Enter Cunningham, Thisbe and her Maid.

Thisbe: Come, now we are alone, sing me the last new song.

BEHN

PAGE 217. "A curse upon that faithless maid." This song, sung to a lute by Elarira, opens the play.

SHADWELL

PAGE 218. "Lovers lament." The stage directions preceding and following this song are interesting:

Enter Urania (in white, with guards; musicians clothed in white, and other attendants in a solemn procession) led between two gentlemen in mourning. As they go, this song is sung, to a solemn tune.

Song. "Lovers lament."

There appears a scaffold covered with black, and Urania led between two gentlemen in black: The King looks to see the execution (above).

SETTLE

PAGE 218. "Let us use time" has the following brief introduction:

Corisca: Celia, convert her with that song I taught you.

RAVENSCROFT

PAGE 218. "Nymphs that now." The Duchess, distracted, calls for "a song to lull my troubled thoughts asleep," and this one is sung.

HOWARD

PAGE 219. "My love and I." A duo; the first verse is sung by Phillidor, the second by Mirida.

DUFFET

PAGE 220. "I never shall." Sung by Clara, disguised as a page. The play from which this song is taken was reissued in 1684 with the new title *The Fond Lady*.

OTWAY

PAGE 220. "Princes that rule." The context of this song is thoroughly Elizabethan or Jacobean, showing how stage conventions linger:

King: Boy, take my lute, and with a pleasing air
Appease my sorrow, and delude my care.

Song. "Princes that rule."

During the singing, the king falls asleep.

DURFEY

PAGE 221. "I'll sail upon the Dog-star." Set by Purcell, this became one of his most famous songs. The title-page of the play states that it contains "all the Songs and Noises to 'em, excellently composed by Mr. Henry Purcell." They are given, eight in all, at the end of the book. The "noises" were a simple bass part. For Purcell's setting, see Jackson, *E. M.*, p. 136.

Durfey adapted the first stanza of this song from *Loving Mad Tom*, one of the variants of *Tom of Bedlam:*

I'll bark against the dogstar,
And crow away the morning;
I'll chase the moon
Till it be noon,
And I'll make her leave her horning.

Cf. Frank Sidgwick, *Tom of Bedlam's Song* in *The London Mercury*, VII, 518-524; Chappell, *O.E.P.M.*, I, 175-178.

PAGE 221. "Celladon, when Spring came on." Sung by musicians, as the stage directions indicate: *They all sit. Here follows comical singing and dancing.*

LEE

PAGE 222. "Weep, weep, you Muses." This song, opening the act, is commanded by Britannicus: "Go sing the song without."

POWELL

PAGE 224. "When Sylvia is kind." Another "song within," to "soft music"; it is a serenade prepared for Urania by Ferdinand, whom she has rejected. Before stanza two is the stage direction: *Here enters Ferdinand who stands gazing on Urania.*

ANONYMOUS

PAGE 224. "Corrinna, in the bloom of youth." The heading of this song states that it was written by a "Person of Quality" and sung "within" by Mrs. Boetler, whose name is not included in the cast. The three songs of this play are all sung off stage. One which we have omitted has the heading: *The King discovered melancholy, some attendants standing by him; a song and symphony of music within.*

CONGREVE

PAGE 225. "Love's but a fraility." The context:

> *Millimant:* Dee say so? Then I'm resolved I'll have a song to keep up my spirits.
>
> *Enter Mincing.*
>
> *Mincing:* The gentlemen stay but to comb, Madam; and will wait on you.
>
> *Millimant:* Desire Mrs.—that is in the next room to sing the song I would have learnt yesterday. You shall hear it Madam. Not that there's any great matter in it. But 'tis agreeable to my humour.
>
> *Set by Mr. Eccles and sung by Mrs. Hodgson.*
>
> *Song.* "Love's but the fraility."

Mrs. Hodgson, whose name is not in the dramatis personæ, was evidently brought in just for this song.

STEELE

PAGE 225. "Why, lovely charmer." Quite in the Elizabethan fashion, this song is performed at Biddy Tipkin's window, apparently by Clerimont's servant, who "has a voice" and sings in the next scene. It is interesting to observe that in Steele's *Funeral*, Act ii, a song is read and then sung, as in Jonson's plays.

COREY

PAGE 227. "Happy was man." Sung by Peggy in reply to a request for "the latest song":

> *Peggy:* I have one to your humor, Mr. Wildish. Gentlemen, you'll excuse my bad voice.

GAY

PAGE 227. " 'Twas when the seas." The context:

> *Kitty:* But I forlorn! This ballad shows my care.
>
> (*Gives Susan a ballad*)
>
> Take this new ballad which I bought at Fair:
> Susan can sing—do you the burden bear.
>
> " 'Twas when the seas."

The air for this song was also used in *The Beggar's Opera*—No. XXVII.

PAGE 228. "Were I laid on Greenland's coast." As the last line indicates, this was set to the old air, "Over the hills and far away."

PAGE 229. "If the heart of a man." Set to "Would you have a young virgin," a song composed by Tom Durfey. It is sung by Macheath.

PAGE 229. "How happy could I be." Sung by Macheath, confronted by both Polly and Lucy. It was set to the air "Give ear to this frolicsome ditty."

PAGE 229. "Cease your funning." Sung by Polly. Its air has not been traced to an older song; possibly it was composed for these words.

PAGE 230. "O ruddier." Sung by Polyphemus in praise of Galatea. Handel composed the music for *Acis and Galatea*.

THOMSON

PAGE 230. "When Britain first." For this famous song, Dr. Arne composed the music. *Cf.* V. Jackson, *E. M.*, p. 166. Mallet claimed the words but modern authorities give the song to Thomson.

In the Masque, this song is sung to King Alfred, with the following introduction:

Hermit: Behold, my Lord, our venerable bard,
Aged and blind, him whom the Muses favour.
Yet ere you go, in our loved country's praise,
That noblest theme, hear what his rapture breathes.

An ode. "When Britain first."

CAREY

PAGE 231. "What though they call me." This does not appear in the first edition of the play, 1728, or in the 1748 Dublin edition; nor in these volumes does any stage direction call for a song. It is printed in the 1753 edition, at the end of the play, and has the title *"Sung by Mrs. Cibber in the Fifth Act. The words by Mr. Carey."* Mrs. Cibber took the part of Jenny. The song became a popular one. Its air is used for Air XII in *The Lover his own Rival. A Ballad Opera,* 1753.

FIELDING

PAGE 232. "How unhappy." Printed before the list of "Persons in the Farce" with the heading, "Song by Mr. Blotpage in the second Act." It is written to the air "Ye commons and peers."

PAGE 232. "The dusky night." This, the eighth song, is set to the tune "There was a jovial beggar." It is sung by Scut:

Badger: Come, let us be merry; we'll have a hunting song. Sir Knight, I should be glad to see you at my country seat. Come, Scut, sing away."

There are fifteen songs in this piece. For a second setting of this song, attributed to Dr. Arne, see Chappell, *O.E.P.M.,* II, 175.

PAGE 233. "When mighty roast beef." Sung by Sancho, who prefaces the song with "Give me a slice of roast beef before all the rarities of Camacho's wedding." The air, printed at the head of the song, is "The King's Old Courtier." In Chappell, *O.E.P.M.,* II, 96, is the statement, unsupported by evidence, "The words and air of this song are by R. Leveridge."

ANONYMOUS

PAGE 234. "While the sweet blushing spring." Solo by Young Boncour: "As Mr. Warble is gone, I will attempt it myself."

The preface of this play speaks of "the very liberal and friendly assistance of Mr. Sheridan" in the production of this recovered play of Fielding's; and this song is quite in the style of Sheridan's lyrics, or of his day. Certainly it is not by Fielding.

GARRICK

PAGE 234. "Come, come my good shepherds." This song Garrick inserted, with the following context, in *Florizell and Perdita*, his version of Shakespeare's *Winter's Tale*.

> *Old Shepherd:* Come, come daughter, leave for a while these private dalliances, and love whisperings, clear up your pipes, and call, as custom is, our neighbors to our shearing.
> *Perdita:* I will obey you.
>
> *Song.* "Come, come."

PAGE 237. "Come cheer up, my lads." The text is from *The Universal Magazine*, pp. 152-153, March, 1760, where it is printed with music (air and bass) under the title "*A New Song, sung by Mr. Chapness in Harlequin's Invasion.*" The author's name is not given.

David E. Baker, in his *The Companion to the Play House, II*, 1764, prints a sketch of Garrick that includes a list of pieces of which "he has been reputed the author." The fifth of these is *Harlequin's Invasion. A Christmas Gambol.* This song is not mentioned. It is generally attributed to Garrick. For its music, written by Dr. Boyce, see Vincent Jackson, *E. M.*, p. 174.

GOLDSMITH

PAGE 236. "Let school-masters." Sung by Tony Hardcastle in an "Ale-house room" to "several shabby fellows, with punch and tobacco."

> *Tony:* Then I'll sing you, gentlemen, a song I made upon this alehouse, The Three Pigeons.
>
> *Song.* "Let school-masters."

C. DIBDIN

PAGE 237. "Then farewell" is sung by Tug. "I'll stick to my word, I assure you; if you wont have me, I'll go on board a man-of-war."

For the music to this and the following song, see Vincent Jackson, *E. M.*, pp. 176-179.

PAGE 237. "Blow high, blow low." One of the most popular of all Dibdin's songs. He wrote "considerably more than a thousand," his melodic gift atoning for their sentimentality. See George Hogarth, *The Songs of Charles Dibdin . . . and their Music*, 1843.

SHERIDAN

PAGE 238. "Here's to the maiden." In Sheridan's MS., reprinted by Frazer Rae, this is sung by Careless, "at table with wine," to Charles

Surface and other companions. In Thomas Moore's edition of Sheridan's plays, 1821, it is sung by Sir Harry Bumper; so also at the first performance, May 8, 1777. In Moore's edition, the third line of the last stanza is not repeated. For the original air to this song, composed by Thomas Linley, Sheridan's father-in-law, see Jackson, *E. M.*, p. 184.

PAGE 239. "Had I a heart." Sung by Carlos to Louisa.

LEWIS

PAGE 239. "Nought avails." *Rich and Poor* is a revision of *The East Indian*, acted 1799, which did not have this song.

TENNYSON

PAGE 241. "Hapless doom." Sung by Queen Mary.

PAGE 241. "Is it the wind." This opens the act. It is preceded by these stage directions:

Rosamund's bower. A Garden of Flowers. In the midst a bank of wild-flowers with a bench before it.

HENLEY

PAGE 247. "We hadn't been." Sung by Pew, "a blind beggar, once boatswain to the *Arethusa*." Kit French, a privateersman, joins him in the chorus. This play was written by Stevenson and Henley; I suspect the song to be Henley's.

LADY GREGORY

PAGE 248. "Yesterday travelling," and "It is pitiful" are sung by "A wandering Songmaker." The airs for both these songs are printed with the play.

PAGE 249. "All round my hat." Sung by Taig, a chimney sweep. The air is printed in the notes to the play.

YEATS

PAGE 249. "The wind blows." Sung outside the cottage by the "Faery Child" calling Maire Bruin to The Land of Heart's Desire. After Maire's death, the play ends with this song, again sung off stage.

HOUSMAN

PAGE 250. "How now." A serenade, at Prunella's window. As Pierrot cannot sing it, Scaramel brings a tenor. This song, with its original music, is published by Messrs. Elkins and Co., London.

GALSWORTHY

PAGE 251. "The windy hours." Sung to Seelchen by the Youth of the Wine Horn mountain, "slowly to the chords of a mandolin." Between stanzas one and two is the stage direction: *His voice grows strange and passionate.*

BOTTOMLEY

PAGE 251. "The bird in my heart's a-calling." Sung off stage by Blanid "to a tired, monotonous tune."

CLEMENCE DANE

PAGE 252. "Come with me to London." Sung by the players of Henslowe's company, persuading Shakespeare to leave Anne Hathaway and seek his fortune. There is much action and dialogue between the stanzas.

PAGE 253. "If Luck and I." Sung by Christopher Marlowe "and two or three men sitting round a table drinking," in "a private room at an inn late at night." Mary is Mary Fitton. As in the previous song, there is action and dialogue between the stanzas.

SOME ASPECTS
OF
SONG IN THE DRAMA

A Musical Contest between *England* and
Wales. Michael Drayton's *Poly-Olbion*, 1613.
The right half of the map of the fourth Song.

Some Aspects of Song in the Drama.

DEVELOPING from the church service, elaborated at festivals into little plays acted by priest and chorister, and from the games and mummings of the folk, it was inevitable that the British drama should abound in song. This lyrical tradition is an unbroken one, from the tenth century trope, *Quem quæritis,* to the songs of Shakespeare, of Dryden, and of Sheridan; even in our own day there are certain playwrights who have enhanced their works by following this old custom.

Though both dramatist and audience desired singing on the pageant or in the hall, from the first the texts of the songs were often slighted by the early scribes and copyists. Frequently they did not deem it worth while to write them down and merely indicated them by "Cantat" or "Intrant cantantes"; yet enough have been saved to indicate that the early playwrights realized many of the dramatic possibilities of singing. The third song in this book, the lullaby sung by the terror-stricken mothers of Bethlehem, is more affecting than dialogue or soliloquy. Furthermore, the priests or clerks who composed the guild plays understood that a lyric may disclose a character as plainly as the conventional speech of self-revelation; Noah's wife is placed by her drinking song. The later writers of interludes made Lusty Juventus, Youngman, Idleness, and other heroes—and heroines—unfold their plans, their motives, their very natures by singing. As a method of procedure, the early writers soon discovered they could win the attention of an audience by beginning or ending a scene, an act, or the play itself, with a song. They found they could introduce a character or take him off the stage effectively by making him sing; while at times, to arouse the expectation of the audience, an actor, before he entered, would be heard singing. To avoid monotony, they varied the songs and used solos, part songs for two, three and four voices, and choruses in which all the actors might join, possibly the audience as well. Other effects were gained by having two groups of singers on the stage reply to each other—the antiphonal singing of the church—or by having certain singers on the stage answered by others off stage; we have even a solo sung in the presence of the audience and its chorus sung "without."[1] Of the music for these early songs very little remains; a few of the airs have been preserved in manuscripts; some of the popular melodies to which the words were set have survived in later music books or dance collections, such tunes as "Sellengers Round" or "Heart's Ease." So fond were the early dramatists of employing song that they frequently included several in one short interlude or play. There are seven in the brief *Tom Tyler*, acted about 1560, seven also in Phillips's *Grissell*, printed about 1566, and eight in *The Trial of Treasure*, printed in 1567. These songs were of all kinds—songs of lovers, of rogues, of soldiers and sailors, drinking songs, serenades, slumber songs, songs of Nature, of joy or mourning, moral songs, didactic songs, "contention" songs—a type Shakespeare used in *Love's Labour's Lost*—and songs that explain some dramatic situation. Thus early in the history of the British drama certain types of song and a certain technique in their use became firmly established in the minds of both playwright and audience.

These types of song and the conventional methods of employing them were accepted by the great Elizabethans, who added new types and new methods of their own devising. As the pages of this book will show, the reign of Elizabeth and of James I was the golden age of song in the drama. Then it was that music and sweet poesy agreed. Inspired song writers collaborated with composers who were unrivaled even by the musicians of France or of Italy. At no other time has the British drama contained so many songs of such grace and beauty; at no other period has singing been used more effectively in plays.

The stage directions of Elizabethan plays call for scores of lyrics that have disappeared forever. Robert Greene has scattered throughout his prose works many tender and charming songs; he had the lyric gift and he would naturally employ it to enhance the artistic effect of his plays, yet they offer nothing for this volume. In his *James IV*, iv, 1. 1598, is the stage direction *"Enter certain huntsmen (if you please, singing)*, but we shall never know their hunting catch. From Peele's plays we have gathered some delightful songs, but many others will

---

[1] All these points are illustrated by songs in this book.

never be found. In his *The Famous Chronicle of King Edward I,* 1593, there are allusions to these lost lyrics:

Friar: Wench, to pass away the time in glee,
               Guenthian set thee down by me,
               And let our lips and voices meet,
               In a merry country song.
Guenthian: Friar, I am at beck and bay,
               And at thy commandment to sing and say,
               And other sport among.

               The Friar and Guenthian sing.

This "merry country song" is gone; lost also is another one the friar sings, sitting alone, the song he "learned long ago," that is "short and sweet but somewhat bold" and which he likes so well:

               "Once let me sing it and I ask no more."

Missing from this same play is the lullaby Joan sings at the queen's command; and the part song the "novice and his company" perform at the queen's tent to the accompaniment of fiddles.[1] And this example, taken from an early Elizabethan play, is unfortunately typical of many other dramas written at this time. In *The Maid's Metamorphosis,* i, 1602, three choruses are called for in rapid succession, yet not one of them appears in the text. In Marston's *Antonio's Revenge,* 1602, the stage directions call for six songs, and in his *Antonio and Mellida, Part I,* 1602, for seven songs, yet we have not a single line from these thirteen lyrics.[2]

Three instances of the disappearance of songs from plays are especially interesting. In the quarto editions of Lyly's plays published between 1584 and 1601 there are many stage directions calling for songs, yet none appear in the text. In 1632 Blount brought out in a collected edition six of these plays and we find in them for the first time twenty-one songs. Here are lyrics, some of them of great beauty, recovered merely because Lyly's plays were reissued; without Blount's edition we might never have known them. For a second instance, Thomas

---

[1] Seven important songs are missing from this play.
[2] It will be remembered that a song called for by a stage direction is missing from Act iv of *Julius Cæsar;* another, from Act v of *Pericles, Prince of Tyre;* and two from the witch scenes in *Macbeth,* Acts iii and iv.

Heywood saw through the press his *Rape of Lucrece*, 1608, and advertised on its title-page that this edition contained all the songs; yet he omitted from it one lyric and in all probability it was his finest one, "Pack, clouds, away, and welcome, day."[1] The third instance is yet more interesting. The second folio of the plays of Beaumont and Fletcher appeared in 1679 with a preface signed by the publishers, Martyn, Herringman and Mariot. In it they explain that their new edition is as "correct as might be," and that they can present a text much better than that of the first folio, 1647, because "we were very opportunely informed of a copy which an ingenious and worthy gentleman had taken the pains (or rather the pleasure) to read over; wherein he had all along corrected certain faults (some very gross) which had crept in by the frequent imprinting of them. His corrections were the more to be valued, because he had an intimacy with both our authors, and had been a spectator of most of them when they were acted in their life time. This therefore we resolved to purchase at any rate; and accordingly with no small cost obtained it. From the same hand also we received several prologues and epilogues, with the songs appertaining to each play, which were not in the former edition, but are now inserted in their proper places." As an additional incentive to buy this volume, on its title-page was inserted the line "Published by the Author's Original Copies, the Songs to each Play being added." As a matter of fact, this friend of the dramatists, this admirer of their works, saved but ten songs for us, all belonging to plays that had appeared without them in the 1647 folio, so in this case songs are restored to their text after an interval of thirty-two years.[2] Unfortunately he by no means added the "songs to each play." Eight lines after the lyric "Welcome sweet liberty," which he restored to *The Chances*, there is the stage direction *"Sing again"*; this song he could not give, nor the one that is called

---

[1] See notes, pp. 266, 289.

[2] These songs are: "Dearest, do not you delay me" and "Let the bells ring" from *The Spanish Curate*; "He ran at me first" from *The Beggar's Bush*; "Merciless love," "Welcome sweet liberty," and "Come away" from *The Chances*; "Weep no more" and "Court ladies laugh" from *The Queen of Corinth*; "Sit soldiers" from *The Knight of Malta*; "A health for all this day" from *The Woman's Prize*. No one of these ten songs appeared in Beaumont's *Poems*, 1640 and 1653, though these volumes contained nearly two score songs from the plays.

for a few lines further on. A better case is found in *The Honest Man's Fortune*, iii, 1.

Viramour: If you please, Madam
              For sure to me you seem unapt to walk,
              To sit, although the churlish birds deny
              To give us music in this grove where they
              Are prodigal to others: I'll strain my voice
              For a sad song, the place is safe and private.
Lady Orleans: 'Twas my desire; begin good Viramour.

Music. A Song.

The reader does not find either this song of the faithful page who later offers all his money to his master—"I pray sir, take it; I'll get more with singing"—or the one he sings in Act iv. Indeed Viramour exists to sing, but his songs could not be recovered even by one who had enjoyed an intimacy with Beaumont and Fletcher.

The stage directions do not indicate all the lyrics we have lost; if by chance we could restore to the plays every song they call for, there would be still many a one missing. It not infrequently happens that in the first edition of a play not merely a song, but all references to it were omitted; and only the fact that the play was reprinted in a more complete edition gives us the song or the allusions to it. The most familiar instance occurs in *Othello*. In the first edition, 1622, two and a half lines directly introducing the "Willow" song and the lyric itself are omitted, though a reference to a song is allowed to remain, a reference, however, which by no means makes it clear that at this point in the play there is singing. In the next year the first folio printed both the song and the lines that immediately introduce it. In the first edition of Beaumont and Fletcher's *Maid's Tragedy*, 1619, the lines that precede the two songs "Lay a garland" and "I could never" are missing, as well as the songs themselves. Three years later both the lyrics and the dialogue introducing them are restored to the text in the 1622 quarto; yet until that quarto appeared, no one would have suspected these songs existed, for nothing pointed to them.[1] A good example of a missing song indicated not by a

---

[1] Undoubtedly songs were sometimes interpolated when a play was revived, but that does not concern the point under discussion. See notes on Heywood and Davenant, pp. 289-290; 316-318.

stage direction but by a speech is found in the opening scene of Massinger's *Duke of Milan*, 1623:

> *Sforza:* I could live ever thus. Command the Eunuch
> To sing the ditty that I late composed
> In praise of my Marcelia. From whence?
>
> *Enter Post.*

In reading these lines, there would appear to be no time for a song; but in presenting the play the situation is made more dramatic if the messenger with the news that tortures Sforza arrives at the very moment he is taking an artist's pleasure in listening to a lyric he had composed. A little later occurs a passage in which the case is not even doubtful:

> *Sforza:*   I was told
> There was a masque.
> *Francisco:* They wait your Highness' pleasure,
> And when you please to have it.
> *Sforza:*   Bid 'em enter.

At this point no stage direction indicates the entry of either masquers or musicians; yet when another post enters with news of defeat, Sforza cries:

> Silence that dreadful music
> 'Tis now unseasonable.

Certainly there was music here, and possibly singing, but nothing in the text shows the entry or the exit of the musicians. Without bringing further evidence, it is plain that we cannot appreciate the use of song by Tudor and Stuart dramatists from the texts of their plays. Could all the songs be discovered and restored to their comedies and tragedies, then and then only could we realize how impassable is the gulf that separates the higher drama of today from the old lyric stage.

Undoubtedly the Elizabethans enjoyed hearing these songs; and it is a fair assumption that they would wish to read them. Why then have so many been omitted from the text? In answer, we must risk a pure conjecture. The publishers or the printers would not delete songs from a manuscript because, as we have seen, they announced as an inducement for purchasers that the songs were included in the book of the play. It would seem probable that the songs were not printed simply because they were not in the copy; and I take it that the songs were missing from so many manuscripts for the following reason. It would be the duty of some musician in every company to be responsible for the musical setting of each song in a play; at times he would compose it himself, or seek the help of some one better qualified, or fit the words to some familiar melody. It would naturally be incumbent upon this same musician to teach the songs to the boy or man cast to sing them in the play, and to see that either the singer played his own accompaniment on the lute, or that the musicians of the company performed it at the right time. This would mean that the text of any song passed into the keeping of this musician; it would be unnecessary to insert it in the manuscripts used by the actors or the prompter, since all that was needed was some cue or warning for actors and musicians that at a certain point in the play a song must be performed. Thus, if my conjecture be accepted, it was the divided interests of two professions—the actor and the musician—that caused the loss of many a song.

There is another reason why at least some of the songs are missing. We know that the dramatists used frequently popular songs so widely sung that it would be unnecessary to write them out. In Wager's *The longer thou livest the more fool thou*, Moros sings a whole page of snatches or refrains from the familiar songs of his day. Surely the song of Vertumnus in Nashe's *Summer's Last Will and Testament*—but two lines are given

> "Sol, sol, ut, re, me, fa, sol,
> Come to church while the bell doth toll"—

was a popular ditty. In *Othello* and *Hamlet* Shakespeare simply followed a recognized custom, as old as the Interludes, when he turned to his purposes songs every one had heard. And if the dramatists drew from such sources there was no reason why they should not turn also to the works of the contemporary madrigal writers and lutanists, for in their song books were lyrics in profusion, suited to many of the situations so dear to the playwrights, serenades, slumber songs, dirges, songs of birds and of flowers. Three songs by Dowland, by Bateson, and by Robert Jones were used in the anonymous *Every Woman in her Humour*, while Campion's "What if a day" was taken by Brome for his *Queen and Concubine*. Surely the

use of lyrics from the song books would not be confined to
these two plays. "Have you never a song of Dowland's making?" asks Philomusus in *The Return from Parnassus, Part I;*
and it seems a reasonable supposition, though we have no evidence for it, that many songs by Dowland, Jones, Weelkes, and
Wilbye were heard on the stage. If that were so, the dramatist
or the musician had merely to select them; there was no reason
for putting them in any manuscript.

Whatever the reason may be, scores of lyrics disappeared;
yet fortunately many remain. Of their music we have but a
few pages, and because we cannot hear them sung, we shall
never realize the full beauty of these songs. Tom Moore ob-
jected to publishing only the words of his *Irish Melodies,* believing that his "verses must lose even more than the *animæ
dimidium* in being detached from the beautiful airs to which
it was their good fortune to be associated." If we are impressed
by the grace of the lyrics by Dekker, by Fletcher, by Shakespeare, we must remember that without their music we know
them only in part. The Elizabethan playgoers desired music
in their theatres, and they heard it. At the private theatres,
there was often both singing and instrumental music before
the play began; and music between the acts was not unknown.[1]
Furthermore, at both private and public theatres, dialogues and
speeches were often given a musical accompaniment that heightened the spoken word and anticipated, in modest measure,
something of the effects Bizet gained in *L'Arlésienne* and
Humperdinck in *Königskinder.* For example, Webster's beautiful lyric in *The Devil's Law Case,*

> "All the flowers of the Spring
> Meet to perfume our burying"

was not sung; it was spoken to "soft music." In Dekker's *Old
Fortunatus,* Fletcher's *Little French Lawyer,* Massinger's
Duke of Milan, Goffe's *Courageous Turk* will be found passages emphasized and heightened by the emotional effect of
music. Small wonder that the Elizabethan drama is so rich in
song.

---

[1] See note to *The Two Italian Gentlemen,* p. 265. There is music
between the acts in Marston's *What you will,* 1607, and Middleton's
The Phœnix, 1607. " 'Tis music 'twixt the acts," says Ronca in *Albumazar,* 1615. For later examples, see Shirley's *Witty Fair One* and *The
Brothers,* in both cases after Act ii.

To an audience that appreciated good singing, in an age of great musicians, these songs were performed to the accompaniment of lute and viol, of harp and flute. Since the days when Thomas à Becket astonished France with the singing boys whom he had brought in his train, England had maintained her reputation for vocal music. Her choirs were famous; then as now English choir masters had a peculiar skill in training boys' voices, and the stage as well as the church profited by it. A great number, possibly the greater number, of the songs in the Elizabethan drama were performed by boys, which would account for the absence of any deep emotion in so many of these lyrics. It would have been a very natural thing if choristers, grown to manhood, joined theatrical companies as actors or musicians, and it could not have been a very difficult matter for an Elizabethan manager to find a singer. When a company possessed an accomplished, or at any rate a popular, one, he might give in a single play what was virtually a short song recital. Shakespeare, who used song rather sparingly, did not have, so far as the stage directions indicate, as many as six songs in one play until *The Winter's Tale*, acted about 1610, in which Autolycus sings five songs and joins Dorcus and Mopsa in a sixth. But in *Every Woman in her Humour*, acted before 1600, Philautus sings at least eight times; in *The Thracian Wonder*, acted probably a little later, Titterus has eleven songs;[1] in Heywood's *Rape of Lucrece*, 1608, there are twelve songs, most of them sung by Valerius; in Shirley's *St. Patrick for Ireland*, acted 1639, the Bard sings eight times.

In many cases the singer in an Elizabethan drama had no part in the action of the play; he was brought in simply for a song or two; yet there were times when a dramatist might wish to give one of his chief characters a song. That would not be so difficult if the character chanced to be a woman, for we remember that the women's rôles were played by boys; but it might be awkward if the part were played by a man who could not sing. There seemed to be three ways of meeting this situation.

In the modern theatre, the musicians are seated immediately in front of the stage; in Shakespeare's day, and long after,

---

[1] Some of his songs are interrupted by the dialogue so he sings more than eleven times. His song against women, iv, 1, ends "Oh, the Devil take you all." Did Suckling know it?

the place reserved for them was not in front of the actors but
behind them and above them.[1] The back wall of the stage was
formed by the tiring house, and here, presumably on the second
floor, was the music room, the place for the musicians, where,
probably behind curtains, they played and sang whenever the
stage directions called for "music within." At times the
musicians came down and performed on the stage for serenades, for dances, for processions; and sometimes they played
there the accompaniment for a song. It was, then, a simple
matter when an actor could not sing and yet was cast for a
song, to take him off the stage, have a song sung "within,"
presumably by him but in reality by one of the musicians, and
then bring him on the stage again. Thus, in *The Spanish Curate*, Landro exclaims:

> Now, if I could but see her; she's not this way:
> I'll in, and strike my lute; that song may call her.
>
> *Lute and Song.*
>
> "Dearest, do not you delay me."[2]

A second method was to declaim the song, not sing it. Probably the dirge in *Cymbeline*, "Fear no more the heat of the
sun," was recited only because the actors taking the parts of
Guiderius and Arveragus could not sing. The third way was
for a character to bid his page or some musician "sing the song
I made"; and there are many examples in this book of what
might be called vicarious singing. Plainly if the actor had been
able to sing, he would have performed his own song himself.
By two of these methods, then, a dramatist was able to employ
song freely, regardless of the question whether a given character could sing or not.

In reading these lyrics, many interesting questions arise,
questions of authorship, of the borrowing of songs from one
play for another, of the use of conventional types; but pos-

[1] See W. J. Lawrence, *The Elizabethan Playhouse and other Studies*,
pp. 90-95, 1912; *cf.* E. K. Chambers, *The Elizabethan Stage*, II, xviii.
Richard Carpenter's *The Pragmatical Jesuit*, 1660 [?], has for its first
song the stage direction *"One sings in the music room." Cf.* Pepys's
diary for March 23, 1661.

[2] See Glapthorne's *Argalus and Parthenia*, ii, 2. 1639, where Parthenia enters with a lute in her hand, speaks two lines and then with-
draws, presumably to sing "within." The villain recognizes her voice
in the song.

sibly nothing is more worthy of regard than the skilful way so many of these lyrics were used to heighten a dramatic situation. The notes of this book will show how often these songs were much more than a charming *divertissement* or an agreeable embellishment. Compared with the modern playhouse, the theatres of our forefathers were small ones and undoubtedly a song, sung in the music room to the delicate, shimmering accompaniment of a lute, would be heard so plainly that the words could be understood perfectly.[1] It is true that in some of his plays Ben Jonson introduced the curious custom of having a song read aloud before it was sung, apparently fearing that an audience might not catch the full meaning or beauty of the lyric;[2] yet this never became a general procedure and there are so many occasions when the words of a song are necessary to the plot that we may assume the text as well as the music made an impression on the audience.

Two examples of the dramatic use of song must suffice; the notes will indicate many others. The first is from Marston's *Malcontent*, ii, 2, where unfortunately we have only the stage direction for the lyric, not the words. Mendoze enters with his sword drawn to murder Ferneze who is with the Duchess "within." She is listening to a song, sung "within," and Ferneze will not leave her until it ends. The last notes are heard; Ferneze appears, and is instantly struck down. The song, which alone delayed his murder, both prolonged and intensified the crisis. Judging from many a passage, it seems probable that Elizabethan actors ranted far more than their modern successors; on the other hand—and this illustration shows it—they understood better than we do the value of a pause even in the most exciting action; and they gained this frequently by a song.[3] The second example, of quite a different nature, is found in two songs from Fletcher's *Valentinian*.

[1] In Cartwright's *The Ordinary*, acted 1634, the song to a lute, "Come, O come," is sung "within," heard on the stage, and comments are made on it between stanzas.

[2] For reading a song, then singing it, see Middleton, *Blurt Master Constable*, 1602; Field, *Amends for Ladies*, 1618; Shirley, *The Changes, or Love in a Maze*, 1632; Etherege, *Man of Mode*, 1676; Steele, *The Tender Husband*, 1705.

[3] *Cf.* Middleton's *Chaste Maid in Cheapside*, acted *circa* 1611, v, 4, the stage direction *"While all the company seem to weep and mourn, there is a sad song in the music room."*

Lured to court by a lustful king who had sent her a forged message from her husband, Lucina finds herself welcomed too effusively. Rich garments, superb jewels, are offered her, and as she stands perplexed, dismayed, realizing her peril, two songs are heard, one immediately following the other:

> Now the lusty spring is seen

the appeal to the senses, the warning to pluck the flower of youth when it is in its prime, while

> Hear, ye ladies that despise,
> What the mighty Love has done

goes further in its sensuous imagery, and Lucina, as she listens, knows why she has been enticed to court. The song ends and she is asked the significant question whether or not she likes it. On her answer depends her fate:

> I like the air well,
> But for the words they are lascivious,
> And over light for ladies.

This is one of the most dramatic moments in the whole play.

To discuss the different effects the Elizabethan dramatists produced by song would prolong these pages beyond reason; yet one cannot leave this subject without mentioning the greatest dramatist of all. A lover of music, Shakespeare used song more sparingly than did many of his contemporaries; and when his characters sing, the lyric is often one of the conventional types of his day—a serenade, a song of nature, a drinking song, a fairy song, a mad song. All these had been used before his time. Pandora, in Lyly's *Woman in the Moon*, acted about 1593, to take but a single case, sings while insane, one of the first of those mad yet tuneful heroines. A type that inspired some of the most beautiful verse in all the songs—the slumber song for a child—he never uses, for he has but one slumber song, sung to Titania. To say that Shakespeare is not an innovator in his use of song does not imply that his lyrics are scattered through his plays ineffectively, nor does this fact concern their art or beauty; it means that Shakespeare did little to enlarge the range of song in the drama. Possibly his most original use of song is in the casket scene in *The Merchant of Venice*, or the lyrics of Ariel in *The Tempest*. On the whole, he is conservative in the effects he seeks and he does not try certain obvious devices his contemporaries and his immediate successors used.[1] Only once, *Macbeth*, iii, v, does he call for a song "within."

Yet in Shakespeare song on the stage reached its highest beauty. Lyly, Dekker, Jonson, Fletcher, all touch certain chords that have no echo in Shakespeare's music, yet none of these writers showed such art or such scope. Within this small garden of song (and for the most part of song remote from the deepest passions) he shows the same quality of creative power that appears in the great world of his plays. Beauty of meter, grace of diction, phrases that haunt the memory, the wood notes wild, the homely realism of the folk, the music of faery or of a spirit purified from earthly taint—all this may be found in his lyrics and yet this does not explain their charm or their appeal. To use Herrick's phrase, there is a "magic incantation" in his verse. And after his death the lyric tradition still continued and inspired songs touched with the old beauty. But the Restoration marked the beginning of the end. Soon the ballad opera and concert gave England what formerly the play alone could offer; the singer had left the stage and the actress had taken his place. A new dramatic technique had arisen, and though song was still heard, the reign of song on the stage was ended. And so this book is concerned with what has become practically a lost art. With all the wonderful variety and complexity of the modern drama, it does not give us a character whose skill enriched English poetry and made the lyrics in this book live in the memory, a character whose name was often put last in the *dramatis personæ*, who frequently came on the stage unheralded and who left it unobserved. He is called by some of the old dramatists "A boy that sings."

[1] Noble, *Shakespeare's Use of Song*, p. 12, thinks otherwise. "Yet while it is true that Shakespeare did not invent the use of song in plays, he it was who made the play with song occurring in it a consistent art form; it was he who first grasped all the possibilities afforded by song for forwarding the action and who made it a vital part in his dramatic scheme."

BIBLIOGRAPHY

A Selected Bibliography

Here are listed only those editions or collections of plays which have been of assistance in amending the text of any song or in preparing the notes for this volume. For a list of the plays from which the songs have been taken, see page 368.

ADAIR-FITZGERALD, S. J. Stories of Famous Songs. 1898.

ADAMS, J. Q., JR. Shakespearean Playhouses. 1917.

ADAMS, J. Q., JR. "Greene's *Menaphon* and *The Thracian Wonder.*" Modern Philology, III, 317; *"Every Woman in Her Humour* and *The Dumb Knight." Ibid.,* X, 413.

ALBRIGHT, V. E. The Shakespearean Stage. 1909.

ARKWRIGHT, G. E. P. "Early Elizabethan Stage Music." The Musical Antiquary. January, 1913.

ARKWRIGHT, G. E. P. "Elizabethan Choirboys' Plays and their Music." Proceedings of the Musical Association. 1913/1914.

BEERS, H. A. "The English Lyric." Points at Issue and some other Points. 1904.

BELL, R. Songs from the Dramatists. 1854.

BRANDL, A. (Edited) "Misogonus." Quellen des weltlichen dramas in England vor Shakespeare. 1898.

BRERETON, J. L. "The Relation of *The Thracian Wonder* to Greene's *Menaphon."* Modern Language Review. II, 34.

BRIDGE, SIR FREDERICK. A Seventeenth Century View of Musical Education. Proceedings of the Musical Association. 1900/1901.

BRIDGE, SIR FREDERICK. Shakespearean Music in the Plays and early Operas. 1923.

BRIDGE, SIR FREDERICK. Songs from Shakespeare, the earliest known Settings. N.D.

BRODMEIER, C. Die Shakespeare-Bühne nach den alten Bühnen-Anweisungen. 1904.

BROOKE, C. F. T. The Shakespeare Apocrypha. 1908.

BROOKE, C. F. T. The Tudor Drama; a History of English National Drama to the Retirement of Shakespeare. 1912.

BROTANEK, R. Die englischen Maskenspiele. Wiener Beiträge. 1902.

BULLEN, A. H. A Collection of Old English Plays. 4 vols. 1882-1885.

BULLEN, A. D. (Edited) Davison's Poetical Rhapsody. 2 vols. 1890-1891.

BULLEN, A. H. (Edited) England's Helicon. 1887.

BULLEN, A. H. (Edited) Lyrics from the Dramatists of the Elizabethan Age. 2d edition revised. 1891.

BULLEN, A. H. (Edited) The Works of George Peele. 2 vols. 1888.

BULLEN, A. H. (Edited) The Works of Thomas Middleton. 8 vols. 1885-1886.

Cambridge History of English Literature, The. (Edited) A. W. Ward and A. R. Waller. 14 vols. 1907-1916.

CARTWRIGHT, W. Comedies, Tragi-Comedies, with other Poems. 1651.

CHAMBERS, E. K. The Mediæval Stage. 2 vols. 1903.

CHAMBERS, E. K. The Elizabethan Stage. 4 vols. 1923.

CHAPPELL, W. Old English Popular Music, edited by H. E. Wooldridge. 2 vols. 1893.

CHELLI, M. Le Drame de Massinger. 1924.

COWLING, G. H. Music on the Shakespearian Stage. 1913.

COLLIER, J. P. (Edited) John a Kent and John a Cumber. Shakespeare Society Publications, No. 47. 1851.

DANIEL, P. A. Much Ado about Nothing, in Shakespeare Quarto Facsimiles, No. 14. Introduction. 1886.

D'AVENANT, SIR WILLIAM. Dramatic Works. 5 vols. Edited by J. Maidment and W. H. Logan. 1872-1874.

DODGE, J. "Lute Music of the XVI and XVII Centuries." Proceedings of the Musical Association. 1907/1908.

DOLMETSCH, A. The Interpretation of the Music of the seventeenth and eighteenth centuries. 1915. Appendix. 1915.

DYCE, A. (Edited) The Works of John Skelton. 2 vols. 1843.

ELSON, L. C. Shakespeare in Music. 1908.

"Elizabethan Lyric, The." The Quarterly Review. October, 1902.

ERSKINE, J. The Elizabethan Lyric. 1903.

EVANS, H. A. English Masques. 1897.

FARMER, J. C. (Edited) Rastell's Nature of the Four Elements. 1908.

FELLOWES, E. H. The English Madrigal Composers. 1921.

FELLOWES, E. H. English Madrigal Verse. 1920.

FELLOWES, E. H. The English school of Lutanist Song Writers. 1920.

FEUILLERAT, A. John Lyly. 1910.

Förster, F. "Shakespeare und die Tonkunst." Jahrbuch der Deutscher Shakespeare-Gesellschaft. 1867.

Furnivall, F. J. Captain Cox, His Ballads and Books, or Robert Laneham's Letter. 1871.

Gayley, C. M. Beaumont the Dramatist. 1914.

Gayley, C. M. (Edited) Representative English Comedies. 3 vols. 1903-1914.

Greg, W. W. A List of English Plays written before 1643 and printed before 1700. 1900.

Greg, W. W. A List of Masques, Pageants, etc. Supplementary to A List of English Plays. 1902.

Greg, W. W. (Edited) Gesta Grayorum. 1914.

Greg, W. W. "The Authorship of the Songs in Lyly's Plays." Modern Language Review. I, 1.

Grove, Sir George. Dictionary of Music and Musicians, edited by J. A. Fuller-Maitland. 5 vols. 1904-1910.

Halliwell, J. O. (Edited) The Moral Play of Wit and Science and Early Poetical Miscellanies from an Unpublished MS. Shakespeare Society Publications, No. 37. 1848.

Hannah, J. The Courtly Poets. 1870.

Hilton, J. Catch that Catch Can, or A Choice Collection of Catches, Rounds and Canons for 3 and 4 voices. 1652.

Hogarth, G. The Songs of Charles Dibdin . . . and their Music. 1843.

Jackson, V. English Melodies from the 13th to the 18th Century. One Hundred Songs. 1910.

Jonson, B. Songs by Ben Jonson. A Selection from the Plays, Masques, and Poems with the earliest known settings of Certain Numbers. The Eragny Press. N.D.

Kittredge, G. L. "The *Misogonus* and Laurence Johnson." Journal of Germanic Philology. III, 335.

Langbaine, G. An Account of the English Dramatic Poets. 1691.

Lawes, H. Airs and Dialogues. 1653.

Lawrence, W. J. The Elizabethan Playhouse and other Studies. 1st Series, 1912; 2d Series, 1913.

Lawrence, W. J. "The English Theatre Orchestra." The Musical Quarterly, III, 1; "Music in the Elizabethan Theatre." *Ibid.*, VI, 2; "Bird Song in Elizabethan Drama." The Stage, October 2, 1919; "First Read then Sing." *Ibid.*, January 29, 1920; "Welsh Song in Elizabethan Drama." London Times Literary Supplement, December 7, 1922; "The Problem of Lyly's Songs." *Ibid.*, December 29, 1923; "The Authorship of *The Careless Shepherdess.*" *Ibid.*, July 24, 1924.

MANLY, J. M. (Edited) Specimens of the Pre-Shakespearean Drama. 2 vols. 1897-1900.

MONCUR-SIME. Shakespeare: His Music and Song. N.D.

MOORE, J. R. The function of the songs in Shakespeare's plays. Shakespeare Studies. Wisconsin University. 1916.

Musical Antiquary, The. 4 vols. 1909-1913. (October, 1909, "Early Elizabethan Stage Music.")

McKERROW, R. B. (Edited) The Works of Thomas Nashe. 5 vols. 1904-1910.

NAYLOR, E. W. An Elizabethan Virginal Book. 1905.

NAYLOR, E. W. "Music and Shakespeare." Musical Antiquary. II.

NAYLOR, E. W. (Edited) Shakespeare Music. 1912.

NAYLOR, E. W. Shakespeare and Music. 1896.

NETTLETON, G. H. English Drama of the Restoration and Eighteenth Century. 1914.

New Shakespeare Society's Transactions. "A Selection of Shakespeare Madrigals, Glees, and Songs . . . to be Sung, etc. 1884. Pp. 19†-67†.

NICHOLS, J. The Progresses and Public Processions of Queen Elizabeth. 2d edition. 3 vols. 1823.

NOBLE, R. Shakespeare's Use of Song. With the Text of the Principal Songs. 1923.

O'NEILL, N. "Music to Stage Plays." Proceedings of the Musical Association. 1910/1911.

Oxford History of Music. (Edited) W. H. Hadow. 6 vols. 1901-1905.

PLAYFORD, J. Catch that Catch Can, or The Musical Companion. 1667.

PLAYFORD, J. The Musical Companion. 1672.

PLAYFORD, J. Select Airs and Dialogues. 1669.

PLAYFORD, J. Select Musical Airs and Dialogues. 1653.

PULVER, J. "The Ancient Dance Forms." Proceedings of the Musical Association, 1912/1913/1914; "The Viols in England." *Ibid.*, 1920/1921.

REED, E. B. English Lyrical Poetry. 1912.

RIMBAULT, E. F. An Historical Sketch of the History of Dramatic Music in England (in his edition of Purcell's *Bonduca*. 1842).

RIMBAULT, E. F. A little Book of Songs and Ballads, gathered from Ancient Music Books, MS. and Printed. 1851.

SEGAR, W. Honor Military and Civil. 1602.
SCHELLING, F. E. The Elizabethan Drama. 2 vols. 1908.
SCHOLES, P. A. "The Purpose behind Shakespeare's Use of Music." Proceedings of the Musical Association. 1916/1917.
SCHULTZ, W. E. Gay's Beggar's Opera. 1923.
Shakespeare's England. An Account of the Life and Manners of his Age. 2 vols. 1916.
SHARP, T. A Dissertation on the Pageants or Dramatic Mysteries anciently performed at Coventry. 1825.
SIDGWICK, F. "Tom of Bedlam's Song." The London Mercury. VII, 518.
SIGMUND, R. "Die Musik in Shakespeare's Dramen." Jahrbuch der Deutscher Shakespeare-Gesellschaft. 1884.
SMITH, J. S. Musica Antiqua. [1812].
SQUIRE, W. B. "Music." Shakespeare's England. II, 15.
STAINER, J. (Edited with H. R. Bramley) Christmas Carols New and Old. N.D.
SYMONDS, J. A. "The Lyrism of the English Romantic Drama." In the Key of Blue. 1893.

THORNDIKE, A. H. Shakespeare's Theatre. 1916.
THOMPSON, E. N. S. The English Moral Plays. Transactions of the Connecticut Academy. XIV.

VIVIAN, P. (Edited) The Works of Thomas Campion. 1909.

WADDY, R. "Elizabethan Lyrics and Love-Songs." Proceedings of the Musical Association. 1911/1912.
WALLACE, C. W. The Children of the Chapel at Blackfriars. 1908.
WELCH, CHRISTOPHER. "Literature relating to the Recorder." Proceedings of the Musical Association. 1891/1898; "Hamlet and the Recorder." Ibid., 1901/1902.
WILSON, C. Shakespeare and Music. 1922.

INDICES

INDEX OF AUTHORS

Figures in italics refer to the Notes.

Anonymous, 1, 2, 10-13, 19-20, 21, 24-25, 27, 45-52, 104-106, 107-108, 126-127, 179-181, 184-185, 203-206, 224-225, 234; *257-258, 261, 263, 264, 265, 272-275, 294, 295, 302, 318, 319, 320, 326, 327, 332, 334.*

Bale, John, 4; *258.*
Beaumont, Francis, 115-118; *297-299.*
Beaumont and Fletcher, 118-119; *299-300.*
Behn, Aphra, 217; *330.*
Belchier, Dabridgecourt, 111-113; *296.*
Bottomley, Gordon, 251-252; *337.*
Boyle, Roger, 199-200; *325-326.*
Breton, Nicholas, 26; *264.*
Brome, Richard, 159-162; *312.*
Browne, William, 123-124; *301.*
Browning, Robert, 242.
Burnell, Henry, 197-198; *325.*

Campion, Thomas, 69-74; *283-284.*
Carew, Thomas, 157-158; *311-312.*
Carey, Henry, 231-232; *334.*
Cartwright, William, 190-193; *321-323.*
Cavendish, William, 131-132; *303.*
Chamberlain, Robert, 181; *319.*

Cokayne, Aston, 182; *319.*
Congreve, William, 225; *332.*
Corey, John, 227; *333.*
Cowley, Abraham, 198-199; *325.*
Cox, Robert, 162-163; *312.*
Crowne, John, 213; *329.*

Dane, Clemence, 252-254; *337.*
Daniel, Samuel, 53-55; *275-276.*
D'Avenant, Charles, 223.
Davenant, William, 174-178; *316-318.*
Davenport, Robert, 166; *313.*
Denham, John, 198; *325.*
Dekker, Thomas, 81-88; *286-289.*
Dibdin, Charles, 237-238; *335.*
Dryden, John, 206-212; *327-328.*
Duffet?, Thomas, 220; *331.*
Durfey, Thomas, 221-222; *331.*

Etherege, George, 212; *329.*

Farquhar, George, 226.
Field, Nathaniel, 122; *297, 301.*
Fielding, Henry, 232-233; *334.*
Fisher, Jasper, 194-195; *323-324.*
Flecknoe, Richard, 201; *326.*
Fletcher, John, 141-157; *306-311.*
Ford, John, 119-121; *300.*

Fulwell, Ulpian, 21-22; *263.*

G. T., 129-130; *302-303.*
Galsworthy, John, 251; *337.*
Garrick, David, 234-235; *335.*
Gay, John, 227-230; *333.*
Gilbert, William Schwenk, 243-246.
Glapthorne, Henry, 196; *324.*
Goffe, Thomas, 128; *302.*
Goldsmith, Oliver, 236; *335.*
Gomersall, Robert, 166-167; *313.*
Gregory, Augusta, Lady, 248-249; *336.*

Habington, William, 170; *314-315.*
Hardy, Thomas, 246-247.
Hausted, Peter, 163-166; *313.*
Heming, William, 168; *314.*
Henley, William Ernest, 247-248; *336.*
Heywood, Thomas, 89-93, 247-248; *289-291.*
Holiday, Barten, 124-126; *301.*
Howard, James, 219; *331.*
Housman, Lawrence, 250; *337.*

Ingelend, Thomas, 20; *263.*

Jonson, Ben, 93-104; *291-294.*

Killigrew, William, 173-174; *315.*

Lee, Nathaniel, 222-223; *331.*
Lewis, Matthew Gregory, 239-240; *336.*
Lodge, Thomas, 38-39; *270.*
Lyly, John, 30-37; *266-269.*

Marston, John, 106-107; *295.*
Massinger, Philip, 113-115; *296-297.*
May, Thomas, 133; *303-304.*

Mayne, Jasper, 168-169; *314.*
Middleton, Thomas, 78-81; *285-286.*
Milton, John, 182-184; *319.*
Munday, Anthony, 28-30; *265-266.*
Nabbes, Thomas, 171-172; *315.*
Nashe, Thomas, 74-77; *285.*

Otway, Thomas, 220-221; *331.*

Peele, George, 39-45; *270-272.*
Phillip, John, 14-15; *262.*
Pickering, John, 15-19; *263.*
Porter, Thomas, 213-215; *329-330.*
Powell, George, 224; *332.*

Quarles, Francis, 131; *303.*

Raleigh, Walter, 27; *265.*
Randolph, Thomas, 172-173; *315.*
Rastell, John, 3; *258.*
Ravenscroft, Edward, 218-219; *331.*
Redford, John, 4-5; *258.*
Richards, Nathaniel, 194; *323.*
Rowley?, Samuel, 108-110; *295.*
Rutter, Joseph, 187-190; *321.*

Sampson, William, 127; *302.*
Sedley, Charles, 215-217; *330.*
Settle, Elkanah, 218; *330.*
Shadwell, Thomas, 218; *330.*
Shakespeare, William, 55-69; *276-283.*
Sharpe, Lewis, 196-197; *324.*
Sheridan, Richard Brinsley, 238-239; *335-336.*
Shirley, Henry, 159; *312.*
Shirley, James, 133-141; *304-306.*
Skelton, John, 3; *258.*

Steele, Richard, 225-226; *332-333.*

Stevenson?, William, 7-8; *259.*

Strode, William, 167-168; *314.*

Suckling, John, 185-187; *320-321.*

Tatham, John, 197; *324.*

Tennyson, Alfred, 240-241; *336.*

Thompson, Thomas, 201-203; *326.*

Thomson, James, 230-231; *333.*

Tomkis, Thomas, 115; *297.*

Udall, Nicholas, 6-7; *259.*

Wager, Lewis, 13-14; *262.*

Wager, W., 9-10; *259.*

Wapull, George, 22-23; *264.*

Watson, Thomas, 38; *269.*

Webster, John, 110-111; *296.*

Wever, Robert?, 5-6; *259.*

Yeats, William Butler, 249-250; *336.*

INDEX OF PLAYS, MASQUES, AND
ENTERTAINMENTS

From which Songs have been taken.

Acis and Galathea, 230.
Actæon and Diana, 163.
Admiral Guinea, 247-248.
Aglaura, 186.
The Airs that were sung and played at Brougham Castle, 74.
Ajax and Ulysses, The Contention of, 141.
Albumazar, 115.
Alcibiades, 221.
Alexander and Campaspe, 31.
All Mistaken, or The Mad Couple, 219.
Alphonso King of Naples, 224-225.
Altemira, 200.
Amends for Ladies, 122.
The Amorous Old Woman, 220.
The Amorous War, 169.
Amphrisa, or The Forsaken Shepherdess, 92.
Amphytrion, 211.
Amurath the First, 128.
Antony and Cleopatra, 68.
The Arcades, 184.
Argalus and Parthenia, 196.
Aristippus, 173.
The Arraignment of Paris, 39-42.
As You Like It, 63-64.
The Author's Farce, 232.

Becket, 241.
The Beggar's Bush, 152.
The Beggar's Opera, 229.
Bellamira, or The Mistress, 217.
The Bloody Brother, 143-144.
A Blot in the 'Scutcheon, 242.
Blurt Master Constable, 78.
The Bogie Man, 249.
The Broken Heart, 120-121.

The Captain, 144.
The Cardinal, 138.
The Careless Shepherdess, 129-130, 140.
The Changes, or Love in a Maze, 134-135.
A Chaste Maid in Cheapside, 79.
Chester Plays. Noah's Flood, 2.
The Second Part of Cicilia and Chlorinda, or Love in Arms, 158.
The Second Part of the Cid, 190.
Circe. A Tragedy, 223.
Cleomenes, 212.
The Tragedy of Cleopatra Queen of Egypt, 133.
A Pleasant Comedy called Common Conditions, 24.
The Conquest of Grenada. Part One, 209.
The Contention between Liberality and Prodigality, 25.
The Contention of Ajax and Ulysses, 141.
Comus, 183.
Corona Minervæ, 181.
The Courageous Turk, or Amurath the First, 128.
Coventry Shearmen and Tailors Pageant, 1-2.
The Crier by Night, 251-252.
The Cruel Brother, 175.
Cupid and Death, 139.
Cupid's Revenge, 118.
A Cure for Jealousy, 227.
The Tragedy of Cymbeline, 68-69.
Cynthia's Revels, 93-95.

The Death of Robert, Earl of Huntington, 30.
Dervorgilla, 248-249.
The Description of a Maske . . . at the Marriage of the Earl of Somerset and Lady Francis Howard, 73.
The Description of a Mask presented before the King's Majesty at White Hall in Honour of the Lord Hayes and his Bride, 71.
The Description, Speeches and Songs of the Lords' Maske, 72.
The Destruction of Jerusalem. Part I, 213.
The Devil is an Ass, 101.
The Discontented Colonel, 187.
The Disobedient Child, 20.
Don Quixote in England, 233.
The Duchess of Malfi, 111.
The Duenna, 239.
The Dutch Courtezan, 106.

Elvetham, The Honorable Entertainment given to the Queen's Majesty at, 26, 38.

The Emperor of the East, 113.
The Emperor of the Moon, 217.
Endymion, 33-34.
The English Rogue, 202-203.
Epicœne, or The Silent Woman, 99.
An Evening's Love, 209.
Every Woman in her Humour, 105-106.

The Fair Maid of Clifton, 127.
The Fair Maid of the Exchange, 93.
The Faithful Shepherdess, 141-143.
The False One, 150-151.
The Famous Tragedy of the Queen of Cornwall, 247.
The Fatal Contract, 168.
The Fatal Dowry, 115.
The Fathers, or The Good-Natured Man, 234.
Fedele and Fortunio, or The Two Italian Gentlemen, 27.
The Female Victor, 213.
The Floating Island, 167-168.
Florizel and Perdita, 235.
A Fool's Preferment, or The Three Dukes of Dunstable, 221.
The Forsaken Shepherdess, 92.
Four Elements, The Nature of the, 3.
Fuimus Troes. The True Trojans, 195.

Galathea, 34-35.
Gammer Gurton's Needle, 8.
The Golden Age, 89.
The Good-Natured Man, 234.
The Gray's Inn Masque, Song from the (In Davison's Poetical Rhapsody), 70.
Grissell, The Comedy of Patient and Meek, 15.
Grissill, The Pleasant Comedy of Patient, 84-85.

Hamlet, 58-60
Hannibal and Scipio, 171.
Hans Beer-Pot, 113.
Harlequin's Invasion. A Christmas Gambol, 235.
Hayes, Lord (See, The Description of a Mask, etc.).
Histriomastix, 106-107.
Horestes, The History of, 15-19.
The Humourous Lieutenant, 149.
The Hunting of Cupid, 43.
Hymen's Triumph, 53-55.

The Imposture, 137-138.
The Indian Emperor, 207.
The Indian Queen, 206.
The Inner Temple Masque, 123-124.
The Italian Husband, 219.

John a Kent and John a Cumber, 28-29.
A Jovial Crew, or The Merry Beggars, 162.
The Just Italian, 174.

The King and Queen's Entertainment at Richmond, 185.
King Arthur, or The British Worthy, 211.
King David and Fair Bethsabe, The Love of, 45.
King Henry VIII, 156.
King John, 4.
King John and Matilda, 166.
The Knight of the Burning Pestle, 117-118.

Lady Alimony, 205.
The Lady Errant, 192-193.
The Land of Heart's Desire, 249-250.
Landgartha, 198.
The Law against Lovers, 178.
Liberality and Prodigality, The Contention between, 25.
The Life and Repentance of Mary Magdalene, 14.
The Life of Mother Shipton, 203.
Like Will to Like, 21-22.
The Little Dream, 251.
The Little French Lawyer, 151.
The Lamentable Tragedy of Locrine, 46.
The Tragedy of Lodovick Sforza Duke of Milan, 167.
The London Chanticleers. A Witty Comedy, 204.
London's Tempe, 86.
The longer thou livest the more fool thou art, 9-10.
A Looking Glass for London and England, 39.
The Lords' Maske (See, The Description, Speeches, etc.).
Lord Knowles, A Relation of the Entertainment given by, 72.
Love Crowns the end, 197.
The Love of King David and Fair Bethsabe, 45.
Love in a Maze, 134-135.
Love in Arms, 158.
Love in a Tub, 212.
The Lover's Melancholy, 120.
The Lover's Progress, 152-153.
Love's Cure, or The Martial Maid, 114.

Love's Kingdom, 201.
Love's Labour's Lost, 56.
Love's Mistress, 93.
Love's Riddle, 199.
Luminalia, or The Festival of Light, 179.
Lusty Juventus, 6.

The Mad Couple, 219.
The Mad Lover, 146-148.
Magnificence, 3.
The Maid in the Mill, 154.
The Maiden Queen, 207.
The Maid's Metamorphosis, 47-49.
The Maid's Tragedy, 119.
The Man's the Master, 176.
Marciano, or The Discovery, 206.
The Marriage of Wit and Science, 21.
The Martial Maid, 114.
The Martyred Soldier, 159.
Mary Magdalene, The Life and Repentance of, 14.
The Masque of Alfred, 231.
The Masque of Beauty, 98.
The Masque of the Gypsies Metamorphosed, 101.
The Masque of the Inner Temple and Gray's Inn, 116.
Measure for Measure, 62.
The Merchant of Venice, 57.
The Merry Beggars, 162.
The Merry Wives of Windsor, 62.
The Tragedy of Messalina, 194.
Metropolis Coronata. The Triumphs of Ancient Drapery, 29.
Microcosmus, 171.
Midas, 35-36.
A Midsummer's Night's Dream, 56-57.
Misogonus, 13.
Mr. Anthony. A Comedy, 200.
The Mistress, 217.
The Montebank's Masque, 108.
More Dissemblers besides Women, 81.
Mother Bombie, 37.
Mother Shipton, The Life of, 203.
Much Ado about Nothing, 58.
The Mulberry Garden, 217.

The Nature of the Four Elements, 3.
The Tragedy of Nero, 223.

Neptune's Triumph for the Return of Albion, 99.
A New Interlude of Vice, containing the History of Horestes, 15-19.
The Nice Valour, or The Passionate Madman, 153-154.
Noah's Flood, 2.
The Noble Soldier, 108.
The Noble Stranger, 196-197.
The Northern Lass, 159-161.

Oberon, The Fairy Prince, 99-100.
The Obstinate Lady, 182.
The Old Couple, 133.
The Pleasant Comedy of Old Fortunatus, 83-84.
The Old Mode and the New, or Country Miss with her Furbelow, 222.
The Old Wive's Tale, 44-45.
The Tragedy of Orestes, 128.
Othello, 60.

Pan's Anniversary, 103-104.
Pastor Fido or The Faithful Shepherd, 218.
The Passionate Madman, 153-154.
Patience, 243-246.
The Comedy of Patient and Meek Grissell, 15.
The Pleasant Comedy of Patient Grissill, 84-85.
The Picture, 114.
Pleasure reconciled to Virtue, 103.
The Poetaster, 95-96.
Polyhymnia, 43.
The Provoked Husband, 232.
Prunella, 250.

The Queen of Arragon, 170.
The Queen of Corinth, 156.
Queen of Cornwall, The Famous Tragedy of the, 247.
Queen Mary, 240-241.

Ralph Roister Doister, 7.
The Rape of Lucrece, 27, 91.
The Recruiting Officer, 226.
A Relation of the late Royal Entertainment given by . . . the Lord Knowles, 72.
The Return from Parnassus, 104.
Rich and Poor, 240.
Richmond, The King and Queen's Entertainment at, 185.

The Rival Friends, 164-166.
The Rivals, 175.
Robert, Earl of Huntington, The Death of, 30.
The Royal Shepherdess, 218.
The Royal Slave, 190-192.

The Sad Shepherd, 102.
St. Patrick for Ireland. The First Part, 136.
Sapho and Phao, 32-33.
The School of Compliment, 134.
The School for Scandal, 239.
Secret Love, or The Maiden Queen, 207.
Selindra, 174.
The Seraglio, 238.
She Stoops to Conquer, 236.
Will Shakespeare, 252-254.
The Shepherd's Holiday, 187-189.
The Shoemaker's Holiday, 82.
The Siege, 193.
The Silent Woman, 99.
The Silver Age, 90.
The Sisters, 137.
Somerset, Earl of (See The Description of a Maske, etc.).
The Sophy, 198.
The Spanish Curate, 155.
The Spanish Friar, 210.
The Spanish Gypsy, 109-110.
The Spring's Glory, 172.
Summer's Last Will and Testament, 75-77.
The Sun's Darling, 87-88.
The Swaggering Damsel, 181.
Swetnam, the Woman Hater, arraigned by Women, 127.

Technogamia, or The Marriage of the Arts, 125-126.
The Tempest, 61.
The Tender Husband or The Accomplished Fools, 226.
Tethys Festival, 53.
The Thracian Wonder, 51-52.
The Three Dukes of Dunstable, 221.
The Tide tarrieth no Man, 23.
Tom Tyler and his Wife, 12.
Totenham Court, 172.
The Trial of Treasure, 20.
The Triumph of Beauty, 136.
The Triumph of Peace, 135.

Twelfth Night, 65-66.
The Two Gentlemen of Verona, 62.
The Two Italian Gentlemen, 27.
The Two Noble Kinsmen, 157.
Tyrannic Love, 208.

The Unfortunate Lovers, 177-178.

The Tragedy of Valentinian, 145-146.
The Variety, 132.
The Villain, 214-215.
The Virgin Widow, 131.
Volpone, 97.
The Vow Breaker or The Fair Maid of Clifton, 127.

The Waterman or The First of August, 237.
The Way of the World, 225.
Westward Ho, 85.
The What d'ye call it, 228.
The White Devil, 111.
The Widow, 80.
Wily Beguiled, 50.
The Play of Wit and Science, 5.
The Witch, 79.
The Winter's Tale, 67-68.
Wit and Science, The Marriage of, 21.
The Witty Combat or The Female Victor, 213.
The Witty Fair One, 135.
A Woman is a Weathercock, 122.
The Woman Hater, 115.
Women Pleased, 150.
The World tost at Tennis, 78.

INDEX OF FIRST LINES

A bonny, bonny bird I had   160
A curse upon that faithless maid   217
A new master, a new!   18
A pox on our gaoler, and on his fat jowl   190
A round, a round, a round, boys, a round   162
Adieu, farewell earth's bliss   76
Adieu, fond love; farewell, you wanton powers   152
Ah Chloris! that I now could sit   215
Ah fading joy! how quickly art thou past!   206
Ah how sweet it is to love   207
All hail fair Phœbus, in thy purple throne   49
All round my hat I wore a green ribbon   249
All ye that lovely lovers be, pray you for me   44
All ye woods, and trees, and bowers   142
Amarillis told her swain   214
Amidst the mountain Ida's groves   48
Am not I in blessed case   19
An eye of looking back were well   102
And let me the cannikin clink, clink   60
And was it not a worthy sight   16
And will he not come again?   58
Are they shadows that we see?   53
Arm, arm, arm, arm! the scouts are all come in   148
Art thou gone in haste   51
Art thou poor yet hast thou golden slumbers?   84
As I out rode this enderes night   1
As light as a fly   24
As little lambs lift up their snowy sides   48
As many as match themselves with shrowes   11
At the Spring   194
Autumn hath all the summer's fruitful treasure   77
Away, away, flatter no more   213
Away, delights, go seek some other dwelling   144

Back and side go bare, go bare   7
Beauty, alas! where wast thou born   38
Beauty, and the various graces   137
Beauty arise, show forth thy glorious shining   85
Beauty, no more the subject be   171
Be not so cruel, fairest boy   181

Be still my sweet sweeting, no longer do cry   14
Better music ne'er was known   118
Beyond the malice of abusive fate   215
Black spirits and white, red spirits and gray   79
Blow, blow, thou winter wind   63
Blow high, blow low, let tempests tear   237
Brave iron! brave hammer! from your sound   85
Broom, broom on a hill   9
But shall I go mourn for that (my dear)   67
But why   165
Buzz, quoth the Blue-Fly   99
By the moon we sport and play   47
By the rushy-fringèd bank   183

Call for the robin-redbreast and the wren   110
Can you blow the little horn?   47
Can you paint a thought? or number   120
Care-charming Sleep, thou easer of all woes   145
Cast away care, he that loves sorrow   88
Cast our caps and cares away   152
Cease warring thoughts, and let his brain   136
Cease your funning   229
Celladon, when Spring came on   221
Chant birds in every bush   105
Charm, O charm, thou god of sleep   197
Charon, O Charon   147
Chloris, we see the offended gods   173
Cold's the wind, and wet's the rain   82
Come ashore, come merry mates   73
Come away, away, away!   135
Come away, bring on the bride   151
Come away, come away death   65
Come, blest virgins, come and bring   168
Come cheer up my lads, 'tis to glory we steer   235
Come, come, away: the spring   161
Come, come, lie down and thou shalt see   21
Come, come, my good shepherds, our flocks we must shear   234
Come follow me, you country lasses   154
Come, follow your leader, follow   109
Come heavy souls oppressèd with the weight   167
Come let the state stay   186
Come let us be frolic and call for our tipple   202
Come list and hark   91
Come, lovely boy unto my court   188

Come, my Celia, let us prove   97
Come, my dainty doxies   80
Come, my Daphne, come away   138
Come, my sweet, whiles every strain   190
Come, noble nymphs, and do not hide   100
Come, shepherds, come   142
Come, shepherds, come, impale your brows   129
Come, Sleep, and with thy sweet deceiving   115
Come thou Monarch of the vine   68
Come unto these yellow sands   60
Come you whose loves are dead   117
Come, you young men, come along   162
Come with me to London   252
Comforts lasting, loves increasing   120
Corinna, in the bloom of youth   224
Cupid and my Campaspe played   31
Cupid, if a God thou art   164
Cynthia, to thy power and thee   118

Day is dismounted on the watery plain   213
Dear, do not your fair beauty wrong   133
Dearest, do not you delay me   154
Did not you once, Lucinda, vow   184
Do not fear to put thy feet   142
Doune from heaven, from heaven so hie   1
Drink to-day, and drown all sorrow   143
Drop golden showers, gentle sleep   128
Drowsy Phœbus, come away   163

Eyes, hide my love, and do not show   54

Fair and fair and twice so fair   40
Fair Iris I love, and hourly I die   210
Fair summer droops, droop men and beasts therefore   74
Fancies are but streams   87
Farewell, adieu, that courtly life   15
Farewell this company   181
Farewell ungrateful traitor   210
Fear no more the heat o' the sun   69
Fie, cease to wonder   115
Fie on sinful fantasy: Fie on lust, and luxury   62
Fine young folly, though you were   170
Flow, flow delight   171
Fly hence, shadows, that do keep   119
Fools, they are the only nation   96

Fortune my foe, why dost thou frown on me?   47
Fortune smiles, cry holyday!   82
From whence was first this Fury hurled   157
Full fathom five thy father lies   61
Full hard did I sweat   37

Get you hence, for I must go   67
Give me fortune, give me health   80
Give me my lute; in thee some ease I find   223
Glories, pleasures, pomps, delights, and ease   121
God Lyæus, ever young   146
Golden slumbers kiss your eyes   84
Good hostess, lay a crab in the fire and broil a mess of souse a   21
Great Pan, to thee we do confine   196
Grieve not, fond man, nor let one tear   129

Had I a heart for falsehood framed   239
Had sorrow ever· fitter place   53
Had those, that dwell in error foul   98
Hail, beauteous Dian, queen of shades   89
Hapless doom of woman happy in betrothing!   241
Happy times we live to see   78
Happy was man ere cheated sense   227
Hark, hark, the lark at Heaven's gate sings   68
Hark, now everything is still   111
Have pity, Grief; I cannot pay   164
Have you a desire to see   159
Haymakers, rakers, reapers, and mowers   87
Hear, ye ladies that despise   145
Helpless wretch, despair, despair   194
Hence, all you vain delights   153
Here's to the maiden of bashful fifteen   238
Hey ho, care away, let the world pass   19
His golden locks time hath to silver turned   43
Holiday, O blessed morn   107
Hot sun, cool fire, tempered with sweet air   45
How blest are they that waste their weary hours   131
How can he sing whose voice is hoarse with care?   104
How happy could I be with either   229
How I laugh at their fond wish   166
How now, everywhere up in air stars stare   250
How round the world goes, and everything that's in it   80
How should I your true love know   58
How unhappy's the fate   232
Hymen, god of marriage-bed   189

I am a poor tiler in simple array   10
I am gone sir, and anon sir   65
I am in love and cannot woo   140
I cannot tell what this love may be   243
I could never have the power   119
I feed a flame within which so torments me   207
I have a pretty titmouse   10
I mun be married a Sunday   6
I neither will lend nor borrow   136
I never shall henceforth approve   220
I will follow through yon grove   197
I'd have her merry, laugh, and smile   132
I'll sail upon the Dog-star   221
If all these Cupids, now, were blind   98
If I freely may discover   95
If love be like the flower that in the night   27
If Love his arrows shoot so fast   134
If Luck and I should meet   253
If the heart of a man is depressed with cares   229
If yet, if yet   103
In a herber green, asleep whereas I lay   5
In a maiden-time professed   79
In the merry month of May   26
In wet and cloudy mists I slowly rise   179
In youth when I did love, did love   59
Is it the wind of the dawn that I hear in the pine overhead?   241
It is a punishment to love   199
It is pitiful and sharp to-day are the wounds of Ireland   248
It was a lover and his lass   64

Jog on, jog on the foot-path way   67

Ladies, though to your conquering eyes   212
Lawn as white as driven snow   67
Lay a garland on my hearse of the dismal yew   119
Let school-masters puzzle their brain   236
Let the bells ring, and let the boys sing   155
Let's meet again to-night, my Fair   246
Let us sip, and let it flip   12
Let us use time whilst we may   218
Lo here we come a-reaping, a-reaping   45
Look out bright eyes, and bless the air   150
Love, a thousand sweets distilling   135
Love and Death o' th' way once meeting   201
Love for such a cherry lip   78

Love is a law, a discord of such force	50
Love is a sickness full of woes	54
Love is blind, and a wanton	95
Love's a lovely lad	51
Love's but the fraility of the mind	225
Love's far more powerful than a king	197
Lovers lament, lament this fatal day	218
Lovers, rejoice! your pains shall be rewarded	118
Lullaby, lullaby baby	128
Lully, lula, thow littell tine child	1
Lustily, lustily let us sail forth	24
Make room for my rich waters' fall	150
Matilda, now go take thy bed	166
Melampus, when will Love be void of fears?	44
Melancholy, hence! go get	134
Melpomene, the muse of tragic songs	41
Merry knaves are we three-a	32
My Daphne's hair is twisted gold	35
My lodging it is on the cold ground	175
My love and I a bargain made	219
My love can sing no other song	105
My shag-haired Cyclops, come let's ply	32
Night as well as brightest day hath her delight	71
No more dams I'll make for fish	61
No, no, fair heretic, it needs must be	186
No, no poor suffering heart, no change endeavour	212
Nor Love nor Fate dare I accuse	159
Not he that knows how to acquire	133
Nought avails thy plaintive crying	239
Now fie on love, it ill befits	139
Now hath Flora robbed her bowers	70
Now, now the sun is fled	191
Now the lusty spring is seen	144
Now wend we together, my merry men all	29
Now what is love I pray thee tell	27
Nymphs and shepherds, dance no more	184
Nymphs that now are in your prime	218
O cruel Love! on thee I lay	32
O Cupid! monarch over kings	37
O, fair sweet face, O, eyes, celestial bright	150
O fly my soul, what hangs upon	137
O for a bowl of fat canary	30

O gentle love, ungentle for thy deed   41
O Ida, O Ida, O Ida, happy hill   39
O Love, how strangely sweet   106
O mistress mine, where are you roaming?   64
O ruddier than the cherry   230
O sweet Diana, virtuous queen   203
O that joy so soon should waste!   94
O, the merry month of May, the merry month of May   82
O yes, O yes! if any maid   35
Oars, oars, oars, oars   85
O'er the smooth enamelled green   183
Of Neptune's empire let us sing   69
Of Pan we sing, the best of singers, Pan   103
Oh, fair sweet goddess, queen of loves   147
Oh no more, no more, too late   121
Oh, sorrow, sorrow, say where dost thou dwell?   108
Oh stay, Oh turn, Oh pity me   52
Oh, turn thy bow   153
Old Tithon must forsake his dear   50
Once Venus' cheeks, that shamed the morn   167
Orpheus I am, come from the deeps below   146
Orpheus with his lute made trees   156
Our prentice Tom may now refuse   226

Pack, clouds, away, and welcome, day   90
Pan's Syrinx was a girl indeed   36
Pardon, goddess of the night   58
Peace and silence be the guide   116
Peace, wayward barne, O cease thy moan   161
Phœbus, unto thee we sing   93
Pinch him, pinch him, black and blue   34
Poor mortals, that are clogged with earth below   206
Princes that rule and empires sway   220
Prithee, pretty maiden—prithee tell me true   243

Queen and huntress, chaste and fair   94

Rise from the shades below   149
Rise, lady mistress, rise   122
Robin is a lovely lad   74
Rocks, shelves, and sands, and seas, farewell   34
Roses, their sharp spines being gone   156
Round about, round about, in a fine ring a   48
Run to Love's lottery! Run, maids, and rejoice   177

Sabrina fair	183
Satyrs sing, let sorrow keep her cell	49
Seal up her eyes, O Sleep, but flow	193
See, see a metamorphosis	172
See the chariot at hand here of Love	100
See where Calisto wheels about	214
Shake off your heavy trance	116
Shall I because my Love is gone	187
Shame upon you, Robin	240
Sigh no more, ladies, sigh no more	57
Sigh, shepherds, sigh	130
Since painful sorrow's date hath end	49
Since you will needs my heart possess	199
Sing care away, with sport and play	12
Sing his praises that doth keep	141
Sing sweetly, that our notes may cause	115
Sing to Apollo, god of day	36
Sister, awake, close not your eyes	104
Slaves are they that heap up mountains	172
Sleep sweetly, sleep sweetly, sweetly take rest	29
Slow, slow, fresh fount, keep time with my salt tears	93
So Beauty on the water stood	97
So, so	205
Somnus, the humble God, that dwells	198
Spite of his spite, which that in vain	20
Spring all the graces of the age	99
Spring, the sweet Spring, is the year's pleasant king	75
Stand back, ye sleeping Jacks at home	17
Stand: who goes there?	33
Steer hither, steer your winged pines	123
Still to be neat, still to be drest	99
Submit, bunch of grapes	203
Sweet Echo, sweetest nymph, that liv'st unseen	182
Take, oh take those lips away	62, 143
Tell me, dearest, what is Love?	117
Tell me gentle hour of night	71
Tell me, Jove, should she disdain	196
Tell me what you think on earth	187
Tell me where is Fancy bred	57
Terlitelo, Terlitelo, terlitelee, terlo	47
The bird in my heart's a-calling through a far-fled, tear-grey sea	251
The black jack	125
The blushing rose and purple flower	114

The bread is all baked   175
The dusky night rides down the sky   232
The faery beam upon you   101
The flude comes flittinge in full faste   2
The glories of our blood and state   140
The God of shepherds, and his mates   40
The hour of sweety night decays apace   107
The merry waves dance up and down, and play   198
The nut-brown ale, the nut-brown ale   106
The ousel cock, so black of hue   57
The poor soul sat singing, by a sycamore tree   60
The princely heart, that freely spends   25
The spheres are dull and do not make   182
The strange effects of my tormented heart   42
The wind blows out of the gates of the day   249
The windy hours through darkness fly   251
Then farewell, my trim-built wherry   237
Then, in a free and lofty strain   96
There's a woman like a dew-drop, she's so purer than the purest   242
They bore him bare faced on the bier   59
They that for worldly wealth do wed   122
Thine eyes to me like suns appear   131
This lady, ripe, and calm, and fresh   174
This way, this way come, and hear   151
Those flowers your infancy did crown   180
Thou more than most sweet glove   94
Though I am young and cannot tell   101
Though little be the god of Love   138
Though Wastefulness and Wantoness   23
Though we contemplate to express   113
Thyrsis, unjustly you complain   216
Time is a feathered thing   168
Time to pass with goodly sport   3
'Tis in good truth a most wonderful thing   177
'Tis late and cold; stir up the fire   153
'Tis mirth that fills the veins with blood   116
To carve our loves in myrtle rinds   192
To Tunis and to Argers, boys   204
Tobacco's a musician   124
Tomorrow is St. Valentine's day   59
Trip and go, heave and ho   75
Trip it, gypsies, trip it fine   108
Troll the bowl and drink to me, and troll the bowl again   21
Turn, turn thy beauteous face away   114
'Twas not his person nor his parts   189

'Twas when the seas were roaring 227

Under the greenwood tree 62
Urns and odours, bring away 157

Victorious men of earth, no more 139
Virtue stand aside: the fool is caught 83
Virtue's branches wither, Virtue pines 83

Wake all the dead! what ho! what ho! 178
Wake, my Adonis, do not die 192
Wake, our mirth begins to die 96
Walking in a shadowed grove 111
Wassail, wassail, out of the milk-pail 4
We care not for money, riches or wealth 173
We cobblers lead a merry life 45
We hadn't been three days at sea before we saw a sail 247
We have great gain, with little pain 22
We that have known no greater state 91
Weep eyes, break heart 79
Weep no more for what is past 174
Weep no more, nor sigh, nor groan 155
Weep, weep, ye woodmen wail 30
Weep, weep, you Muses, drain the springs 222
Welcome, mine own! 4
Welladay, Welladay 42
Were ever chaste and honest hearts 54
Were I laid on Greenland's coast 228
What a dainty life the milkmaid leads 172
What are earthly honours 159
What bird so sings, yet so does wail? 31
What need we use many beseeches 201
What sing the sweet birds in each grove? 124
What thing is love? for (well I wot) love is a thing 43
What tho' they call me country lass 231
Whenas the rye reach to the chin 44
When Britain first, at Heaven's command 230
When daffodils begin to peer 66
When daisies pied and violets blue 55
When from the wars I do return 127
When I go out of door 244
When icycles hang by the wall 55
When mighty roast beef was the Englishman's food 233
When Sylvia is kind, and Love plays in her eyes 224
When that I was and a little tiny boy 65

Wherever I am, and whatever I do   209
Where the bee sucks, there suck I   61
While dancing rests, fit place to music granting   73
While the sweet blushing spring glowing fresh in her prime   234
Whilst we sing the dolful knell   126
Who is Sylvia? what is she?   61
Why art thou slow, thou rest of trouble, Death   113
Why, lovely charmer, tell me why   225
Why should not youth fulfill his own mind   6
Why so pale and wan, fond lover?   185
Why was I doomed by fate to prove   200
Will you buy any tape, or lace for your cape?   68
Wind, jolly huntsmen, your neat bugles shrilly   88
With fair Ceres, Queen of Grain   90
With fragrant flowers we strew the way   38
With ye, marry Sirs, thus should it be   3
Woo her, and win her, he that can   72
Woodmen, shepherds, come away   133

Ye little birds that sit and sing   92
Ye sacred fires, and powers above   46
Ye should stay longer if we durst   116
Yes, were the Loves or false or straying   98
Yesterday travelling Connacht   248
You charmed me not with that fair face   208
You say my love is but a man   159
You spotted snakes, with double tongue   56
You stole my love; fie upon ye, fie   28
You that seek to sunder love   28
You virgins, that did late despair   137
Your hay it is mowed, and your corn is reaped   211
Your pretty person we may compare to Lais   13